THE SEA

the SEA
a cultural history

John Mack

REAKTION BOOKS

Published by Reaktion Books Ltd
33 Great Sutton Street
London EC1V 0DX, UK

www.reaktionbooks.co.uk

First published 2011

Printed and bound in Great Britain
by CPI/Antony Rowe, Chippenham, Wiltshire

British Library Cataloguing in Publication Data
Mack, John, 1949–
   The sea : a cultural history.
   1. Ocean. 2. Ocean and civilization. 3. Seafaring life.
   I. Title
   551.4′6-DC22

ISBN 978 1 86189 809 8

Contents

Preface

There are two separate strands which have come together in the planning of this book – or rather two separate, but in the end related questions. The first is a negative one: why did no one apparently think it worth settling on the large island of Madagascar in the western Indian Ocean until late in human history? It is an island well-endowed by nature and, other than being inhabited by ferocious mosquitoes along its coasts, not inconvenienced by the lions, leopards or other predators that stalk the hinterlands of the nearby African continent. Its famous lemurs are benign residents posing no physical threat to human settlement. A second question is why – coincidentally at about the same time as Madagascar was finally being colonized – did the people of East Anglia take to burying a leader in a huge ship on the top of a hill? Sutton Hoo is a pleasant place above a sheltered inlet, a good place to bury a prominent person who would have been familiar with the maritime world along this part of the English coastline. But why drag a huge ship all the way up there to do it?

The questions occurred in this sequence but at different moments several decades apart. The first obliges a reconsideration of what it means to be at sea and how the maritime world is constituted; the second implies bringing the subject back onto land to think about how the maritime and terrestrial worlds interact. The movement of the book that follows reproduces that sequence: it starts by thinking about human engagement with the sea in maritime terms, rather than merely as an extension of the activities of the land; and it ends by seeking to bring together the argument round a consideration of the grand ritual gesture of ship-burial. In between it ranges widely across the literature on the human experience of the different oceans and seas.

After working in various inland parts of eastern Africa – and having had the opportunity to spend time along the Swahili coast of Kenya and latterly Tanzania – the outbreak of civil war in southern Sudan in the early 1980s made it inadvisable to continue working with pastoralist communities in what was to become a war-torn area. The opportunity arose to begin an ethnographic survey on the island of Madagascar, which in those days was mostly approached by plane from Nairobi. The route lay over the north-west coast of the island with a clear sight of the soils leeching off the central highlands and turning the rivers and a wide semi-circle of the waters of the Mozambique Channel a distinctive brownish-red colour. Flying in to land in the highlands near the capital of Antananarivo has become the usual way of getting there. However, on subsequent visits I have been able follow an older practice and approached by sea from Zanzibar entering the ports at Mahajanga, Antsiranana (previously Diego Suárez) and, on the east coast, at Toamasina (Tamatave). What this experience makes entirely evident is both the proximity of 'la grande île' to inhabited lands and islands in the vicinity and also the availability of a number of sheltered harbours. So the island is vast, neither remote, lacking appropriate harbours (albeit dispersed ones) nor short of resources. True, it lies at the extremities of the monsoonal system which linked together the trading practices of the wider Indian Ocean world. Being off the beaten track, however, was not a criterion which limited the exploration and settlement of the Pacific, the North Atlantic or other areas which were colonized much earlier than Madagascar. Madagascar was not occupied until very late in human history – probably only within the last 1,200 to 1,500 years.

The big question which has preoccupied those concerned with the antiquity of human activity in this part of the Indian Ocean concerns the question of *who* first colonized the island in the context of increased precision about *when* the event might have happened. Even if we set aside the questionable assumption that it was a single event, the whole detective cast to this search is hard to avoid. There are a limited number of candidates who might have committed the deed, and, while the scenarios are conflicting, all have persuasive aspects. Much is down to the imaginative powers of reconstruction of the researcher and the assessment of new pieces of information as they arise. However, as in the standard

mystery story, none of the current occupants is saying anything definitive: Madagascar stands out amongst island populations in retaining
virtually no oral tradition about sea voyaging from anywhere else. Even
relatively recent arrivals retain only the vaguest history of having come
from elsewhere. And for inhabitants of an island nation with an
immensely long coastline, very few contemporary Malagasy derive a living
from the exploitation of the sea itself.

Contrast that with, for instance, the Polynesians' sense of their
origins and connectedness. There, the accounting of ancestral voyaging is an established part of oral tradition and distinctions between
first occupants and later arrivals is part of the understanding of hierarchical relationships. Individual clans may be identified, as in Fiji,
as people of the sea rather than the land, expressing – or at least implying – their more recent arrival. In New Zealand the Maori recount
their genealogical descent, linking themselves across the generations
to the voyagers who first settled the islands, and thence backwards
in time to the divinities from whom the Maori derived.

So there are other fundamental questions to be posed than those
of a 'whodunnit' kind. '*Why not?*' is surely an equally pressing and
complex issue to be raised – why was an island the size of Madagascar
running parallel to the coast of Africa at a distance of only 400 kilometres, lying within the compass of the Indian Ocean's monsoonal
winds, not occupied much earlier than it was? And, beyond that,
why does the sea not feature in symbolic or political contexts amongst
the peoples of Madagascar in the way it does elsewhere? The fact of
Madagascar being both accessible and thinly occupied was, after all,
precisely what made it so attractive to the pirates who based themselves
in the Bay of Antongil as late as the early eighteenth century, returning
for what would nowadays be called 'rest and recreation' from preying
on merchant shipping in the rest of the Indian Ocean or pilgrim ships
heading to or from Mecca. It is in trying to understand the answers to
these questions that the wider treatment in this book arises, for what is
implied is not a specific set of historical reflections but a more fundamental rethink of the ways in which maritime cultures are configured
by scholars.

Teaching at the University of East Anglia led to the second reflection which brackets this volume. East Anglia has a rich maritime context
and at Sutton Hoo in Suffolk a major archaeological site of international
significance, now run as a National Trust site. In a way it is actually

rather a disappointing place to visit since one of the most exciting finds there was only recovered in skeletal form – the ship-burials discovered beneath several mounds, the excavations now backfilled and the mounds reconstructed on the hill overlooking an inlet near Woodbridge. They were Anglo-Saxon burials, not Viking ones, but none the less conform to the practice otherwise characteristic of elite burials in Scandinavia. The large and impressive grave goods are also missing from the site, being regarded as of much greater importance than their local context might imply and now placed under the stewardship of the British Museum – though parts are lent back for temporary exhibition at the site on an annual basis. Interestingly, the body of the deceased was not found in the excavation either, having apparently succumbed to being buried in less than favourable environmental conditions. So what remains is enigmatic. But the fact of the burial being of a ship, a very large one at that, and apparently one which once sailed on the local stretches of water and possibly more widely in the North Sea, has attracted less attention than the sumptuous cargo with which it and its human occupant were buried. The voluminous literature on the site and the finds discovered there has very little to offer in explanation of the ship. Who was buried there in such splendour has seemed a much more pressing question. Ships are a very familiar image in coastal communities and no doubt have emblematic and other significance. But why go to all the effort of decommissioning one from maritime usage and burying it in a difficult location? As with the issues surrounding the occupation of Madagascar, to understand the significance of a ship when not in its normal milieu at sea seemed to direct investigation back to what it meant to be on the seas in the first place.

One overriding reflection was that an understanding of the pre-industrial engagement with the sea is considerably hampered by assumptions derived from the experience of steam ships and modern developments in cartography and marine survey. These can quite unwittingly colour understanding of how people find their way at sea, how they conceptualize it, the kinds of relationships to the maritime environment implied and the observational skills appropriate to being on it. Furthermore, the reasons why people might be at sea in pre-industrial contexts may not be immediately perceptible and interpretation of the social relationships which sustain people inhabiting the sea may be skewed. The introduction of steam to the maritime world may seem to have added speed, efficiency and perhaps increased safety to the business of being on the oceans; but in practice it did much more than that. This has all led me to take as a theme the creative and imaginative implications of being on the sea rather than – some might say, at the expense of – a more conventional approach through an account of the technology of ships and boats. Indeed, in some of what follows it is contrasting understandings of technological means and their efficacy which is at issue. Even the compass, which would seem a fundamental technological innovation transforming human experience of the maritime world in paradigmatic ways, was far from being recognized as such by all navigators.

Thus two questions, arising at different times and in quite different situations, directed attention back to the human engagement with the sea in a variety of cultural and temporal contexts. Exploring the implications of these questions was the starting point for the voyage recorded in the chapters that follow.

Introduction

People on land think of the sea as a void, an emptiness haunted by mythological hazards. The sea marks the end of things. It is where life stops and the unknown begins. It is a necessary, comforting fiction to conceive of the sea as the residence of gods and monsters – Aeolus, the Sirens, Scylla and Charybdis, the Goodwins, the Bermuda Triangle. In fact the sea is just an alternative known world. Its topography is as intricate as that of land, its place names as particular and evocative, its maps and signposts rather more reliable.
JONATHAN RABAN, *Coasting* (1987)[1]

This is a book about the sea and about the ways in which human beings interact because of it, navigate their course across it, live on and around it. It is, in short, about the variety of ways in which people 'inhabit' the sea. Its milieu is that of salt water as opposed to fresh water and it takes as its terrestrial limit the interface between the sea and the land, the inter-tidal regions, the beaches, promontories, estuaries and ports which abut the sea, rather than the activities which take place further inland. We might define the subject as the sea itself and the places where the sound and 'smell' of the sea are pervasive. The book is, to a significant extent, concerned with a sensory world for it is fundamentally about the *experience* of the seas and the oceans. It is concerned, in short, with what have been described elsewhere as 'saltwater people'.[2]

Of course, what happens around or even on the sea is often strongly coloured by what happens on the land. People cannot live entirely at sea without some access to the land and its products. Perhaps the closest to an exclusively maritime culture is that of the Bajau Laut, the so-called 'sea gypsies' of the waters of south-east Asia. Their life is led almost entirely on boats or in houses raised on stilts above salt-water estuaries, exploiting the resources of the surrounding lagoons and reefs or moving goods from place to place (illus. 1).[3] There are very few occasions on which they are obliged to set foot on terra firma. Although in modern

1 'The Floating Home of the Sea Gypsies', from Walter Grainge White, *The Sea Gypsies of Malaya* (London, 1922).

times fewer people pursue this maritime life, those who do remain reliant on the historical role of middlemen who arrange essential supplies of fresh food and water and conduct all negotiations with land-based populations on their behalf. Likewise, sea ports around the world have adapted to catering for the needs of mariners who develop a passing acquaintance with the land, its pleasures and resources, but rarely stray far beyond the immediate confines of harbours, other than when docked at their home ports.[4] Those, indeed, who have spent significant periods exclusively aboard ship and out of contact with land, especially before the days of refrigeration, were exposed to the risks of scurvy and other conditions resulting from a lack of ready access to the fresh food and drinking water available on land. As they were obliged to restock when the occasion presented itself, many of the encounters between the European explorers who took to the seas in the so-called Age of Discoveries and indigenous peoples occurred close to coasts and were occasioned by the need of provisioning. None the less whilst the relationship to the land is essential to the habitation of the sea, being at sea is not simply a version of being on land.

Furthermore, although the experience of the sea may be different from that of the land, the historical engagement with it is itself far from uniform in different maritime contexts. The exploitation of marine resources, the techniques and strategies devised to meet the challenges of being at sea – even the ways in which it is conceptualized – are necessarily highly variable for different maritime peoples. Despite this, in writings about the sea the experience of western Europeans – and of Mediterranean mariners in particular – has tended to predominate. The voyaging was itself inspired by a complex of essentially terrestrial factors amongst which commerce, exploitation and empire have always been identified as prominent. The implicit understanding has usually been that people set off in boats inspired to do so by some compelling rationale deriving from their experience of the land.

In European terms, the eighteenth century might at first glance seem to be the exception in the story of this engagement with the sea. Enlightenment thinkers were to elevate 'curiosity' in the roster of intellectual motivations – the British Museum, for example, was established in 1753 as a resource for the 'curious' and its galleries are an index of where such maritime voyages of exploration led. Yet such explorations as those undertaken by Captain Cook and contemporaries of different European nationalities and backgrounds were not acts of pure inquisitiveness. The modern idea of curiosity as an intellectual indulgence with no more worldly inspiration misrepresents the historical circumstances.[5] *Inquisitiveness* and *acquisitiveness* were intimate bedfellows. Being at sea for long periods, then as now, was not something envisaged for the pure thrill of it. The very acts of commissioning and funding such prolonged voyages of exploration in the first place implied the need to open up new markets, to gain access to scarce resources and to move goods between distant ports and their hinterlands. It was not the sea itself which was to be explored and charted; the goal was to first establish and then to realize the potential of the islands and coastlines which provided its margins.

Thus, voyagers like Captain Vancouver, who set sail from Falmouth, England in 1791 bound for the north-west coast of the Americas, were essentially charged with charting the islands and the inlets through the so-called Inland Passage. It took all of twelve months to get there sailing the length of the Atlantic to the tip of Africa, traversing the breadth of the Indian Ocean to Australia and New Zealand, and travelling northwards again by way of the islands of Polynesia, to make landfall on the American coast north of San Francisco, then a Spanish enclave. But that was, in a way, precisely the point. The inconvenience of a route which was so prolonged – especially so in the days of sail – compelled the search for other solutions. The British and the Spanish had already been in conflict over the right to trade with the indigenous populations, particularly from the base established at Nootka Sound on the seaward side of what was to become Vancouver Island. For the British the lack of ready contact between the north-west coast and the trading stations at Hudson's Bay and elsewhere in Canada was problematical. An earlier survey by Captain Cook had failed to reveal any linkage by sea across or around the continent. Captain Vancouver was sent to settle the matter, entrusted with the mission of obtaining

> accurate information with respect to the nature and extent of any water-communication which may tend, in any consider-able degree, to facilitate intercourse, for the purposes of commerce, between the north-west coast, and the country upon the opposite side of the continent.[6]

His conclusion after three months of detailed charting was that no such routes existed. It is perhaps no surprise that, writing in 1817, Mary Shelley chose to locate the last sighting of her Frankenstein monster on the frozen wastes of the Arctic as it/he rushed off, loosed forever as another adventurer – the fictional Walton – was forced to turn back, unsuccessful in the quest for the apocryphal North West Passage. However, the possibility of a way through the frozen waters was a prize that continued to obsess European powers – notably, in the early nineteenth century, the Russians.

The sea, then, was as much somewhere to be endured as some-where to be explored in the quest for distant coasts and passages – and, arguably, it was as much the very acts of endurance on such extended voyages, which for most could only be imagined, that elevated argonauts such as Captain Cook to lionized status. They returned with tangible witness to their discoveries – the natural and artificial (or man-made) 'curiosities' which they had assembled on voyages to distant foreign shores and which were to be bestowed on museums, botanical gardens and zoos, many established specifically to receive these cargos. Whalers were to explore the same seas, but for the moment the voyages of explor-ation were more about the exploitation of the land than any resources located in the oceans themselves.

The sea, in these constructions of it, was empty: a space not a place. The sea is not somewhere with 'history', at least not recorded history. There are no footprints left upon it; it consumes and secretes those who come to grief on its surface and the vessels in which they have sailed. It is not monumentalized. Literature and hymnology are replete with such reflection, rendering the sea a symbolic and metaphorical narrative device rather than a real place. The predominant Western view of the sea might be characterized as that of a quintessential wilderness, a void without community other than that temporarily established on boats crewed by those with the shared experience of being tossed about on its surface, and a space without ruins or other witness to the events which may have taken place on its surface. Victor Hugo remarks in *The Toilers of the Sea* (1866): 'The solitudes of the ocean are melancholy: tumult and silence combined. What happens there no longer concerns the human race.'[7] Sea, in the words of the Caribbean poet Derek Walcott, needs to be historicized.

> Where are your monuments, your battles, martyrs?
> Where is your tribal memory? Sirs,
> In that grey vault. The sea. The sea
> Has locked them up. The sea is History.[8]

Or again, in a stanza from Mary Oliver's poem 'The Waves':

> The sea
>   isn't a place
>   but a fact, and
>   a mystery[9]

The possibility of realizing a 'history' of the sea is neatly presaged in another and much earlier literary context. In an evocative passage in *Gargantua and Pantagruel* François Rabelais, writing in the mid-sixteenth century, talks of a ship approaching an ice bank in the frozen waters of the north. The passengers gather on deck and imagine they can hear indistinct voices and cries. As the noises become clearer, they realize that what they are hearing are the sounds of a great sea battle of the past, frozen in the Arctic ice as they were uttered and only now being slowly released with its melting.[10]

However, if a primary purpose of this book is to reflect on the human engagement with the sea, it is only partly a matter of recovering forgotten archival histories. Indeed, many of the parts of the world considered here had no systems of writing until more recent times.

They may escape 'history' in the sense of not being participant in objective documentary accounting until brought into contact with literate mariners; and even then it is more likely to be their terrestrial activities than their maritime ones which are the focus of documentation – the land-based Bajau are more completely documented than their maritime namesakes. None the less, many maritime or partly maritime peoples do preserve detailed oral chronicles of the sea which may go back across the generations. For instance, Maori chronicling of the voyaging which brought them to the islands of New Zealand may list the achievements of twenty or more generations, the recounting aided by a notched stick on which each indentation has a distinctive pattern representing one generation. In some aspects such narratives may be regarded as merging into the mythological; the Maori trace their maritime origins back to the divinities from whom they ultimately derive.[11] However, to recount this past is not simply to recite a dispassionate list of historical events; for Maori, as for other Polynesians, it is to be filled with a profound sense of a maritime ancestry, to be infused with a past which is fundamentally linked to the sea in a way which diverges from the Caribbean sense of the absence of appropriate linkage. Even without contemporaneous written accounts, this is the sea as revelatory of history, not as an instrument of its concealment. Such assertion of ancestral connection to the sea is in itself one of the ways in which people 'inhabit' it, even if they are otherwise largely terrestrial. In contemporary times this may be less a physical connection than it was in the past, but for Maori it remains for all that a deep-seated – we might even say, an 'existential' – bond.

Histories of the Seas

None the less, if the historical disciplines have struggled to match Polynesian genealogical detail in their accounting of human engagement with the sea, it is still historians and historically inclined geographers who have been able to assemble the richest material through which to think about the phenomenon of the sea as a social, cultural and especially a commercial space. The inspiration for some of this derives from the influential writing of Fernand Braudel, which has attracted proponents and critics in equal measure.[12] Either way, his work stands as a significant moment in historical thinking about the seas – or rather about one sea in particular, the Mediterranean. In many accounts of the region it has seemed more appropriate to refer not to a single sea but to the many which arguably make up the Mediterranean basin and the surrounding regions, each of them already with a separate geographical name. But that would be to misrepresent Braudel's basic thesis which, whilst recognizing diversity, comes in the end to assert the fundamental unity of the Mediterranean. It is also, perhaps, to misrepresent his topic, for the sea (or seas) is less his focus than the wider region which includes an extensive hinterland, *The Mediterranean and the Mediterranean World in the Age of Philip II*[13] as he entitled his major work (1949). What this encouraged is attention to the distinctive and interrelated historical continuities of the Mediterranean region as a whole. His approach was less preoccupied with the narrative aspects of history – with anything associated with the initiatives of Philip II as an individual actor, for instance – and more concerned to ascribe causal priority to the environment. Thus, as city states develop and decline, as regional economies boom and bust, the underlying disparities of resources across the region remain the same and set in motion the need for extensive trading networks as far north as the Baltic and, via the Black Sea, deep into the Russian heartlands. The Mediterranean is expanded by the river systems which penetrate deep into Europe – and Braudel's focus is principally directed northwards rather than towards Africa. Thus, the merchant ships with their polyglot crews which criss-crossed the Mediterranean itself throughout recorded history were responding to the diverse hands which nature had dealt out across a vast region, not just of islands and coastal areas, but of the continent itself. The Mediterranean, as the word itself implies, was simply the space in between these lands.

Of course, much of this historical debate has centred on the Mediterranean to the exclusion of other seas and oceans, though there have been some attempts to apply the same approaches elsewhere, notably to the Indian Ocean.[14] Yet, in practice, the seas are portrayed either as the backdrop to the stage on which the real action is seen to take place – that is, the land – or they are portrayed simply as the means of connection between activities taking place at coasts and in their interiors. The characteristics of the sea itself, the nature of man's interactions with it, the alliances and liaisons which take place on it and because of it, the contacts effected, cemented or cast asunder, are all largely absent from this historiography.[15]

In parallel with this, a form of national history writing has also conspired to diminish the attention to the seas as globalized transnational spaces that might have developed. This history is largely focused on the emergence of national navies, imperial ambitions and to some extent merchant shipping which, because they are instruments of statehood, tend to be cast in terms of admirals and captains, their deeds in defence of the nation and the sea battles in which they and their fleets have participated. Whilst the work of historians such as N.A.M. Rodger stands apart,[16] there is otherwise an inherent triumphalism evident in some of this literature, especially in more popular writing. The extensive documentation of the transgressive history of pirates gives some sense of alternative aspects to the recounting of maritime history. Yet it too is often cast in terms which, in the same vein, can appear overly romantic.

To explore the range of cultural experience of the seas we need to move beyond the confines of any individual sea or oceanic system. In a world where Eurocentric preoccupations have found their way to the very heart of historical thinking, an attention to oceans in a wider context immediately opens up a globalized perspective, for oceans have themselves exercised the major role in this process. Their history may be clouded, but their part is unarguably one of major importance.[17] Well before Europeans had set out on journeys of circumnavigation, the Phoenicians had sailed round Africa and back again to the Mediterranean; the Pacific islands had been explored by Polynesian mariners who criss-crossed the Pacific occupying Rapa Nui (Easter Island) by AD 400 and Hawaii possibly a century later, and who had found and settled New Zealand by AD 1000; the Norsemen mastered the challenging waters of the North Atlantic to arrive in Newfoundland by way of Iceland and Greenland by the eleventh century; and the Chinese had sailed to the east coast of Africa a century before Vasco da Gama ventured round the Cape and into the Mozambique Channel. The history of any one sea or ocean quickly becomes the history of others. The history of the seas has, thus, a major contribution to make to the contemporary project of seeking to understand the mechanisms of globalization.[18]

Given this degree of interaction and exploration even in more distant historical times, it is difficult to sustain the idea of any single oceanic identity – nor should we expect such cohesiveness of culture or of historical experience. Oceans do not necessarily function to promote uniformity. They are, rather, arenas of transnational interchange.[19] If Braudel saw the influence of the maritime world of the Mediterranean as contributory to a *longue durée*, an imprisoning conception in which human activity is seen as constrained and directed by the environment, this comparative approach imparts to the seas a critical agency, revealing them as a dynamic engine of historical change.

Among the historical pursuits it might be argued that maritime archaeology has a certain priority for its consistent attention to questions of the role of the maritime world in promoting cultural diffusion. Yet it, too, is restricted in its approach, being, after all, reliant either on the remains of seaborne activity preserved on land, or on seeking the marks of man's passage not on the surface but at the bottom of the sea in the vicinity of coasts and ports. The very location already compels a perspective which is unavoidably terrestrial.[20] Yet, there is certainly recognition in recent archaeology of the value of adopting a perspective which is imaginatively as much in the sea as on land. Barry Cunliffe has explored the role of the peoples of the north-west Atlantic coasts in shaping what might be called a European sense of identity and of the role of the maritime sea routes in forging it.[21] A number of archaeologists working beyond Europe have been inspired by other models of human engagement with the sea to suggest expansions to European technological understandings of the engagement of coastal peoples with the sea, with their emphasis on harvesting maritime resources and enabling safe passage across its surface. A comparative approach draws attention to the richness of maritime cultures with their mix of spiritual and ontological investment in the environment of the sea. And, indeed, the stories examined by Cunliffe and others of the Irish monks who explored the north-west Atlantic in the first millennium AD already suggest that such an ideological – or theological – engagement with the sea also has its parallels in Western experience. Through the cross-fertilization of ideas which arises from a comparative approach – and often one drawing on the insights of ethnographic accounts – a traditional archaeological focus on landmarks and shipwrecks is expanded. What some envisage is an archaeology of 'seascapes', an approach to the sea that incorporates the land rather than the other way round.[22] On this basis Paul Rainbird, an archaeologist with extensive field experience in Micronesia, has made the case for an island archaeology which he sees as implying a shift from material and environmental evidence towards the lives and experience of mariners. Braudel's approach concentrates on the influence the environment has had on historical circumstances but not on the influence man has had on the environment. In his understanding, the underlying historical realities are unified and continuous because the interactions of man and environment are portrayed as static. The focus, Rainbird suggests, needs to be placed on the people who create the material world in the first place and their perceptions of the environment, rather than the reverse.[23]

The ambition, however, remains a future prospect and would seem to foreshadow a move beyond the materials conventionally assessed by archaeologists. Unaided by other disciplinary approaches, archaeology would not seem to be capable of taking the decisive step offshore on its own. Geographers provide one stimulating resource to turn to; and oceanography in particular is attracting increasing interest and sophistication in analysis as the impact of climate change on sea levels, temperature and the movements of currents becomes evident.[24] Geographers, indeed, have been at the forefront of developing a sophisticated interdisciplinary critique of the extent to which seas and oceans can be objectively regarded as units with a common narrative in any meaningful sense at different periods of history.[25] The notion that seas might be constructed as communal spaces which differ significantly from the terrestrial concepts embedded in the idea of the nation state has gained some currency in recent years. To Braudel's somewhat static view of the Mediterranean as a trading space has been added an understanding of seas and oceans as unstable dynamic entities. New constellations of common interest emerge and dissolve as coalitions are forged; and these themselves have a bearing on the whole process of state formation itself. Some of these emergent coalitions are trans- and inter-oceanic in scale and extend well beyond any terrestrial conception of territoriality. Attention to the seas thus challenges the otherwise reifying conceptions of nations and continents. Geographical perspectives also highlight a continuing tension in approaches to the governance of the sea, notably that between strategies which seek to build up a practice of regarding the sea as common territory, and that which sees the exploitation of its resources or its geopolitical implications as susceptible to national claims to territoriality. The issue revolves around the changing approaches to stewardship in an international context and, in cartographic terms, around whether the lines drawn on the ocean connect or divide. Clearly this in itself has a changing historical and spatial context.[26]

First-hand accounts

But, if we are to take seriously the observation that the understanding of the sea is predicated on an understanding of the people who inhabit the sea, accounts of mariners must clearly play a large part in what follows here. Some of these are explicitly ethnographic (or more broadly anthropological) in content; others are first-hand autobiographical accounts, some in the guise of fiction. In truth, though, ethnography has rather less to offer than literary sources. It has rarely reported on the experience of being on the seas; instead, to the extent that reference is made to the sea at all, it has almost always focused on the implications of being close to the sea, of having a relationship to it, not actually of being *on* it. Roland Barthes once described the beach as a place bedecked in flags and bunting, as a symbolically charged environment. It is a frontier marked by colour and noise, the interface between a world which is celebrated and enriched and one which is devoid of such overt signification. If the sea risks becoming an ahistorical zone for historians, for many anthropologists the sea is, in parallel, culturally barren. Yet, of course, Barthes is talking only of the European beach – and, given that the European engagement with beaches and swimming in the sea has its own distinctive history, he is only talking of the beach as he encountered it in the first half of the twentieth century at that.[27] As cultural spaces beaches are far from uniform in their significance across time and across cultures – and so too, it might be surmised, must be the seas further offshore. There is, however, no established anthropology of seascapes to complement the burgeoning anthropological attention to the perception of landscape.[28]

There are, of course, innumerable ethnographies of coastal populations, of fishermen and traders who are none the less largely land-based. But, if fishermen provide one kind of trope and farmers another, it still remains the case that most fishermen, even those who exploit the resources of the seas rather than freshwater lakes or rivers, return home to unload their catches at the end of the day and spend their evenings in coastal villages. Likewise farmers are not restricted to tilling the soil if their resources can be supplemented from the rivers or the seas. The tropes interrelate and interpenetrate. Plato famously commented: 'We inhabit a small portion of the earth . . . living round the sea like ants and frogs round a pond.'[29] His observation, of course, was mostly stimulated by the experience of the eastern Mediterranean. Yet it is in the anthropological accounts of the Pacific that the fullest exploration of maritime lore is to be found.[30] In addition to more conventional descriptions, much of it emphasizing indigenous ideas of astronomy and its relation to navigation, there is one source on which we draw which stands out. David Lewis, a New Zealand-born medical doctor and round-the-world yachtsman, worked with indigenous navigators in 1968–69 in various parts of the Pacific. His practice was to sail with local mariners whether in outrigger canoes or in his own boat, but to undertake journeys without the aid of compasses or other instrumentation. The resulting account – *We, the Navigators: The Ancient Art of Landfinding in the Pacific* (1972) – is a readable, personalized ethnography providing comparative data on navigational systems from Fiji to the Admiralty Archipelago off the north of Papua New Guinea and the Carolines.[31]

Suggestive as this literature is, it is limited in extent. A leading feature of this book is thus the value it places on literary sources to expand these perspectives and re-site discussion as far as possible on the sea rather than on land. Many academic authors might read novels of the sea as a means of 'warming up', of getting into the mindset of the mariner alongside more formal reflections and historical accounts. Captain Marryat or Patrick O'Brien might sit on the shelves alongside N.A.M. Rodger, Felipe Fernández-Armesto or Jonathan Raban. Here, however, we take advantage of the many fictional accounts of life at sea which are none the less based on actual experience and act as a form of ethnographic text.

Joseph Conrad's enigmatic old sea dog in his story 'The Nigger of the "Narcissus"' (1897) – named, significantly, Singleton – is described as having spent 45 years afloat during which he had been ashore for barely 40 months.[32] He is, in fact, based on a sailor called Sullivan who crewed with Conrad. Herman Melville's Captain Ahab, obsessive hunter of Moby-Dick, was 40 years at sea and only three ashore. This intensity of human interaction with the sea, which both Melville and Conrad witnessed at first hand before beginning their literary careers, is largely absent from conventional academic accounts of 'maritime cultures'. Novels of the sea can, of course, be about subjects in addition to seafaring – indeed their value as literature is precisely that they do embody larger themes. *Robinson Crusoe* (1719), often identified as the first work of fiction in a modern sense, is not just about the hardships of an isolated, shipwrecked sailor; it has been regarded as both a religious narrative and an allegory of early capitalist imperialism. *Moby-Dick* (1851) is about a whaling expedition; but it is also both a spiritual treatise and a study of obsession which at least one author has analysed as an anticipation of the rise of fascism in the twentieth century.[33] None the less the passages on man's relationship to the sea remain. A selective use of literary sources enables us to retrieve this aspect of seafaring.

Much writing about the sea, of course, employs the idea of the sea as metaphor rather than as lived reality. It is revealing, for instance, that in a definitive anthology such as *The Oxford Book of the Sea* (1992), which focuses explicitly on writing about the sea itself, there are no texts by William Shakespeare reproduced despite the fact that he, above all authors, has penned some of the most memorable lines in the English language – some 26 examples being listed in the sister publication the *Oxford Dictionary of Quotations* under the word 'sea'.[34] Of the late plays several have explicit scenes set at sea – notably the two plays which are actually set at sea, *Pericles* and *The Tempest*, whose opening scene is well-informed on handling ships in a storm. It seems Shakespeare was conversant with reports of voyages and shipwrecks, and certainly he was well placed to seek out the company of the mariners of his day. Yet, almost all Shakespeare's allusions to the sea are poetic analogies between the human condition and the boundlessness of the oceans, its moods of storm and calm, or its capacity to utterly consume those lost in its wastes. Likewise his use of nautical language is not in itself any indication of an engagement with the sea since the English language is replete with phraseology which derives from seafaring. Indeed there is no evidence that Shakespeare himself ever went aboard ship. This is the case with much writing about the sea; it is rarely observational in the way that, for instance, the naturalist Rachel Carson is in her beautifully crafted descriptions of the life of the coastal areas of the American east coast.[35] Even in a recent novel by Richard Collins whose title – *The Land as Viewed from the Sea* (2004) – suggests a perspective very close to that advocated here (and which

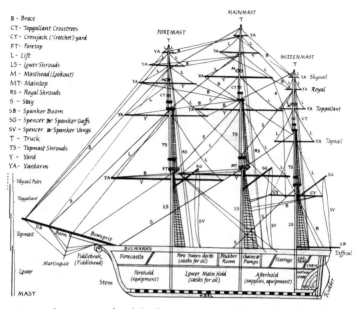

B - Brace
CT- Topgallant Crosstrees
CY- Crossjack ('Crotchet') yard
FT- Foretop
L- Lift
LS - Lower Shrouds
M - Masthead (Lookout)
MT- Maintop
RS - Royal Shrouds
S - Stay
SB - Spanker Boom
SG - Spencer & Spanker Gaffs
SV - Spencer & Spanker Vangs
T - Truck
TS - Topmast Shrouds
Y - Yard
YA- Yardarm

2 *Rigging and Cross-section of a Whaler*, from Herman Melville, *Moby-Dick; or, the Whale* (New York, 1851).

is echoed in an article of my own which foreshadows the contents of this book),[36] the sea remains essentially a metaphor for terrestrial experience. The movement of the tides, the storms, the residues washed up on beaches, the experience of sailing are all counterpoints to the development of a tempestuous relationship taking place on land. The sea is a place of contemplation of the vicissitudes of lives otherwise played out on land. As Herman Melville wrote: 'Meditation and water are wedded forever.'[37]

That said, many literary sources never the less have what we might call a strong ethnographic element to them. *Moby-Dick* is known as a classic novel of the sea by virtually every child brought up in an English-speaking education system, even if it is not necessarily read cover to cover. The focus on the doomed, single-minded search for the great white whale – and the implications of such fixation – have no doubt been recommended principally as imaginative drama and instructive material through which to reflect on the moral implications of grand obsession. Less well-remarked is that the original version is accompanied by a map showing the voyage of the ill-fated *Pequod* and by a series of illustrations which show in great detail and with named parts a cross-section of the rigging of a whaler, the 26 different sails (illus. 2), the layout of the deck and all the different implements carried on a whale boat of the mid-nineteenth century (illus. 3). The implements used to cut up a successfully 'landed' catch are illustrated and accompanied by detailed drawings to demonstrate where the incisions are made on different types of whale. This is no formal manual of the techniques of the whaling industry, yet even so Melville has felt compelled to portray the mariner's life aboard such a ship. For half of a very long book the 'plot' disappears as Melville effectively stands down narrative structure in favour of long descriptive and meditative passages. What Melville has done in *Moby-Dick* is to paint 'a body of men at work, the skill and the danger, the laboriousness and the physical and mental mobilization of human resources, the comradeship and the unity, the simplicity and the naturalness'.[38] The book has all the apparatus of an ethnographic monograph before the discipline of anthropology was yet underway, drawing on Melville's 'participant observation' as a professional seaman on whalers and frigates operating principally between New England and the Pacific between 1839 and 1844. The book's theme, indeed, was itself suggested by a real event in which an American ship was rammed and sunk by a whale in the middle of the Pacific Ocean.

Melville, of course, was not alone in his close attention to the lived experience of the sea. Richard Henry Dana, Jr might be accounted

Implements Belonging to a Whale Boat

1. Oar   2. Boat-waif   3. Boat-hook   4. Paddle   5. Boat-sails   6. Sweeping-line-buoy   7. Lead to Sweeping-line
8. Chock-pin   9. Short-warp   10. Boat-piggin   11. Boat-keg   12. Lantern-key   13. Sweeping-line   14. Boat-hatchet
15. Lance-warp   16. Boat-grapnel   17. Boat-knife   18. Fog-horn   19. Line-tub   20. Boat-bucket   21. Drag
22. Nipper   23. Boat-crotch   24. Boat-compass   25. Boat-anchor   26. Row-lock   27. Tub-oar-crotch

3 *Implements Belonging to a Whale Boat*, from Melville, *Moby-Dick; or, the Whale.*

more of a diarist than a writer of fiction. Son of a famous New England poet, Harvard student and member of the Massachusetts elite, Dana set out in 1834 as an ordinary seaman on the *Pilgrim*, a little brig engaged in the trade of hides from the Californian coast back to his native Boston. He learnt en route that the *Pilgrim*'s voyage would take them longer than imagined. So he determined to transfer to another ship and eventually returned, rounding Cape Horn a second time, on the *Alert*. Even so he was at sea for two years, during which time he forewent the society of his Harvard contemporaries entirely. His method compares favourably with that of the present-day ethnographer. Dana lived life 'before the mast' as a common sailor, taking notes as he went along and developing it into a larger narrative. The resulting book gives a comprehensive picture of initiation into American seafaring life – with all its pleasures and its discomforts.[39] As an objective autobiographical account of the life of an ordinary merchantman it received popular acclaim, its effect enhanced by a simple narrative style rather than informed by any self-regarding literary intent. Indeed, in an epilogue written when Dana returned to California 24 years later he reports that he re-met many of the people he had known as a sailor and that his book was much in circulation amongst ordinary seamen with experience of the life of the merchant seamen involved in the early nineteenth-century hide trade. He was to be one of Melville's main inspirations. Like many an ethnographer since, he went on to champion the cause of those amongst whom he had worked, deploying a legal training picked up when he returned to improving the conditions of merchant seamen.

The documentary turn of these accounts is notable in American writing about the sea. Raban makes the interesting point that for American authors the wilderness was not so much the sea as the interior of the continent itself.[40] It was terrestrial wastes that obsessed many of them. The direst of experiences tended to be relocated to the mountainous wilds of the Rockies rather than at sea. Not that the seas were uniformly regarded as benign; but they are approached without the baggage of the European 'sublime', that potent mix of awe and sheer terror which haunted so much British writing about nautical experience from the vast Gothic novel of Ann Radcliffe, *The Mysteries of Udolpho*, to the verse of Lord Byron.

Byron, of course, was a serious yachtsman who maintained a professional crew on his boat in the Mediterranean. Shelley was an amateur enthusiast, though the boat he commissioned famously sank in a storm in the Gulf of Spezia barely two months after he came into its ownership, his inexperienced pursuit of the thrill of sailing in a gale leading to his demise. Experienced authorial mariners, however, abound both major and minor in literary terms. Other than Shakespeare, the most significant exception is perhaps Coleridge, whose classic Romantic poem of the sea *The Ancient Mariner* (1798) vividly evokes maritime experience. It was conceived against a background of deep interest in accounts of sea voyages and a long-standing fascination with ideas of the spirits of the deep, but in fact it predates his first proper sea-voyage – a crossing from Yarmouth to Hamburg which he reportedly found disappointing.[41] And there are some which focus rather on their characters' complete lack of seamanship, as in Redmond O'Hanlon's *Trawler* (2004): when the man on the Clapham omnibus takes to sea, his account of the whole physical challenge of nautical experience, the confrontation with seasickness, the nauseous smell of fish, the disruption of routine – especially sleeping patterns – vividly brings into focus the distinctiveness of maritime experience.[42]

From these sources, all of which are drawn on below, we learn not just about the sea and the handling of ships but also about the society of seafarers. As with those described by Braudel in the Mediterranean, the crews on the ships described by Dana, Melville, Conrad and others were truly cosmopolitan. Indeed, it is not just that major long-distance migrations took place by ship and that sea ports were amongst the first urban centres to develop cosmopolitan populations; the ships themselves, regardless of the nationality of their owners or their home port, were very often sailed by crews which were multi-ethnic in composition. This is not just true of the European or American shipping which is the context of most maritime literature. There is evidence that Muslim ships trading in the Indian Ocean in the thirteenth century were also crewed by multi-ethnic sailors. Despite differences in language and culture, the ways in which the discipline and mutuality on which successful voyaging depended was achieved (or not) is also suggested by many informed literary sources. Sometimes survival itself is the issue. Stephen Crane in his short autobiographical story about being shipwrecked off the coast of Florida on New Year's Day 1897 found himself – inexperienced as he was – afloat in a life raft and rowing for a distant and dangerous shore with the four survivors of the ill-fated ship. They formed a motley crew with their range of skills and some, notably the captain, injured and unable to assist. Crane reflects:

> It would be difficult to describe the subtle brotherhood of men that was here established on the seas. No one said that it was so. No one mentioned it. But it dwelt in the boat, and each man felt it warm him. They were a captain, an oiler, a cook and a correspondent [Crane himself, who at the time was a war correspondent], and they were friends, friends in a more curiously iron-bound degree than may be common.[43]

It is only by concerted efforts, setting aside personal discomfort and overcoming incipient exhaustion to take turns at the oars, that, finally, they make shore – and safety.

Ships' companies were also marked by another feature which distinguishes them from terrestrial society: the almost complete absence of women, or at least their occasional – but almost always transgressive – presence aboard ship in the days before passenger ships and cruise liners. Ships are, very largely, 'manned'. Again, the implications are prominent in much nautical literature. Scottish trawlermen, even before embarking on a dangerous passage to fish in the seas of the North Atlantic, need to observe many taboos. Women are not allowed on ship or even to touch the guard rails when in port.[44] Conrad writes of another 'old sea dog', very much in the mould of Singleton, whom he met at a funeral:

> I learned afterwards that he was looked upon as the terror of sailors, a hard man; that he had never wife or chick of his own, and that, engaged from the tenderest years in deep-sea voyages, he knew women and children merely by sight.[45]

Gender relations relocated to the seas are reordered in complex ways – and this is so in many cultures, as we shall see.

Pictorial sources

Cartography and marine painting share a common beginning, and, arguably, they are in origin fundamentally ideological rather than strictly representational forms of imagery. Some of the first 'maps', indeed, are more readily described as ideograms than as replications of objective geography and as such were of little or no use in terms of planning prospective long-distance journeys. So-called T-O maps are essentially circles with a T in the middle dividing them into three sections representing the three known continents in the Middle Ages: Asia, Europe and Africa. The point of their intersection was centred on Jerusalem with the area beyond the circle occupied by the seas and the heavens. The Christian conceptualization of space gave a strong sense of centre and periphery with the oceans as the limiting factor of the known world.[46] In Europe more accurate sea charts emerged with lines to show the connections between different ports in the Mediterranean, the portolan maps familiar to medieval sailors. However, the lines themselves were straight, making no allowance for the reefs, winds and currents. Mariners' logs therefore began to include indicative outline drawings of prominent parts of the coastline, sometimes including ships to give an impression of scale. Being images produced from the sea, they are the precursors of subsequent marine painting but produced initially for navigational rather than aesthetic purposes.

If these appear to be devoid of ideological contents, subsequent imagery of the sea often has a nationalistic context. Discussions of marine art have mainly been restricted to discussion of pictorial representations – and inevitably have not included indigenous cultures around the world.[47] Although representations of the sea are to be found on Egyptian tomb painting and on ancient Greek vases, amongst the first images of the coastline are those done by European mariners. Marine painting as a category of European art was developed principally by the Dutch in the seventeenth century, of whom Jan van Goyen, Aelbert Cuyp and Simon de Vlieger were amongst the most prominent. From thence a practice of sea- and ship-painting spread to other countries, often being taken up by artists who otherwise specialized in landscape painting. The scenes depicted are sometimes beaches and strands; and ships are often included, especially in the representation of naval encounters. However, the boundless sea itself is rarely portrayed in pictures. The artists usually had direct experience of the sea and of sailing and this emerged in their various depictions. Jan van Goyen made innumerable trips along the Dutch coastline, hiring fishing boats for the purpose and coming back with sketchbooks

filled with scenes drawn on the spot. By the mid-1600s it was cus-
tomary for seascape painters to be included in naval fleets and they
often sketched battle scenes as they were occurring. Their depictions
reflected a knowledge of how sailing ships of the period responded to
the winds, how they handled in various weather conditions, and a direct
observation of the labours of seafarers. Scenes which showed ships
riding on seas in tumultuous fury substantiated popular conceptions
of the sea as an untrammelled force of nature.[48]

A cardinal moment in the development of a parallel British tradition of practice was the emigration of the van de Veldes from their
native Netherlands to England in 1672.[49] Willem van de Velde the
elder would make sketches of marine scenes which were turned into
impressive canvasses by Willem the younger. Their influence on the
British marine painting tradition associated particularly with Isaac
Sailmaker and Peter Monamy was significant and by the eighteenth
century included painters working in the Romantic tradition who were
equally adept at landscape and seascape painting.[50] An interesting
example is the link between Richard Wilson, the distinguished painter
of landscapes portraying scenes in both his native Wales and in Italy,
and William Hodges, the artist who accompanied Captain Cook on
his second voyage to the Pacific between 1772 and 1775. Hodges had
studied with Wilson and transferred the practice of enlivening
landscape by dramatic use of light and shade to depictions of the sea,
which is evident in pictures of, for instance, Cape Town, the Antarctic
and Polynesia.[51]

J.M.W. Turner is often identified with the Romantic tradition.
Turner's exploration of sea painting included adaptations and 'improve-
ments' on the works of the Dutch masters, producing pictures which
play on the construction and themes of familiar marine paintings but
significantly dramatizing their composition.[52] Turner's later celebrated
seascapes extend this and take atmospheric painting into a new realm
which is at times almost wholly expressive in conception. That Turner
should be drawn to the sea is readily explicable. Its many different
moods, from raging turmoil to reflective calm provide a ready palette
of effects through which to explore the possibilities of light, whilst
water itself provides a reflective surface which even in his landscape
painting he exploited to full effect. The 'sublime' in its literary sense
of a confrontation with the savage grandeur of nature found ready
expression in Turner's sea pictures.[53]

Art historians have focused mostly on discussions of a Euro-American tradition of pictorial representation. Even Japanese works such as some of those by the print-maker Katsushika Hokusai or the evocative work on the seas by the contemporary photographer Sugimoto Hiroshi are rarely included in reviews of representations of the sea. Other forms of visualization associated with maritime practice, such as the Marshall Islands so-called 'stick charts' from Micronesia or pageants in various parts of the world which involve floats in the form of highly decorative ships, have escaped attention altogether and are not mentioned in any broader survey of the arts of the maritime world – a project which, in truth, has yet to be embraced in such inclusive terms.

The character of what follows, therefore, is promiscuous in terms of its sources and wide-ranging in terms of the seas and oceans it considers. It reflects on accounts which go beyond my own immediate areas of academic interest – in anthropology and latterly art history – and immediate experience in the Irish Sea and the western Indian Ocean. The purpose here is neither to repeat nor to attempt a detailed overview of the rich and varied literature on which the different disciplines draw. The questions it asks are of a more comparative kind dictated by the themes it addresses. These include such issues as: what the knowledge base of the sea might be in different cultures, and how it is acquired; how the conventional trade-based model of the interactions of mariners and land-based peoples is transformed by this refocusing; how seascapes are understood by those who derive their livelihood from them; conversely, what the conception of the land amongst mariners might be and the relation of seafarers to it; how ships become embodied social spaces or 'homes'; and finally, how the sea is configured on land and what the symbolic usages of the material culture of seafaring are in different cultures. To pursue its themes it certainly draws on archaeological and historical sources but it is also founded on the limited ethnographies of maritime peoples, on literature and on representations of the sea both in art and in more technological and functional contexts.

Each of the chapters tackles a different aspect of the subject of man's engagement with the sea: the extent to which they interconnect culturally (or not); the ways in which the seas are conceptualized;

ships and boats as social spaces; the ways in which the seas are navi
gated and related processes of enskilment; different practices i
visualizing the sea; beaches as sites of interaction and the topics c
language, gender and material culture in a maritime context. Finall
we move back onto land and consider the significance of ships in
terrestrial context looking at the link between ships and churche
and ship-burials. Conceived as a series of themed chapters they non
the less overlap and flow into one another – like the salt-water se
themselves.

Yet we cannot ignore the fact that seas themselves have differer
moods. Some have combinations of current and wind which mitiga
against sailing in open water and oblige 'coasting', moving slowly alor
the shoreline from the safety of one harbour to the next. In others th
conditions close to the coast are rough and being out of sight of lar
is the surer way to achieve longer voyages. Many have seasonal chang
obliging a 'closed' period each year when boats are laid up until mo:
favourable weather conditions resume. Navigation may often requi
a sight of the night sky and is hindered by persistently cloudy cond
tions; and many systems are most effective in facilitating east-west
west-east journeys and need to be adjusted to sail accurately in an
other direction. Similarly, the experience of the sea is fundamental
related to the kind of craft used to sail across it. Some are most effe
tive when sailing before the wind; some tack easily where others ca
only change direction by 'wearing', going round by sailing in long loop
The engagement with the maritime environment is as varied as th
with the land. Its understanding amongst contemporary comment
tors is further hampered by a number of modern developments whic
because we take them for granted, threaten to obscure the realities
many peoples' experience of the sea in pre-modern times. Two star
out: the first is the invention of the steamship. When steam was fir
introduced into the maritime world, it was regarded by many as th
devil's work. Where sail ships worked with nature and responded
its vicissitudes, by the mid-nineteenth century steam had allowed shi
to cut their course directly through the waves. The experience of th
sea was to change utterly. It was a Rousseau-esque moment when ma
relationship to elemental nature was irrevocably changed or, as son
regarded it, 'violated'.

If, then, one defining difference between the pre-modern an
the nineteenth- and twentieth-century experience of the sea is th

invention of steam and iron-clad shipping, a second, paradoxically, is the invention of flight, and latterly of satellite imagery. The sea seen from the air is a different place from the sea regarded at water level. Many mariners in the pre-modern world would not necessarily have had a concept of a unified sea for the simple reason that they did not experience it as a whole. There were no overhead views which encouraged it to be visualized in its entirety. In Europe, as we have remarked, portolan maps were simply that, sailing lines between ports, and even the most sophisticated, such as those in the famous Catalan Atlas of 1375, gave a fragmentary view of the coastline as a whole. The mariner's view in pre-modern times was strictly experiential, restricted to an image of waters and shorelines born of familiarity – to what the Romans knew as *mare nostrum*, our sea. We begin, therefore, by exploring the characteristics of different seas, what 'our sea' in its various guises was and is to those engaged with its challenges.

one

Different Seas?

Wind is full of this mystery. So, too, is the sea.
Like wind, it is composite in nature; under the waves of
water, which we can see, are waves of force, which we
cannot see. Its constituents are — everything. Of all the
jumbles of matter in the world the sea is the most
indivisible and the most profound.[1]
VICTOR HUGO, *The Toilers of the Sea* (1866)

Where our subject is not a particular sea or ocean but seas in gener
and the diverse human interactions which they have facilitated, a
immediate question arises: are the characteristics of different wate
really comparable? Is the experience of the sea the same thing to some
one born alongside a Mediterranean or Baltic seaway as it is to on
brought up, say, on the fringes of a lagoon in Micronesia? How are the
great 'Voyages of Discovery', celebrated in the seventeenth and eig
teenth centuries as achievements of European seafaring and maritim
know-how, to be placed beside the arguably comparable feats of the
Oceanic voyagers who explored and colonized remote islands an
atolls in the farthest Pacific well before Europeans were even aware
their existence?

I was brought up within the sight, sound and smell of two adjacen
salt-water areas. In one direction was the spectre of the cranes in the
Harland and Wolff shipyards, now sadly depleted in business, whe
the *Titanic* was built. This is Belfast Lough, where in the mid-twentie
century the sound of the hooters of passenger and cargo ships comin
and going up the estuary of the River Lagan was the backdrop to ever
day life. Modern shipping is more discreet and instead of stea
billowing from funnels sleek giants ferry cars and their occupants fro
Belfast to Stranraer in nearby Scotland, cruising smoothly down t
Lough several times a day, their passage slowed to a gentle pace to redu
the wash from their bows which would otherwise impact on the coas
line and its marine environment. Looking southwards was another se

Strangford Lough, where my father sailed a yacht of a type which, I have been told, was originally developed by local shipbuilders using offcuts from the shipyards themselves and is specific to that part of Northern Ireland: the so-called 'lightning' class. They are two contrasting interfaces between the land and the sea. Belfast Lough, though it had to be dredged to get the *Titanic* out in preparation for its ill-fated maiden voyage across the Atlantic, gives ready access to the deeper waters of the Irish Sea. Strangford Lough, by contrast, is a kind of miniature Mediterranean, being a partially enclosed sea with a strong tidal flow at the narrow straits where it meets the open seas beyond. Even in the 1950s and 1960s, the twin harbours of Strangford and Portaferry on either side of the tidal race were every bit as definitive of the range of our sailing experience as the Pillars of Hercules were to the Mediterranean sailors of antiquity. The Straits of Strangford Lough were our Straits of Gibraltar and we rarely penetrated beyond them. So strong are the currents here that the world's first commercial tide-stream turbine, the Seagen Turbine, has been successfully installed in Strangford narrows and is selling electricity to the national grid.

Different seas, different shipping – a different experience of the maritime world; yet the idea that different seas might have different histories is, at first sight, puzzling. After all, as a matter of straightforward hydrological fact all the seas of the world run into each other, at least all those composed of salt water. They are in that sense fundamentally connected, 'indivisible' in Victor Hugo's words. However, each sea does have its own characteristics; indeed depending on the breadth of perspective adopted each has its own combination of characteristics. If, as we have seen, a sea like the Mediterranean is conventionally regarded as one entity, its northern shores are very different physically and culturally from its southern coastline; the Adriatic on one side of the Italian peninsula is not the same as the Tyrrhenian on the other. The Black Sea, though from some points of view part of the same Mediterranean system, has its own historical and geographical pinch-point at Constantinople. This lent a particular distinctive configuration of religious and political issues even when the Byzantine Empire developed relations with first Venice and later Genoa.[2] This is not to argue deterministically; but it does show up the fact that maritime experience is variable. Coasting requires a very different set of skills and knowledge from sailing on the open oceans. It also requires a different kind of ship, one able to manoeuvre in shallow waters, to tack into the wind as readily as to run before it. Ships which work well in one kind of maritime context turn out to be deficient when transferred elsewhere; and it is not necessarily just a matter of technical characteristics – as the Romans found when taking their oared galleys into the Red Sea where water supplies were insufficient to support a large crew in searing temperatures. To provide the context for exploring the variability of maritime experience this chapter looks at the conditions which obtain in different seas and oceans.

The Mediterranean

The Straits of Gibraltar is a good place at which to begin a general account of the characteristics of different masses of water – and their interconnection. It is the choke point at which what from a cartographic point of view looks like an inland sea proves not to be. On one side are relatively calm and predictable waters; on the other, the Atlantic with its storms and crashing rollers, and the especially treacherous waters of the Bay of Biscay. The architectural implications of the promontories which 'guard' its entrance – the so-called Pillars of Hercules – express the classical idea of a magisterial gateway leading from an enclosed space to the dangers of the ocean wastes beyond. Controlling its narrow passage implied controlling all ingress and egress – hence the disputed history of the Rock of Gibraltar itself. Without the characteristics imposed by the Straits the iconic status of the Mediterranean as a bounded space would dissipate: there would be no 'Atlantic Mediterranean' or 'Mediterranean Atlantic', no 'Mediterranean of the North' (in other words, the Baltic),[3] 'transoceanic Mediterranean' (that is, the Caribbean)[4] or 'Japanese Mediterranean'.[5] The Pacific could not be conceived as an emerging version.[6] H. J. Mackinder could not refer to the Irish Sea as the 'British Mediterranean'.[7] Captain Vancouver would have been robbed of analogy in talking of the so-called Inside Passage along the north-west coast of the Americas as that 'expansive Mediterranean Sea'.[8] The metaphor even extends to deserts.[9] The habit of thinking in terms of the Mediterranean to express the idea of seas as contained – culturally rather than geographically (which plainly they are not) – is a pervasive trait in European writing, and not just because of the more recent influence of Braudel.

Yet, if the Straits of Gibraltar are a kind of portal, going in is much easier than coming out. One underlying reason for this is the difference in salinity between the Mediterranean and the Atlantic and the strength of the currents in the narrow Straits themselves. The water flowing into the Mediterranean from the Atlantic is lower in salt content than that in the Mediterranean itself. Here there are only three main river systems which introduce significant amounts of fresh water into the seas which comprise the Mediterranean basin: the Nile, the Po and the Rhône. With evaporation, salination in the Mediterranean is thus significantly increased from that which obtains in the Atlantic. The denser outflow from the Mediterranean therefore passes underneath the Atlantic waters coming in. Unlike an oceanic estuary where the tides effect a reversal in the direction of flow of the sea water, there is a relatively small tidal flow in the Mediterranean at Gibraltar and only in one direction. Julius Caesar's fleet was reportedly astonished by the tidal range they encountered along the coast of Britain. It is said that when they beached their ships in 55 BC it was beyond the high-tide line. However this was the period of neap tides. When the spring tides came some ships floated off and still others were damaged.[10] Pytheas of Massalia seems to have voyaged further north sometime before 320 BC and, according to Strabo, reported tidal ranges of up to 30 cubits (approximately 6 metres or 20 feet). This may be something of an exaggeration but tides of 3 metres (10 feet) do occur at the Isle of Wight, 6 metres at Dover and up to 9 metres (30 feet) at Liverpool, which compares with barely 90 cm (3 feet) at Gibraltar. Beyond the obvious points about the restrictions imposed by foreign political and naval control of the Straits, these physical characteristics also conspire to restrict shipping within the Mediterranean, or at least to render passing into the Atlantic problematic.

Once in the Mediterranean, the Atlantic waters move anti-clockwise, setting up currents which skirt the seas in that direction around the Mediterranean shores. Usually the direction of currents is aligned with the characteristic direction of the winds; if the predominant wind direction changes so too may the direction of the prevailing currents, as in the Indian Ocean. The Mediterranean is an exception. Here there are a complex series of local winds and indeed the Greek compass of antiquity was based on wind directions rather than the day or night sky. A number of these seasonal winds are well-known. The *mistral* blows into the Gulf of the Lion off the coast of southern France, whilst the *maestrale* blows into the Gulf of Genoa and passes over Corsica and Sardinia into the Tyrrhenian Sea off the western coast of Italy bringing strong westerly or north-westerly winds. In the northern Adriatic the *bora* blows down the length of Italy, where it is known as the *tramontana*, the name given to the rhumb line which forms the northerly direction of the Classical compass. As it moves into Sicily and Malta it becomes a north-easterly. The dominance of these and other northerly winds is compromised only by the *sirocco* which in the spring and autumn blows from the Saharan belt across the full length of the southern coastline of the Mediterranean. These hot, dust- and sand-ridden winds produce violent storms which render maritime activity particularly hazardous in these periods. Lighter sea and land breezes in the morning and the evening add to the local range of winds. However, despite local and seasonal variations, the predominant winds in the Mediterranean basin are those that blow from the north and the north-west – that is, in broadly the opposite direction to the characteristic movement of the currents. For completeness we should add that water gains from the Danube and the Russian rivers that enter the Black Sea set up strong and consistent currents which flow through the Bosphorus and Dardanelles into the Aegean supported by northerly winds.[11]

All this has important implications for the character of human engagement with the sea; and, since it is the experience of the Mediterranean which has coloured much writing about maritime cultures, its particularities are significant. Perhaps the most influential impact of climate and sea conditions from antiquity through until at least the early modern period is the encouragement it gives to practices of coasting rather than maritime expeditions across the open expanses of the Mediterranean. The easiest and longest journeys undertaken were those from north to south or from west to east. Here favourable winds sustained passages made from Marseilles out towards the Balearic islands or towards Sardinia; Genoa and Pisa down to Sicily and points in between was straightforward; Venice was in ready contact with the whole of the Adriatic, whilst Constantinople benefited from the Black Sea outflow and supporting winds to be in ready contact with Crete and on towards Cyprus. Routes were facilitated by access to some of the chain of islands lying especially off the northern coast – the Balearics, Sardinia, Corsica, Sicily, Corfu, the Greek islands and Malta. All had an important part to play in sustaining maritime trunk routes and their possession was critical to ensuring safe passage.

Whilst the northern Mediterranean was largely a Christian shore throughout the last millennium and the southern shores were largely Muslim, the activities of Spanish Moors and the changing fortunes of the Balearic islands in the western Mediterranean indicate the extent to which any generalization is immediately corrupted. In the seventh century, for instance, Muslim pirates operated there with impunity. In AD 707 the Balearics were taken by Tunisian forces and then in 789 Spanish Moors raided the islands. In the mid-ninth century they fell under the authority of the Umayyad caliphate of Córdoba, and by 902 they were again subject to further repression from Spanish Muslims. One way or another the islands were regarded as critical to sustaining Islamic influence over the western Mediterranean in these periods. In the eastern Mediterranean Crete occupied a parallel position to the Balearics in the west and likewise has a turbulent and diverse history, falling under Byzantine, Muslim and Christian control at different times. Even Athens, after all, came under a host of different sways. The Parthenon shifted between being a temple dedicated to the goddess Athena, through various incarnations as a Catholic cathedral; it was a mosque, a munitions store and a ruin before it finally emerged as a national symbol of the modern Greek state.[12] The generalized model of a Christian north and a Muslim south is flawed, which is in itself witness to the connectivity of the Mediterranean.

It is interesting that even for a lengthy expedition in medieval times, such as a diplomatic mission which set out in 1369 from Genoa destined for Alexandria (a journey of some 81 days), only one in three nights were spent at sea and most of these on the crossing from Rhodes to Egypt, the passage assisted by the wind behind. The first parts of the route down the Italian coast, round the foot of Italy, across to Corfu and thence via the Greek islands, were mainly achieved by port-hopping.[13] Journeys in the opposite directions, from south to north or from east to west, had the assistance of the currents, but not of the wind. In these cases it was even more essential to claw a route around the coast. In the fourteenth century the safest route from Alexandria back to northern Italy would, as it had been since antiquity, have been by way of the Levantine coast rather than straight across to Cyprus or Rhodes and onwards. A century later the Florentine galleys that traded with Egypt and the Lebanon went first to Alexandria and only subsequently to Beirut, following the logic of prevailing sea conditions. Oared galleys, of course, needed to be low in the water or to have portholes so that the oars could most effectively propel the vessel, bringing with it the dangers of being swamped in more exposed seas. To remain within reach of sheltered anchorage was by far the most advantageous strategy.

It is one indication of the predominance of coasting along Mediterranean shipping lanes that discussions of navigation are very largely couched in terms of the features of the land rather than the sea, the sun or the stars. Coastlines with distinctive promontories or high mountains behind – and preferably with islands and harbours to match – were the vital components of navigational knowledge, a strong contrast with, say, navigational practice in the Pacific. Thus, for instance, the strongly accented topography of the Balkan coast of the Adriatic made it the preferred route to or from Venice rather than the route along the Italian coast. It provided both landmarks by which to set a course and shelter should that prove necessary. The Greek islands and coast with high mountains in the interior provided prominent features by which to set course. Mount Ida on Crete was one such – at 2.4 km (8,000 feet), it is visible on a clear day at a distance of 161 km (100 miles).

Comparison with the coast of North Africa is revealing. Here the flatness of the coastline provides few ready natural features to guide shipping. At more important ports or prominent hazards artificial aids were sometimes constructed, such as the famous tower on Pharos island at the approaches to the Nile delta, which according to tradition was in effect an early form of lighthouse with flares lit on it to guide ships at night.[14] Otherwise the combination of northerly winds or the squally seasonal conditions produced by the *sirocco*, the presence of low reefs and shelves in many places and the lack of natural harbours or fresh water supplies conspire to make the southerly routes the least favourable to shipping. However, there is no inevitability about this. Clearly a great deal of shipping did pass along the southern routes. Those inveterate mariners of antiquity, the Phoenicians, controlled the central Mediterranean from their base in Carthage on the coast of what is now Tunisia as long ago as 814 BC according to most sources. At this port city with inlets from the sea the distinctive Punic culture developed, an urban elite with strong links to the sea and to the other

Phoenician settlements as far east as Tyre, in Sicily, Corsica, the Iberian coast and beyond the Mediterranean to Cadiz.[15] The documentation of shipping and navigational practice in European sources dealing with pilgrimage, crusading and the development of mercantile maritime traffic in general may be both more substantial and better known than that dealing with the Muslim shores of the southern Mediterranean; but that does not mean that places like Tripoli, Carthage/Tunis and Algiers – let alone Alexandria – were not busy ports from early times sustained in part by sea-going mercantile interests around the wider Mediterranean world. The Straits between Sicily and north Africa – well known during the Second World War as a dangerous area for shipping due to the presence of German U-boats – could also be controlled effectively from bases on the North African coast.

Nor was shipping irrevocably confined within the Mediterranean itself. The Phoenicians not only passed through the Pillars of Hercules to investigate the Atlantic beyond; they also explored the Red Sea and circumnavigated the whole of the African continent probably around 600 BC, that is two millennia before the feat was to be repeated. Around 425 BC Phoenician settlements seem to have been established somewhere around the mouth of the Senegal River with exploratory missions going beyond possibly as far as Mount Cameroon.[16] Likewise, whilst it is usually suggested that the sailing season in the past was limited to a shortish period between spring and autumn, when circumstances demanded some shipping did certainly brave the risks of Mediterranean storms, the fog and overcast skies which restricted the visibility of the coastlines. There could be advantages, militarily or commercially, in taking to the seas when others thought it more prudent to remain in port. Whilst some such voyages may have ended disastrously – as in the shipwreck which sets in motion the drama of Shakespeare's *Tempest* – advances in sailing technology and the safety net provided by the development of the mariner's compass had by the late medieval period decreased the risks. The Mediterranean was to all intents and purposes becoming more of an all-weather prospect.

The North Atlantic

Of all the oceans, the exploration of the Atlantic was the exclusive achievement of Europeans. True, indigenous occupants of the Americas explored the islands off the coasts of Central America and when Columbus arrived there it was already occupied by Carib peoples, now known generically as the Taino. However, native North and South Americans did not otherwise venture to explore the wider expanse of the oceans. The Phoenicians by contrast not only explored the African coastline, they also sailed northwards setting up settlements along the Atlantic coast of Iberia. However, the first named explorer of the waters of the northern Atlantic was the Mediterranean traveller Pytheas of Massalia, referred to above. That he kept a journal and published his observations in a work now lost is evidenced by the extensive references to him and the reports of his voyaging by other ancient authors. In the early fourth century BC he set sail either from the western Mediterranean in a Greek ship or possibly from a port in the Bay of Biscay having crossed by land and taken local vessels, as has been plausibly argued by Barry Cunliffe.[17] It is suggested that amongst his motivations was the possibility of tracing the importation of a valuable resource, tin, back to its origins in the mines of Cornwall. If so, he certainly took advantage of local knowledge and local craft to travel further, circumnavigating Britain and calculating its probable dimensions before exploring parts of the adjacent coast of western Europe. In addition, secondary quotation from his writings refers to a land of Thule which is said to have been six days journey from Britain by boat, a place with volcanic activity, frozen seas and darkness for half the year. It is also speculated that it may have referred to Norway. Yet whether Pytheas visited its coastlines, set foot on the island of Shetland or indeed Iceland (as some unequivocally suggest),[18] or whether he merely reported what others told him, remains uncertain. If Cunliffe is correct, his method would seem to have been to capitalize on the understanding of the seas by local mariners rather than exploring for himself and making his own 'discoveries' for the first time.[19] He may, indeed, not have been a mariner at all but a passenger taking advantage of existing coastal traffic. His observations on geography and astronomy are those of a scientific observer but not necessarily a mariner recording sailing directions for others to follow. In the various reports of his writing only those on tidal range seem to chime with a mariner's concerns.

If we set aside the possibility of Pytheas personally sailing north to the Arctic Circle, his experience of the sea was, in practice, largely that of coasting. The exploration of the open seas of the North Atlantic was largely undertaken at later periods by Irish monks and by the Norsemen. The journeys involved a northerly sailing direction from Ireland and a westerly one from Scandinavia. Since, for reasons that become clear in future chapters, latitude sailing is the predominant navigational direction in the northern hemisphere, the voyaging of the so-called *peregrine*, mariner-monks, from the coasts of Britain, was potentially the more complicated and hazardous. Some of this voyaging by the faithful seems not to have been motivated by informed navigational assessment of the likelihood of finding land and more by a sense of submitting to the will of God. Monks found washed up on the coast of Cornwall after drifting aimlessly at sea in their skin-covered currachs reportedly explained to King Alfred's court that they cared not where they would end up. Their intention was to seek solitude and the certainty of the life of eternal resurrection.[20] Whatever the ultimate fate of their souls, such objectives would, no doubt, have resulted in disaster and shipwreck more often than in the chance discovery of otherwise unknown and unsettled islands in the seas. But clearly many journeys by sea were informed by the practised arts of navigation without the attendant risks of throwing yourself at the mercy of the waves (or the Divine). During the monastic diaspora of the sixth to eight centuries, the remote places around the British coast where monastic settlements were established – Iona, Lindisfarne, Whithorn or most spectacular of all Skellig Michael off the coast of County Kerry in Ireland – would have been settled with similar religious intentions of self-sacrifice, but were evidently more motivated by acts of seamanship. Likewise the currents and winds would not, other than in exceptional circumstances, have conspired to wash aimless monkish mariners northwards to Shetland and the Faroe Islands around AD 700, let alone Iceland which was also colonized by Irish clerics.[21] For these longer voyages across the open oceans other methods suggest themselves.

Apart from the confirmations of direct archaeological evidence of ecclesiastical buildings in remote places, the principal source of information on the mariner-monks occurs in the *immrama*, the tales of voyages. Although many of these have something of a legendary quality to them – notably the 'Voyage of St Brendan', a hagiographic text much reproduced and popular through into medieval times – they nevertheless contain a number of useful navigational and technical observations. Firstly, the boats used for longer journeys seem to have been sea-going versions of the currach memorably described by the Irish playwright J. M. Synge as the boat which ferried him to and from the Aran Islands over a number of years in the late nineteenth century. The currach is a light skin-covered craft constructed around a wicker frame which is usually rowed in proximity to coastlines and whose survival until very recent times along the west coast of Ireland is witness to its manoeuvrability close to the most rugged of shores and in the turbulent seas of the western Atlantic. In modern times it has generally been made of canvas rather than hide and painted over with tar to make it seaworthy. Its lightness allows it to ride rollers which would swamp heavier vessels, so long as it remains pointed in the direction of the waves. Synge gives a vivid portrait of the process:

> Every instant the steersman whirled us round with a sudden stroke of his oar, the prow reared up and then fell into the next furrow with a crash, throwing up masses of spray. As it did so, the stern in its turn was thrown up, and both the steersman, who let go his oar and clung with both hands to the gunnel, and myself, were lifted high above the sea.
> The wave passed, we regained our course and rowed violently for a few yards, when the same manoeuvre had to be repeated.[22]

Further out to sea towering waves are encountered. Yet, although there is a great deal of bailing out, the buoyancy of the boat when kept straight into the line of the waves ensures safe passage. The boat described by Synge (and those still to be seen along the coast of Co Donegal in the 1950s and '60s) lacked sails but did have the keels and rudder which their basin-shaped cousin, the coracle, lacked.

The currachs in use in the so-called Age of the Saints would have been large seagoing ships capable of carrying routinely not just around twelve to fourteen monks, their belongings and ecclesiastical equipment, but also the means to sustain them on the challenging island niches they sought to colonize. We know these will have included livestock from the presence of sheep at abandoned Irish settlements rediscovered by the Vikings on the Faroes. The 'Voyage of St Brendan' talks of a sailing currach carrying a crew of seventeen with sufficient provisions for 40 days. In addition to a keel, the ships were also furnished with a central mast, a square-sail and rigging, all referred to in Adomnán's *Life of St Columba*. Evidently they also had iron anchors.

The *immrama* contain no definitive description of the discovery of the most northerly of the islands known to have been occupied by these pious Irish clerics. There is, however, a reference to a voyage made northwards by the monk Cormac ua Liatháin which, though apparently not resulting in successful landfall, does give an indication of the conditions under which such journeys might be undertaken. We learn that Cormac sailed for fourteen summer days and nights under full sail, thereby suggesting a southerly breeze and a preference for sailing with wind behind and at more clement times of the year. This was clearly preferable to, for instance, rowing against the wind or tacking, which as we have seen carried risks – even with a keel – of being swamped by waves hitting the vessel broadside. It is worth remarking that the idea of sailing with the wind is also entirely consistent with the theological imperative of submitting to God's will. Similarly, it has been suggested that the monks may have followed the annual migration of geese flying northwards in noisy flocks from winter breeding grounds in the Shannon estuary and round the northern coasts of Ireland towards their summer feeding grounds at the time of the spring equinox.[23] This too might be interpreted as another example of priests following divinely inspired signs to discover routes not just towards previously undiscovered lands, but into eternal life.

Cormac did not achieve these ambitions on this expedition. Whether he and his fellow voyagers were intending to visit some distant colony in a land already familiar to them, or whether this was a genuine voyage of discovery, we do not know. The texts suggest that Cormac only turned back when confronted by a large shoal of jellyfish – which was actually rather a minor hazard compared with the fearsome leviathans that were popularly understood to lurk in the oceanic depths. If, as described, the journey out might have had something of an opportunistic aspect to it, that back must have been more precisely calibrated. The chronicles of Irish adventuring indicate that navigation by celestial observation and attentiveness to signs such as portents of changing weather conditions, the sound of breaking waves or the flights of birds, were common. We hear of the importance of sailing on 'luminous nights'. There are also indications that professional pilots and experienced seamen were employed on these expeditions, though the disposition of responsibilities and authority within the vessel is not clear.

The successors of the Irish in the exploration and colonization of the northern Atlantic, the Vikings, came from a different direction. Their journeys of discovery were mostly against the prevailing westerly winds. This has seemed to some a hindrance to voyages of discovery as the distances covered and the speed of voyaging is so much reduced from that achieved when sailing before the wind. However, in practice journeys of exploration *de nuovo* make sense when undertaken in this direction. In the Pacific, as in the north Atlantic, it has seemed less hazardous to head into the wind in the surety of a swift and safe restoration to home base should circumstances require it. Sailing before the wind can only normally make sense when the destination is already known and perhaps when a reversion to more favourable conditions for a return journey can reliably be anticipated – as in the Indian Ocean with its seasonal monsoons. Once the Atlantic islands had been discovered no doubt Norse pilots would have taken advantage of the less frequent easterly or south-easterly breezes to hasten their journeys westwards.

However, it is a question whether or not the Vikings discovered first the Faroes and then Iceland, which they began to settle around AD 860, for themselves.[24] By the end of the eighth century the Vikings had already begun attacking the isolated monastic communities around the coast of Britain, especially in the north-east, from bases in the Shetlands and Orkney. By the mid-ninth century they had become established in Dublin and Cork and were exploring the west coast of Ireland and attacking the monasteries established there. Viking raids were also beginning along the English Channel coasts and were eventually to extend into the Mediterranean. Irish knowledge of the routes to the Faroes might have been readily available to the Vikings and from thence onwards to Iceland. It is reported that they found Irish monks there on their first voyages of reconnaissance; though, when Norse settlement began in earnest, the Irish were in the process of abandoning Iceland, leaving it as empty land ripe for Scandinavian settlement. Yet, even then, the Irish remained a part of the story since a large number participated in the re-colonization either as slaves or as concubines. This fact alone indicates that the Norse settlement was led by the aristocratic tier of society whose households contained people in servitude, and this is further endorsed by the evidence that they were mostly ship-owners themselves coming from chiefly families along the western seaboard of Norway.

Parts of the history are recounted in the *Landnámabók* ('The Book of Settlement'), an otherwise largely legendary account, known from the thirteenth century in various versions. This gives the sailing directions (by then, established) into the North Atlantic and tells us that the time of the voyage from the Norwegian coast to Iceland passing close to Shetland and the Faroes was seven days. There is an evident symmetry between the stories of settlement and various aspects of the saga as recounted. The method seems to have been one of surveying the distant islands, settling them and moving on to explore further into the Atlantic. The tripartite process is paralleled by the story of one of the first settlers of Iceland, Flóki Vilgerdason. It is recounted that he sailed with his three daughters and his livestock. His first port of call was in the Shetlands where his first daughter died. On reaching the Faroes his second daughter was given up in marriage, leaving him to go on to Iceland with his remaining daughter. Likewise he carried with him three ravens. Birds were often carried on ships as an additional navigational aid, being released in the hope that they might fly in the direction of otherwise unseen landfall. Noah himself had released the raven and the dove from the Ark to try and find shore. In this instance the first bird to be sent up flew back home, the second took flight but returned to the ship. Meanwhile the third flew off in the direction of Iceland, giving them confirmation of the bearing along which to sail.[25]

The trip westwards from Iceland is facilitated by the East Greenland current which passes northern Iceland to run down the south-eastern coast of Greenland itself, meeting the contrary Labrador current at the southern tip of the island. It was known to the Icelandic settlers from accounts of one Gunnbjorn Ulf-Krakason who was driven there by an unexpected north-easterly wind, assisted no doubt by the favourable current. However, the settlement was eventually undertaken by an outcast from Norwegian and then Icelandic society, Erik the Red, expelled twice by his fellow citizens for his murderous practices. He is said to have sailed with 25 ships filled with potential colonists in 982; apparently fourteen arrived, establishing a foundational community.

When the Atlantic was first crossed definitively is not recorded. From Greenland it is not an immense task to go onwards to Newfoundland. Within five years of the settlement of Greenland reports of another potential landfall further to the west were already in circulation. Leif Erikson, the son of Erik the Red, followed up the reported sighting as the new century dawned. The broad accuracy of the saga in which the story is retold was confirmed in the early 1960s when Columbus's priority in the discovery of the Americas was displaced by the excavation of what proved to be a Viking dwelling dating to the eleventh century at the northern tip of Newfoundland – the correct time frame for the reports of this first crossing of the Atlantic.

The contrast between Norse and Irish experience of the sea is striking. The Irish came from a different direction, as we have seen. They were motivated less by a desire to colonize or a thirst for fame and potential wealth than by the search for religious solitude; their ships were light but manipulable. The Vikings are known for the sleek vessels with high prows which ferried them swiftly on their voyages of conquest in the eastern sea lanes of the Atlantic. However, their westerly migrations appear to have been achieved in broader and heavier ships made of oak clinker-built with the planking held in place by iron rivets and caulked with animal hair and pitch. These ships were double-ended and steered with a rudder-pole on the starboard side. They were not oared boats but true sailing ships furnished with one square sail suspended from a T-shaped mast. Such ships were reportedly capable of carrying approximately 50 people, together with requisite livestock, provisions and the basics to start up a new settlement. Unlike the seas further south, the prevalence of climatic depressions even at the most propitious times for sailing allowed rainwater to be collected at sea. Indeed, the changing wind direction in the wake of passing rain-ladened low pressure systems allowed the recalibration of sailing directions if ships had been blown off-course by storms.

The reason for this exploration and settlement of distant islands was largely turmoil in Norway itself and the perceived need of those not in the ascendancy to find alternative bases beyond the immediate shores of Scandinavia – from which no doubt Viking raids on the Norwegian homelands could periodically be launched. For such voyages in these northerly latitudes, of course, navigation by the sky was a different proposition to that further south. The summer solstice with almost complete daylight is an advantage in terms of seeing where you are heading but it makes it difficult to navigate by the sun as it is not straightforward to tell the time of day. Likewise sailing by the stars is hindered by the fact that closer to the pole the circles of the stars are at an increasingly oblique angle to the horizon. The Great Bear in particular arced across the sky and was not the reliable navigational star it was regarded as being in the Mediterranean, for instance. The Pole Star was probably used as the more reliable guide.[26] Presumably sailing in the winter was not a realistic proposition.

Apart from the activity of seabirds, other indications of the proximity of land in the North Atlantic were provided by the prevalence of marine activity in the waters over the continental shelf which surrounds Iceland. The most obvious of these would have been whales attracted by the abundance of crill, herring and squid. It would have been relatively easy to pass directly to Greenland by charting a course to the south of Iceland with the assurance of all this to confirm latitude. The crossing to Greenland itself is barely 160 miles at the shortest point. Reports that in exceptionally clear weather both coasts could be visible at the same time do seem credible for there are high peaks especially in the direction of Greenland. Finally, cloud formations on the horizon can be read by experienced mariners, as the Norsemen undoubtedly were, as signs of land.

Along the North American coastline other phenomena obtain and became well known to later mariners. Perhaps the most significant is the Gulf Stream flowing north from the Caribbean before it fans out across the Atlantic to pass the northern coasts of the British Isles. Richard Dana, returning to Boston from California by way of Cape Horn in 1836, records his impressions:

> *Thursday, September 15th.* This morning the temperature and peculiar appearance of the water, the quantities of gulf-weed floating about, and a bank of clouds lying directly before us, showed that we were on the border of the Gulf Stream. This remarkable current, running north-east, nearly across the ocean, is almost constantly shrouded in clouds, and is the region of storms and heavy seas . . . At noon, the thermometer, which had been repeatedly lowered into the water, showed the temperature to be seventy; which was considerably above that of the air, – as is always the case in the centre of the Stream.[27]

The disproportionate warmth of the Caribbean currents has other effects. Where the Gulf Stream meets the Labrador Current to the south of Newfoundland the colder waters sink underneath.

This results in dense fog banks which straddle the approaches to the St Lawrence Seaway.

Into the South Atlantic

The central Atlantic explored by Columbus is a different proposition altogether.[28] Again, as with the progression from island to island which ultimately led to the settlement of Newfoundland, the discovery of islands was critical to wider ambitions. The real point of departure for the early Atlantic crossings was not Lisbon or Cadiz – or indeed Palos, the continental port from which Columbus originally set out – but the Canaries off the coast of north-west Africa; the real point of return was not the western Iberian shoreline but the Azores off the European coast at the same latitude. It was not just that the islands acted as staging posts. They both also benefited from winds favourable to the journeys being undertaken. At the latitude of the Canaries the north-east trades blow off the land and allow an Atlantic crossing to be effected with the wind behind. Further north, westerlies pick up blowing back from the northern Caribbean towards Europe. From the Canaries the winds take an outgoing ship reliably into the Caribbean at the other side of the ocean; the Azores provide a check on latitude as Europe is approached on the homeward journey by a more northerly route. Both, indeed, had already been of use in the exploitation of the African trade. The Canaries lay on the route south and were an obvious staging post off an arid coast. Interestingly all of Columbus's initial financial backers had interests in the Canaries, then under Castilian control.[29] It is less obvious, however, why the Azores should have been significant. After all, they lie some 700 miles off the coast of Europe and are in effect in mid-ocean. Yet it is here that mariners could pick up the westerlies and the confirmation of achieving the correct latitude that would bring them safely back to Portugal. Indeed their discovery in the first place is to be attributed to mariners sailing north and east in search of the westerlies they knew to blow onto the Iberian coast at the appropriate latitude.

These checks were important, for the evidence is that Columbus was not an especially gifted navigator. His ship carried a quadrant on its voyages, but it does not seem to have been used.[30] Like Arab mariners who, as we will see in a subsequent chapter, may have carried

compasses as much for ostentation or as a back-up as for any immediate practical use, Columbus relied more on the time-honoured
sensory methods of sailing than on any more scientific set of skills
or technologies. And, unlike Captain Cook or Captain Vancouver,
chosen in part for their voyages of exploration because of their abilities as surveyors, Columbus did not record his voyages on any precise
chart which could reliably aid subsequent exploration. Indeed, for
such reasons it remains a mystery where landfall was actually made on
12 October 1492. Columbus no doubt hoped he had hit upon some of
the outlying islands of the Japanese archipelago. His backers, and he
himself, were intent on finding a sea route to China. They knew
from Marco Polo's account that Japan lay off the Asian coast. Indeed
another reason why the Canaries was chosen for the Atlantic crossing
was that it was thought to lie on the line of latitude of Guangzhou,
identified as a major Chinese port. On successive voyages Columbus
tried to persuade himself and his crew that Cuba was indeed part of
continental Asia and the anticipation that he had stumbled upon a
maritime link to the riches of China, if only the best point of entry
could be found, was what kept the funds flowing in support of four
voyages of exploration. In truth, the native Caribs with whom he
returned, the examples of plants and the meagre amount of gold –
interesting and exotic as they were – gave scant enough encouragement. But now that the method of using the winds to aid successful
crossing of the ocean was known, it always seemed as if one more
voyage, one more act of discovery, would unlock the route to direct
trade with China.

Yet an Atlantic route to Asia round the African continent also
remained an alluring prospect. It was eventually to be discovered that
the key to the southern Atlantic and the rounding of Africa from
Europe was actually by way of Brazil, discovered in 1500 by Pedro
Alvares Cabral. By then, other routes had already been explored.
Bartolomeu Dias, technically the first (after the Phoenicians 2,000
years earlier, of course) to round the Cape, had done so by hugging
the African coast at first before heading out into the ocean in search
of the westerlies which, south of the equator, blow from beyond
the bulge of South America across the south Atlantic and round the
Cape of Good Hope. There he found the turbulent seas where the two
ocean systems meet, naming it the Cape of Storms, a discouraging
name subsequently dropped in favour of the less disparaging term by

which history was to know it, the Cape of Good Hope. Dias, of course, did not penetrate far into the Indian Ocean but turned back on encountering the adverse currents emerging from the Mozambique Channel, having made the first successful essay into the wind system of the Atlantic beyond the equator and peeked round the corner of the southernmost point of the African continent.

He had set out in the summer of 1487, several years before Columbus's pioneering voyage. Dias's achievement did not immediately attract eager imitators; however, one feature of his achievement stands out. Whereas most of the voyaging we have been discussing involved latitude sailing – and the available navigational methods encouraged it – Dias had foregone the common practice of hugging the coast on north–south journeys and set out into the open ocean. Unlike the Indian Ocean traversed by navigators whose home ports were within the monsoonal system, Dias had to find the winds which would facilitate a southerly passage with none of the fixed points of navigational reckoning familiar in the northern hemisphere and an unknown set of sea conditions.

History has treated his successor in the southern Atlantic, Vasco da Gama, rather better – at least, until recently. Another island group came into play – the Cape Verde Islands lying further south than the Canaries and at a latitude where the south-easterly and north-easterly trade winds converge. It is from here that Columbus set out on his third voyage, which took him to Trinidad, the most southerly part of the Caribbean that he was to visit in his decade of trans-Atlantic exploration. Da Gama's departure was almost exactly ten years after Dias's, in July 1497. On leaving the Cape Verde Islands da Gama set out into the open ocean and was to spend fully three months out of sight of land before sighting the coast off what is now Namibia. His square-rigged ships were intended to sail before the wind, taking advantage of the westerlies Dias had found in the South Atlantic to carry him round the Cape.

Vasco da Gama had shown that sailing west was the clue to ultimately arriving in the south. He may not have landed in South America but the triangular route which involved doubling across the Atlantic to reach the Cape had been established. With advice from da Gama, Cabral set out to capitalize on these observations. Leaving Lisbon in March 1500, Cabral had reached the Brazilian coast after just over six weeks sailing. Amerigo Vespucci extended the knowledge of the South American coast, naming the most propitious of its harbours Rio de Janeiro, probably in 1502. Whether these lands were merely large islands or continents was yet to be clear. Where China had gone, if this was not it (or at least its outlying islands) remained a puzzle in the early sixteenth century. If the earth was round and the estimates of latitude were even approximately correct then it should be possible to find it by these routes westwards. But how big the earth might be, and how long such a voyage might take, remained controversial – Columbus and subsequently Ferdinand Magellan both thought it was much smaller than it was and that Asia was always just beyond the horizon. That a whole other continental mass stretching from the polar regions of the north to the cold waters of the south blocked the way was yet to be realized.

Rio's historical development was in large measure due to its pivotal role in the trans-oceanic sea routes as they became established. Five or six weeks sailing time away from Iberia and possibly as little as a further four weeks to Cape Town were statistics that would be hard to better by any other route. Apart from the winds, which change direction to the south of the bulge of Brazil, so too the currents crossing the Atlantic divide when they hit the shoulder of South America. One part is deflected off to the south before it settles into circling round in the dead seas of the horse latitudes at about 30 degrees south. The other goes northwards reinforced by the outflow from the Amazon as it passes into the Caribbean where it circles, parts of it escaping past the Florida peninsula and joining the Gulf Stream up the coast of North America. If it facilitated journeys round the Cape of Good Hope, Rio also in due course provisioned ships heading for Cape Horn and the equally treacherous waters around Tierra del Fuego. Captain Cook, for instance, surveyed parts of the bay and the port when the *Endeavour* called there in 1768 en route to the Pacific Ocean, writing a more extensive account than his usual journal descriptions of its navigational intricacies and its fortifications – perhaps in part because Rio was by then a sovereign port and, despite Anglo-Portuguese treaties, not readily surveyed by ships sailing under foreign flags; perhaps, also, because the viceroy of Brazil was so suspicious of Cook's motives as to keep him under constant surveillance and others might, no doubt, need the benefit of what he could record if they, too, were restricted in what they could do.[31]

No one takes risks unnecessarily in moving with a royal family and their courtly entourage, even if it is to escape impending risks at home. When in 1807 the Portuguese royal family took to the seas to escape the Napoleonic threat in the Iberian peninsula it was across the Atlantic to Brazil that they relocated, establishing Rio de Janeiro as the *de facto* capital of the Portuguese empire. By then, however, the sailing directions had been established and the route to the South American coast had become entirely familiar.

The Red Sea and the Indian Ocean

The Red Sea was potentially amongst the most problematical of all for early mariners. It was here that one of the most notable of Arab navigators, Ahmad b. Mājid al-Najdī, to whom we return in a later chapter, honed his skills over a period of 40 years in the fifteenth century.[32] His grandfather had been trained in these waters, and so too his father who was known, he tells us,[33] as Rubbān al-Barrain, meaning 'Captain of two coasts'. The reference, presumably, was to his knowledge of both the African and Arabian shores of the Red Sea. His father was also the author of a poem of over 1,000 verses describing the intricacies of his various sea routes. Arguably, being adept at way-finding in the Red Sea was an excellent preparation for criss-crossing the Indian Ocean, which, if larger and with a much more intensely inhabited coastline in some areas, is in many ways a less challenging nautical proposition. To Ibn Mājid it was known as the Sea of Qulzum al-'Arab, and, because it was on the pilgrim route to Mecca, was of sufficient importance that he devoted a final chapter to its maritime lore in the *Fawā'id*, a compilation of texts otherwise focused on navigation in the Indian Ocean proper.[34]

The Red Sea was extremely hazardous for the unwary. Ibn Mājid gives a comprehensive listing of the shoals and reefs for the voyages he describes, concluding:

> The dangers of this sea are so numerous that they cannot be mentioned not even in a few individual cases. As for all the well-known places on this route which we have mentioned it is necessary to know them because the pilgrim finds them essential, especially the knowledge of which places are opposite each other [on the two sides of the Red Sea].[35]

The central part of the Red Sea has a deep narrow trough; but, on modern calculations, up to about 40 per cent is quite shallow with shelves and coral reefs to contend with. However, as a Muslim, Ibn Mājid ends on a more reassuring note, remarking that '[a] man can easily ask for divine help in all matters for he is always near the Ancient House [Mecca]'.[36] Ibn Mājid's experience coincided with later European opinion, João de Castro remarking in 1541 that 'the sea presents more hazards to navigation than the whole of the great ocean [presumably the Indian Ocean].'[37]

Ibn Mājid's remark about needing to know which places are opposite each other on the African and Arabian coasts is revealing. We have already seen that the simplest way of navigating is mainly by sailing north or south until the known latitude of a distant port is reached and then to sail along it in an easterly or westerly direction. In the northern hemisphere this is achieved by observing the altitude of the Pole Star and sailing so it is at a constant height above the horizon of the night sky. In open oceanic waters this is readily achieved because east-to-west or west-to-east passages can usually be achieved without encountering any hindrances in the form of reefs or islands. Unlike the Red Sea, there is no maze of shallows to be negotiated requiring changes of course and direction. The Red Sea is aligned north-west to south-east and acts as a funnel for the winds which blow consistently from the north-west, except around the Gulf of Aden and adjacent areas where it is less predictable. Variable local winds in July and August and again in January and February blow off the coast of Sudan; however, they are not a significant influence on the Arabian side. With the additional complications of negotiating shoals these factors add a whole new tier of difficulty to navigating in the Red Sea.

Like the Mediterranean, the Red Sea is also an area of higher salinity than the seas to which it is connected. This is caused by the lack of significant rainfall in the surrounding area and of any resulting river systems which might introduce significant amounts of fresh water into the seas. As evaporation is very high, the effect is to raise salinity to some of the highest anywhere in the world. Like the Straits of Gibraltar, the Straits of Bab el Mandeb – those at the mouth of the Red Sea – are particularly treacherous; the saline water sinks beneath the incoming seas, making it easier to enter, in terms of tidal currents, than to leave. Added to this wind direction is far from favourable.

The north winds (the so-called *Shamāl*) which characterize the more northerly parts of the Red Sea only extend to the area of the southern straits during a brief period between May and September. At that time, and despite counter currents, it is possible to sail out into the Arabian Sea beyond. For the rest of the year, however, conditions favour sailing in rather than out. Trading missions, then, needed to be carefully calibrated to link up with the monsoonal system in the Indian Ocean and the Arabian Sea which, as we shall see, imposed a closed and an open season for sailing.[38] As for Mediterranean sailors entering the Atlantic, tides are another factor to be negotiated by those leaving the Red Sea. In the Red Sea itself the tides range between 60 and 90 cm (two and three feet) and in the central parts are virtually negligible. The coastlines beyond experience quite different tidal conditions.

None of this is insuperable, of course, and there were many notable explorations of the Red Sea and beyond in antiquity, often undertaken by mariners whose home waters were in the Mediterranean. The Ancient Egyptians are known to have sent expeditions into the Red Sea in the middle of the second millennium BC as witnessed by a funerary painting associated with the female pharaoh Queen Hatshepsut which depicts such a maritime expedition. Their goal was to establish commercial relations with the fabled land of Punt, source of incense, ivory and other exotic goods. It has never been authoritatively identified, but modern-day Eritrea and Somalia are the prime candidates. The Egyptians are known to have established a settlement on the Red Sea coast to facilitate the incipient trade with the peoples at the end of their known world.[39] The Persians explored it in the reign of Darius I looking to connect his Empire to the Indus valley civilizations by sea, and then the Greeks sought to supplant Persian merchants when Alexander the Great sent naval expeditions down the Red Sea to open up a route to the Arabian Gulf and the western shores of India. A Greek document dated to the first century AD, the 'Periplus of the Erythraean Sea',[40] is replete with detailed information on the navigation and trading opportunities in the Red Sea, the Arabian Sea, the Persian Gulf and down the east coast of Africa to Rhapta, a coastal town possibly in the area of modern-day Dar es Salaam. A periplus was a kind of handbook compiled for the owner of a merchant ship and this example seems, like Ibn Mājid's works, to draw on a wealth of other sources. Thus, what to some scholars have seemed to be detailed observations based on first-hand experience is supplemented by information on the Indian coastline and the southern parts of the East African coast which is derived from other merchants' accounts.[41] However that may be, it does at least confirm the crucial role of a knowledge of the navigational idiosyncrasies of the Red Sea in linking up the Eastern Mediterranean with Arabia and thence to India and beyond. A canal linking the Red Sea to the Nile was opened up in antiquity and this was refurbished by Ptolemy II in the third century BC.

With the reign of Augustus at the beginning of the Christian era Roman interest in the Red Sea as a route to India was ignited. The Emperor Trajan reopened the older canal and extended it with a new port, Clysma, growing up at the Red Sea end and linked to the site of old Cairo and to Alexandria. Apart from navigational issues, the other initial problem confronting Roman vessels in the Red Sea was, of course, the lack of drinking water. Whilst this is an issue for all mariners in the Red Sea, it was especially pertinent in the case of Roman galleys whose oarsmen were both more numerous than the crews on sailed ships and also obliged to expend a great deal more energy in some of the most demanding of climates. The Romans were, however, eventually able to maintain a fleet in the Red Sea, partly to give protection against pirates who were active especially in the northern parts of the region. Thereby Graeco-Roman trade flourished with the Greeks sailing to Sri Lanka and up into the Bay of Bengal by the second century AD. This only came to an end when in the third century the Roman currency depreciated and, as the economy went into decline, the route was further impaired by the development of the Christian kingdom centred on Axum in northern Ethiopia with access to the Red Sea at Adulis in modern Eritrea.

Although an awkward proposition for the navigator, the Red Sea is the critical corridor which links the cultures and activities of the Mediterranean with the Indian Ocean. However, if the passage out of the Red Sea is seasonal, so too are the sea conditions beyond. The monsoonal system in the Indian Ocean is the mechanism which supported the development of Arab-Swahili culture, which permitted Chinese fleets to explore the East African coast and Indonesian pirates to extend their regime of pillage as far as Madagascar in the first millennium AD. The presence on the East African coast in pre-modern times of seamen originating from the Far East and South East Asia suggests that the vast distances involved in sailing the Indian Ocean were not an insurmountable barrier to direct contact. Across an empty ocean it is fully 4,000 miles from the Indonesian islands to the East African coast. The presence of people who speak a language, Malagasy, to which the nearest cognates are languages spoken in Borneo and nearby areas remains a puzzle; yet it is at least witness to long-distant contacts and influences. The occupation of Madagascar may have been late in the process, probably only in the second half of the first millennium AD, but the evidence of similar dispersed populations right round the Indian Ocean in antiquity is legion. Mesopotamia was in contact with the Indus valley civilizations 5,000 years ago; the Romans were in contact with India 2,000 years ago. There were Armenians originating from Persia right round the littoral, though whether they are to be definitively identified with the 'shirazi' of oral tradition, who in eastern Africa are said to have preceded the development of Islamic trading populations along the coast, is perhaps doubtful. There were significant Jewish populations in western India; Arabs traded up as far as China whilst pockets of Hindu settlement extend round the Indian Ocean.

With such extensive networks from early times it is not surprising that a Braudelian model of the Indian Ocean as an integrated unity has emerged. It is already foreshadowed in the archaeological reflections of Neville Chittick who wrote of the Indian Ocean as 'arguably the largest cultural continuum in the world during the first millennium and a half CE',[42] that is before the Portuguese first sailed round the Cape and began to move up the African coast, ultimately striking out for India itself. What is distinctive is the presence of maritime populations who, though they may have significant links inland, subsist very largely along the coasts. One highly suggestive piece of evidence – which would have been entirely familiar to Chittick, a prominent coastal archaeologist – is the fact that there were no mosques along the East African coast situated more than a mile inland until the nineteenth century when South Asian settlers colonized further in. The Omani sultanate, when it moved its capital southwards in 1837, established itself on the island of Nguja, the largest of the Zanzibari islands. Apart from Chittick, other archaeologists have used suggestive images to suggest this system of integrated coastal cultures. Paul Sinclair has invoked the idea of a trading wheel;[43] Mark Horton has deployed an explicitly Mediterranean analogy in talking of *mare nostrum*.[44] Among historians K. N. Chaudhuri has owned to an explicit debt to Braudel in his writings on the Indian Ocean.[45]

What makes this model of an integrated oceanic system viable is the underlying system of winds with its consequences for the pattern of currents. This is already extensively described.[46] A north-easterly monsoonal wind begins in November each year blowing from the Arabian Sea in the direction of the African coast, enabling a voyage to, say, Mogadishu or Mombasa to be effected in about four weeks under sail. However, storms afflict the Arabian waters in October and November, so the optimum time to set out on such a passage effectively begins in December. By April journeys in this direction should have been completed because the system begins to break up and the winds conveniently reverse direction, blowing from the south-west from May until September. Again stormy conditions prevail in the period of June and July so that journeys should be planned either in May or later into August. Currents follow the switches in the direction of the wind. A similar monsoonal pattern obtains in the Bay of Bengal off the eastern side of India. The ships which plied their trade between the ports of the Arabian Sea and those along the East African coast were typically equipped to run before the wind but less able to tack into it. Their effectiveness was therefore adapted to the conditions of these parts of the Indian Ocean but would be less so outside of the monsoonal waters in which they operated.

The idea of an enclosed sea on the model of the Mediterranean would seem to be impaired by the lack of a southern limit. However, in effect this boundary is established not by land but by the winds and currents. The monsoonal system extends southwards to approximately the latitude of Cape Delgado on the coast of northern Mozambique, or of northern Madagascar. At this latitude south-east trade winds take over, until – to the south of Madagascar – the so-called Roaring Forties, strong westerly winds, are encountered, which the Dutch were to exploit to effect a rapid transit from the Cape to their territories in the Dutch East Indies. Arab ships seem never to have explored this far south. They knew of Madagascar but further south and especially into the Atlantic was a world of 'darkness'. No doubt part of the answer to the question posed in the Preface – why the large landmass of Madagascar was not colonized until late in human history – is related to its position: it stretches for over 1,000 kilometres in a north-south direction between these two wind systems, both lying at or beyond the southern limit of conventional Arab shipping routes given the characteristics of the boats in use. Instead, the south-western reaches of the Indian Ocean were explored rather by European mariners coming round the Cape from a southerly direction.

Once ships rounded the Cape, however, progress from a southerly direction was frustratingly slow with contrary winds and currents. Bartolomeu Dias, as we have seen, turned back in the face of the difficulties. Vasco da Gama penetrated further. He succeeded in passing through the Mozambique Channel to reach at least the site of Mombasa on what is now the Kenyan coast. Beyond that, he relied on locally retained pilots to help him find his way up the coast to the north of Mombasa and thence directly across the Indian Ocean to Calicut in south-west India. But the impact of da Gama's 'eruption' – as European history, encouraged by da Gama's own account, would portray it – into the Indian Ocean with its lucrative trading system is now regarded as of minimal significance locally.[47] From the point of view of Arab-Swahili history, let alone that of the merchants deriving from the Indian subcontinent, the Portuguese intrusion into their world was hardly of major significance. Fort Jesus, overlooking the entrance to the old port at Mombasa, survives as a testament to the Portuguese presence in this part of the Western Indian Ocean. Its interior walls, preserved by the Kenyan museum authorities, show wistful images of ships drawn by the would-be colonists and record the sense of isolation of the Portuguese seamen garrisoned here. Yet there were probably no more than 30 here at any one time and – local skirmishes notwithstanding – the disruption to the wider Indian Ocean trading wheel was relatively minor.

The Pacific

In moving from the Atlantic onwards to the vastness of the Pacific we are following the routes of the first mariners to circumnavigate the world. Notable amongst these was the small fleet assembled by Ferdinand Magellan for such an ambitious voyage. The whole enterprise, however, was far from an unrivalled success. In the event only one of Magellan's ships limped home to Spain in 1522 – and it did so without him after Magellan himself had been killed in a conflict in the

Philippines. However, much of the exploration of the Pacific had already been undertaken by others well before Magellan's day, albeit unseen and otherwise undocumented. What are recorded are only the voyages of exploration mounted from Europe. Yet we can reconstruct something of what was achieved in pre-European times and in particular by the Polynesians. Polynesian mythology and oral history consistently identify ancestral voyaging as being from other islands than those they currently occupy rather than suggesting they have always been there or still less that they originated on continental shores. Despite Thor Heyerdahl's alternative theories, it is generally accepted that the Polynesians had arrived at the most remote island of all – Rapa Nui (Easter Island), off the coast of Chile – by about AD 400, having sailed there across the Pacific rather than setting out from the coast of South America. Hawaii was in an equally inaccessible and isolated place but had been reached by AD 500. New Zealand and the Chatham Islands took a little longer since they were only approached from the north and sea conditions tended to favour east–west or west–east voyaging rather than north–south. None the less they were both settled by the end of the first millennium. The Polynesians did not maintain regular contact across all the islands they settled; but they did have the means to set out on long-distance voyaging on a regular basis – voyages which have seemed incomprehensible to those not aware of the sophistication of indigenous knowledge of the seas in which they lived.[48] This more than compensated for the apparently simple maritime technologies involved: outrigger canoes and none of the familiar technical equipment whether in the form of charts or other navigational devices.

The underlying pattern of currents and winds in the Pacific duplicates that in the Atlantic and the Indian Oceans. In other words, the area around the equator is a continuation of the doldrums which, famously, can becalm sailors for weeks on end. South-east trade winds blow in the southern hemisphere and north-east trades in the northern hemisphere originating in the horse latitudes lying at 30 degrees south or north. As in the Atlantic the most reliable winds are the trade winds closest to the equator, with the stormiest being those in higher latitudes. However, the intervention of landmasses produces different results in the two ocean systems. In the Pacific one of the most significant effects is the result of the landmass of Australia and New Guinea and of the continental shores of South East Asia. On the familiar principle that the directions of the current broadly follow that of the winds, the basic current direction across the Pacific within the tropics is from east to west. These may vary locally in both strength and direction as water streams round intervening islands. When the seas meet the larger landmasses they tend to funnel back rather than being split, as happens when the Atlantic currents hit the bulge of South America. Thus in the Pacific they reverse and stream back along the line of calmer winds at the equator itself. This sets up a west to east equatorial current. North of here the wind and currents turn along the coasts of Japan and China and circulate in a clockwise direction passing across the North Pacific and down the coast of North America to form the Californian current moving southwards before turning out to sea again at about 30 degrees north. South of the equator is a mirror image with the currents circulating in an anti-clockwise direction from Australia across to the South American coast where it moves northwards as the Humboldt and the Peru Currents turning out to sea again at around 30 degrees south. Further local variation is introduced by the monsoonal system whose effects are not restricted to the Indian Ocean. They reach as far south as northern Australia, affect South East Asia and the waters up round the rim of the northern Pacific, with the characteristic reversals of direction between the summer and winter and complex effects on the underlying pattern of currents. There are also the effects of El Niño and La Niña, periodic fluctuations in the temperature of the waters in the eastern Pacific with its effects on the global climate but especially in the waters off the coast of South America where turbulent weather makes voyaging all but impossible.

The seasonal variations, the local currents set up by islands and reefs and the less perceptible oceanic currents, were all known to local Polynesian mariners. The effects of the presence of land were evident even when land itself was not in view. As we will see in a later chapter, sailing directions in terms of the rising of different stars were memorized and adjustments made to account for the strength and variability of wind directions and currents. Even in overcast conditions the 'feel' of the canoe and the close observation of the sea and the skies ensured a successful outcome. Indeed the use of the past tense is barely justified since until very recently such practised navigational skills were extensively in use and passed on from generation to generation.

Much of this is at odds with practice elsewhere. Coasting, the characteristic navigational procedure of European mariners along both the Atlantic seaboard and in the northern Mediterranean in the pre-modern period, is of little relevance in a sea studded with islands, many well out of sight of each other. The sea connected islands rather than separating them – a fundamental difference between European and Pacific perceptions of the maritime world. When Western explorers ventured into the Pacific in the sixteenth century their ambitions, by contrast, were, as they had been for Columbus, to find new routes to known lands. The islands that they encountered were stumbled upon; they were important especially as a potential source of fresh water and for any other resources they might have, but the fundamental purpose of the voyaging was not their 'discovery' as such.

Once established in the Pacific, however, understanding the wind systems became a priority. The Spanish with their bases in South and Central America had particular interests in comprehending how things worked. There had not been any historical connections across the North Pacific – no Chinese voyages to the eastern coasts of the Americas, as there had been across the much greater distances to eastern Africa. Yet despite the remarkable success of Zheng He's Chinese fleet in mastering the monsoonal wind system and undertaking journeys over vast distances, internal considerations brought a halt to such maritime ambitions. The shipyards whose skills and capacity had supported the potential to establish a seaborne empire were reduced to supporting voyages to neighbouring islands, notwithstanding the marvels with which the fleets of the early fifteenth century returned: spices, hardwoods, herbs and medicines and, most sensational of all, a giraffe. Japanese mariners were more restricted in their operations. Their boatbuilders, however, were unable to sustain the ambitions once entertained by the Chinese state. Japanese mariners had considerable difficulty in breaking out of the system of contrary winds and currents which make the waters around the Japanese archipelago especially treacherous.

The first circumnavigation of the North Pacific seems, therefore, to have been that by the ships commanded by an Augustinian priest and mariner Fray Andrés de Urdaneta, setting out in 1564. The problem had been that whilst a route across the ocean in lower latitudes had been achieved sailing westwards, the return passage to Spain's American possessions in Peru and Mexico had proved impossible.

Urdaneta cracked the system by heading north from the Philippines on the summer monsoon to pick up the North Pacific currents flowing eastwards again, allowing him to sail down the coast of California to make port at Acapulco. In due course the Dutch, coming round the Cape of Good Hope rather than Cape Horn, worked out the system in the southern oceans, crossing to Australia and finding routes to the East Indies which avoided the voyage across from Mombasa to India – the route originally shown to Vasco da Gama, and where competition with the Portuguese, let alone Arab and Indian shipping interests, would be unwelcome.

The most complete account of the wider Pacific, however, was the work of one man – Captain James Cook, whose three voyages in the late eighteenth century took him both to the Antarctic and up the north-west coast of America to the Arctic Circle. He visited more islands than anyone had done before in Polynesia and Melanesia, charted the east coast of Australia and made the first detailed survey of the complete coastline of New Zealand's two main islands. Most of these routes from Europe into the Pacific favoured the passage round the Cape of Good Hope and different nationalities tended to stick to the sea lanes they knew. Their stimulus was largely to engage in profitable trade rather than either the lure of acts of discovery or that more nebulous Enlightenment inspiration, 'curiosity'. Captain Cook was an exception. After all, when he set out on his initial voyage in 1768 he was not sailing south and into the Pacific to find any new routes by which to tap into the wealth of Asia. He sailed first to Rio, then passed round the tip of South America – the less favoured route – and into the southern latitudes of the Pacific. He was there ostensibly to observe a transit of Venus from the vantage point of Tahiti. This was a real enough objective: if Venus could be observed from several different locations it might be possible to work out the distances between the earth and Venus and between Venus and the sun, giving for the first time a measurement of the earth's relationship to its parent star. George III himself helped fund Cook's expedition on the basis of this possibility and Cook was accompanied by a scientific team led by a passionate and wealthy young natural scientist, Joseph Banks. However there was also another, albeit less overt, purpose assigned to the voyage: to settle the issue of whether a southern continent, which had become established in European consciousness as a tenacious myth, really existed. His instructions ran:

You are to proceed southward in order to make discovery of the continent above mentioned until you arrive at the latitude of 40°, unless you sooner fall in with it. But, not having discovered it or any evident signs of it in that run, you are to proceed in search of it westward . . . until you discover it, or fall in with the eastern side of the land discovered by Tasman and now called New Zealand.[49]

Recording the passage of Venus was a serious project; but Plan B was more than just a nice add-on. It had national and international significance. The possibility of discovering 'Terra Australis' had already attracted other expeditions in the earlier years of the 1760s with this same secret mission – those by John Byron and by Samuel Wallis, the latter having 'discovered' Tahiti, but not much else. Both were also instructed not to leave it there but also to seek for another fabled geographical phenomenon right at the other end of the world: the North West Passage that would once and for all establish a link between the North Pacific and the North Atlantic, making the great trips down the Atlantic and round one or other of the Capes redundant. Neither Byron's nor Wallis's voyages made any serious progress on that front. Cook was to pursue and finally lay to rest both myths in the course of his three voyages, though the naval authorities still hung onto the dream of a North West Passage and sent George Vancouver to test Cook's conclusion that there was no way through. Cook's voyages were undertaken in 1768–71 aboard the *Endeavour*, and in 1772–5 and 1776 aboard the *Resolution*. His ill-fated third expedition ended with him being battered to death at Kealakekua Bay on Hawaii in February 1779, in circumstances we return to discuss below.

In terms of the exploration of the Pacific, Cook's first expedition, after the astronomical questions that brought him to Tahiti had been addressed, was southwards to try and settle the matter of the missing continent. The *Endeavour* sailed further south than anyone had so far gone, however Cook was obliged by tempestuous weather to reset his course west and north again. Thereby he made landfall at New Zealand which, though identified before, had not been surveyed and was still thought to be possibly of continental dimensions. A thorough survey conducted over six months confirmed that what had been found were two islands of similar dimensions to Britain. That issue solved, there was also the question of whether New Holland (Australia) and

New Guinea formed one landmass or whether they were separated by Straits. The result was a survey of the coast of eastern Australia, near-disaster on the Great Barrier Reef, and the identification of the Torres Strait. A Polynesian navigator, Tupaia (whose involvement with Cook's first voyage is explored in chapter Three), joined the *Endeavour* and helped locate over 70 islands in Polynesia – but still no southern continent.

The second voyage took up the challenge once again. The *Resolution* went in the reverse direction to the *Endeavour*, by way of the Cape of Good Hope. Cook had come to the conclusion that it was more expeditious to round the treacherous waters of southern Africa with the wind behind and to take advantage of the Roaring Forties to traverse the Indian Ocean at higher latitudes. From the Cape, however, he first went directly south venturing far into the Antarctic Circle, skirting the line of pack ice and running the gauntlet of the icebergs. Crisscrossing the area as close to the ice floes as was safe produced no new discoveries; but this did not prevent Cook from striking out once again for the Antarctic the following year, this time from New Zealand. Negative evidence may not have been welcome but at least the matter of 'Terra Australis' had been resolved. If it did exist it was in the polar region and neither viable for settlement nor possessed of riches that would repay exploitation. He wrote:

> the greatest part of this Southern Continent (supposing there is one) must lay within the Polar Circle, where the sea is so pestered with ice, that the land is thereby inaccessible. The risk one runs in exploring a coast in these unknown and icy seas, is so very great, that I can be bold to say, that no man will ever venture farther than I have done and that the lands which must lie to the South will never be explored.[50]

That issue settled, the third voyage turned to tackle the remaining question of the fabled North West Passage. Round the Cape of Good Hope once again, and across to New Zealand for a third time, Cook struck out north by way of Tonga, Tahiti and found Hawaii, seemingly the first European to do so (though the discovery that the Hawaiians had some iron tools was – and remains – a puzzle). He ultimately made landfall at Nootka Sound on Victoria Island and began his survey of the coastline northwards along the coast of Alaska and through the Bering Straits. When ice caused him to turn back he had penetrated as far as 70 degrees north, just short of the latitude he had already reached in his exploration of the fringes of the Antarctic. Another ghost had, in his eyes at least, been laid to rest: there was no North West Passage. This, of course, gave even more significance to all the careful charting and surveying he had undertaken across the length and breadth of the Pacific, for it would continue to be necessary to travel round one or other of the Capes to maintain the links which had now been firmly established between the Atlantic and the Pacific. Accurate maps were essential.

Cook had said he wished to travel as far as it was possible for man to go and with his ventures into the Arctic Circle from the North Pacific he could be said to have achieved that ambition. His demise, just over four months later, robbed him of what would certainly have been a hero's homecoming. Cook was the very embodiment of late eighteenth-century virtues: intensely curious, thorough, obsessively interested in accurate measurement and documentation and with an irrepressible determination to encompass the vastness of the seas. Where Diderot sought to comprise human knowledge with his encyclopaedia or Chambers to document the English language with his dictionary, Cook's geographical and hydrological ambitions were equally large, literally global. His voyaging, too, was a quintessential Enlightenment project.

Captain Cook or his descendants, together with Joseph Banks, donated much of their collections to different museums, especially in Britain. The British Museum was also a product of the eighteenth century and saw itself as a repository of cultural achievements worldwide and across time. Banks himself became a Trustee of the British Museum and was instrumental in setting up the so-called 'South Seas Room' in Bloomsbury, which rapidly became the most popular and visited of the displays of world cultures through the first half of the nineteenth century – the Parthenon marbles and the Egyptian collections notwithstanding.

The Changing Experience of the Sea

It will be argued below that with the production of accurate maps, the mariner's relationship to the sea changed irrevocably. Navigation

by sensory means alone, or by the senses informed by simple instrumentation, was to become less essential to successful way-finding. Seas,
which in the days of sail and of purely observational techniques of
navigation could be portrayed as 'different' in terms of their characteristics and the demands made on ship technology and skills,
were all to be rendered as much more similar than they once seemed.
Knowledge of the currents and the winds would continue to be significant in terms of the speed of progress and the amount of drift;
stormy conditions were always to be avoided; watchfulness was still an
unavoidable duty of seamen – but now less to remark variations in the
behaviour of the sea or the clouds as to anticipate the dangers posed
by other vessels as the shipping lanes filled up with traffic.

The introduction of the magnetic compass placed the navigator
at a significant remove from the environment, whose close observation had until then been the method of engagement which allowed
complex acts of way-finding to be effected. A compass course, in the
words of Jonathan Raban,

> is a hypothesis. It has length but no width. It can't be seen or
> felt . . . It cannot even be steered. The autopilot on my boat
> leaves a cleaner, straighter wake than I can manage, yet it keeps
> 'on course' – as I do – only by making continuous mistakes.[51]

This revolution in the experience of the sea is one for which
Polynesian, let alone other, mariners using observational methods were
unprepared, nor was it to be one to which they were readily converted.
Its implications were devastating – it threatened to

> render obsolete a great body of inherited, instinctual know-
> ledge, and rendered the sea itself – in fair weather, at least
> – as a void, empty space to be traversed by a numbered
> rhumb line.[52]

The compass and later iron shipping had the effect of rendering all
seas the same. Yet, in practice, the Polynesian navigator traversing the
Pacific in a dugout canoe with a simple sail and a float attached on one
side was not sailing on the same sea as Captain Cook and his ships.

However, beyond these technical means – or better, in parallel
with their development – the extent to which seas and oceans have

acted as integrated historical and geographical units has also influenced the ways in which the waters flow into each other in a cultural and commercial sense. This in its turn is dependent on the extent of interaction between the local and the regional or global – and, indeed, whether this is characterized by genuine exchanges or simply down-the-line transmission. However that may be, arguably the distinctiveness of individual seas was significantly changed at the moment when sixteenth-century European mariners set out on their extensive voyages of 'discovery'. From the early modern period globalization effectively had already brought into question the separateness of different bodies of water.

two

Concepts of the Sea

> *The sea, in fact, is that state of barbaric vagueness and disor-*
> *der out of which civilization has emerged and into which,*
> *unless saved by the effort of gods and men, it is always liable*
> *to relapse. It is so little of a friendly symbol that the first*
> *thing which the author of the Book of Revelation notices*
> *in his vision of the new heaven and earth at the end of time*
> *is that 'there was no more sea.'*
> W. H. AUDEN, *The Enchafèd Flood* (1951)[1]

> *'Oceania' connotes a sea of islands with their inhabitants.*
> *The world of our ancestors was a large sea full of places to*
> *explore, to make their homes in, to breed generations of sea-*
> *farers like themselves. People in this environment were at*
> *home in the sea.*
> EPELI HAUʻOFI, 'Our Sea of Islands' (1993)[2]

In English the phrase 'all at sea' carries with it the sense that someone is completely and utterly lost. This is the sea as wilderness, as a place without paths or distinctive marks. Once in its midst, the fear of becoming irretrievably disoriented is inescapable. Auden clearly had such a conception in mind when writing *The Enchafèd Flood*. A few pages on from the passage quoted above he continues:

> The sea is no place to be if you can help it, and to try to
> cross it betrays a rashness bordering on hubris, at which
> a man's friends should be properly concerned.[3]

Similar ideas obtain elsewhere. Amongst the maritime Bajau Laut of the Philippines, for instance, to be lost is not a matter of being at sea but of being at sea 'without sightings' – that is, with the landmarks used to thread a route through a complex of island archipelagos and reefs, or used to identify the correct location of fishing grounds, being obscured. If that happens, a fisherman will retrace his route as best he can until he regains a sight of familiar features prominent on the land and fixes his position anew. Spirit mediums talk of being in trance as like being 'without sightings'.[4]

In Fiji, by contrast, the student magazine of the University of the South Pacific at Suva is called *Wansolwara*, a Pidgin term which translates as 'one ocean, one people'.[5] Elsewhere in Oceania, a Torres Strait elder is quoted as remarking: 'I am part of the sea and the sea is part of me when I am on it.'[6] Nonie Sharp, who recorded the comment, interprets it as meaning that 'his sensibilities are shaped by the salt waters to which he belongs so that he and his kin themselves become the salt waters speaking.'[7] The Pacific scholar Epeli Hau'ofa made a similar point that, rather than just being an objective physical resource to be exploited, the sea has ontological implications for many of those who live near it and trace their ancestry to voyages made across it. The ocean, he said, is 'in us':

> That the sea is as real as you and I, that it shapes the
> character of this planet, that it is a major source of our
> sustenance, that it is something that we all share in
> common wherever we are in Oceania, are all statements
> of fact. But above the level of everyday experience, the
> sea is our pathway to each other and to everyone else,
> the sea is our endless saga, the sea is our most powerful
> metaphor, the ocean in us.[8]

He himself was a good example of this conception of the sea as an integrative cosmopolitan medium: born in Tonga, he was brought up in Papua New Guinea and spent much of his professional life at university in Fiji. Such ideas of an ocean which connects and has been the means of ancestral voyaging have led to the formulation of a concept not just of seascapes (in contradistinction to landscapes) but of 'spirit-scapes', notably for maritime groups of Australian Aborigines living in northern Queensland and for Torres Strait islanders.[9] The experience of Coleridge's Ancient Mariner, who famously despairs of his predicament – 'Alone, alone, all alone / Alone on a wide, wide sea!' – is far from replicated by truly maritime peoples elsewhere. The conception of a sea that is energized, motivated and inhabited by spirit entities lessens any dimension of loneliness and isolation. In an

Aboriginal context, a 'saltwater person' can, in Ian McNiven's words, 'never be alone while out at sea'.[10]

Here, then, are two alternative cultural views of the sea: one which constructs it as an unwelcome and unwelcoming wilderness where the land is a reassuring point of reference; the other which sees it as entirely familiar and unthreatening. These are, however, only characterizations of two extremes. Arguably there are no completely maritime cultures any more than there are completely terrestrial ones. Sea-going peoples cannot sustain themselves without access to the resources of the land. Even the so-called 'sea gypsies' of South East Asia, who live entirely on salt water to the extent of even raising their houses up on stilts in estuaries if not actually living on boats, need fresh water and agricultural products to sustain them.[11] Likewise places remote from the shoreline may none the less use maritime products, even in prehistoric times. The currency of Central Africa in pre-colonial times was cowrie shells from the Indian Ocean; even in the High Andes Inca used shells and other products from the Pacific coast in burials at the peaks of the highest mountains.[12] It is clearly inappropriate to draw up any thorough-going distinction between maritime and terrestrial domains, and those who have studied the maritime world have largely been reluctant to do so.

Furthermore, even island communities can hardly be characterized as having a uniform approach to the sea. Auden is far from speaking for the whole of Britain. Conceptions are multiple. Thus, although Britain was to turn its attentions to the command of the oceans,[13] in eleventh-century England it was common for the leading men of the kingdom, whether they were bishops or aristocrats, to serve for a period at sea. They were described as 'steersmen', which referred at once to their role as leading statesmen and also to their literal role at the helm of ships at sea. Likewise the means of procuring an army or a fleet at the time was by conscription for service at sea, known as 'ship-soke', a system whereby landowners were obliged to provide men for the navy. When the land forces were on manoeuvre they would often march close to the shore and would be supplied from the sea. The same officer would take command of both the land army and the parallel fleet offshore.[14] Little had changed by the mid-seventeenth century. Naval affairs were still seen in a distinctly land-based context. Cromwell's New Model Army was distrustful of the navy which they regarded as a regrettable necessity. Thus, as they commissioned new ships they gave them the names of their successful civil war battles on land. The *Naseby* even had as a figurehead the image of Oliver Cromwell mounted on his horse. Likewise the fleet was commanded not by an admiral but by a general, or rather by three colonels who together fulfilled the role.[15]

Whilst an element of generalization is unavoidable in a book which takes a comparative approach, even the two extremes sketched out here are only characterizations of particular attitudes or tropes which may be found in any culture. These medieval and Cromwellian attitudes to seafaring are thus only moments in the history of Britain's engagement with the sea, and in any case coastal fishing communities would have held different views. It is also an interesting contrast with those Tanimbar islanders near Papua New Guinea discussed in our final chapter who conceptualize and, in a reversal of the New Model Army's approach, even construct their village in terms of a ship and adopt maritime titles and roles as the model of their social organization.[16]

We have here one conceptualization which constructs the sea in terms of the land and another which constructs the land in terms of the sea; and both may be found side by side. If the preponderance of northern hemisphere academic discussion has been one-sided, the practice of 'coasting' which we have noted as dominating maritime experience of the Mediterranean (and to some extent the North Atlantic and the Baltic) throughout much of history would seem to be at the root of the issue. In a sense, the land was not just a navigational reference point but a conceptual one. It is suggested here that there is a case for positive discrimination which is located in the nature of the maritime experience rather than representations of it which draw on terrestrial expectation. One way this is pursued is through an attention to the sea itself and how people engage with it technologically and socially, which are explored in the next two chapters. Another way is to take the discussion beyond the immediate sphere of the European experience of the sea. Before the days of steam and diesel, before ocean liners and sophisticated technical developments in cartography and navigational equipment, sea voyages of comparatively large range were routinely undertaken in some of the world's oceans with no sophisticated technological aids, yet with no unassailable sense of the precariousness of the journeying either – and in some cases they still are. The sea was neither unknown nor unknowable. It may have been regarded as the habitat of Rainbow Serpents off the coasts of north-east

Australia, or of Komogwa, familiar of killer whales off the islands of western Canada; but these were not capricious leviathans which limited seagoing or rendered it a seemingly reckless enterprise.

Several distinctive propositions immediately suggest themselves. These monsters of the deep might need to be propitiated but they do not constitute a barrier. Taking to the seas not only provides food, it connects people up. The seas are a resource and a pathway. Being at sea is normal. Although it encourages specialized skills and accords appropriate status to those who prove most adept, it is not necessarily an exclusive profession or a career: in many places it is what everyone does, at least if they are male. The distinction between 'coasting' and taking to the open seas which some societies have seemed to character-ize as somewhere between a necessary evil and outright foolhardiness – or between the merely courageous and the positively heroic – means less in such circumstances. In a sea of islands, like that settled by the Polynesians, the land is the limiting factor, not the waters. The same goes for heavily forested continental shores, such as those occupied by the Kwakwa or the Tlingit on the north-west coast of the Americas. Inland is the impenetrable space, the site of wilderness.

A comparative approach is essential to any wider exploration of the complex range of relationships between the sea and the land, the land and the sea. We begin this chapter not with the complexities of European attitudes to the seas but in the southern oceans, starting off the coast of north-eastern Australia.

The ancestral sea

The fundamental Aboriginal understanding of landscape as a creative outcome of the Dreaming or the Dreamtime is now widely familiar, not least from Bruce Chatwin's sympathetic popular account in his book *The Songlines* (1987).[17] Less obvious is how this mythical formulation of origins pertains to the sea and the islands off the coasts of Australia. Yet the same broad principles apply. Seascapes are also spiritscapes because they too are imbued with equivalent qualities of empowered ancestral energy which animate ideas of the land. Beyond that, indeed, identifiable features of the seas – reefs, shoals, sandbanks or islands, the tides and currents, even seawater itself, together with notable sea creatures – are understood to have been created in ancestral times and to retain their sentient characteristics. The creation of sea channels separating the mainland from the offshore islands is attributed an ancestral origin – an interesting maritime inversion of Moses' act in parting the waters of the Red Sea to create a terrestrial route. Ancestral journeys similar to those familiar on land are also plotted at sea and the sites are linked up as part of a network of seaways that may incorporate 50 or more identifiable places of ancestral significance in the sea routes traversed by Aboriginal mariners and Torres Strait islanders. Indeed, the Goemulag who live on the small island of Mabuiag reportedly enumerate up to 100 named places across 600 square kilometres of sea.[18]

But this is no passive description of seamarks. The sea is charged with continuing ancestral force which is linked both to mythic beings and to Aboriginal people who have died and become 'old people'. Their spirits are said to reside in certain remote islands, real and mythical, and in caves. Islanders off the coast of Arnhem Land identify shallow submerged seabeds as islands of the dead. Three rocks off the end of Mornington Island are cited as the bodies of ancestors who first came to the area. Sometimes it is asserted that pregnancy is the result of a spirit child entering the body of a woman. Amongst coastal peoples, these spirit children have their own particular known locations in the sea and these are often marked by submerged rocks or other features. Likewise maritime conditions and sea creatures are attributed ancestral significance. Mabuiag islanders associate waterspouts with the voyages of 'ghost' people hunting dugongs and turtles.[19] Off the Gulf of Carpentaria waterspouts, cyclones and rainbows alike are all linked to the mythical Rainbow Serpent. In the Torres Strait strong offshore currents which discourage outsiders from invading are said to have been put in place by an ancestral warrior, whilst on the Kimberley Coast of north-west Australia the tidal flow is associated with the actions of a large seawater snake.[20] The sea is thereby suffused with spiritual vigour. It is not an undifferentiated space; it is not emptied of cultural reference, but is replete with it.

There is, however, ambiguity in the Aboriginal experience of the sea for it is not wholly benign either in conception or in practice. It has, therefore, to be placated – or rather, the spiritual forces which animate it have to be. This may take the form of a propitiatory act at a specific maritime site with particular mythological significance or perhaps on a particular body of sea. Typically, it is cigarettes (often lit) together with food which are thrown overboard, though fatty meat is usually avoided as it may attract the attentions of the Rainbow Serpent which is otherwise better left alone beneath the waves.[21] On the coast itself inter-tidal areas or the high-water mark are significant in-between places which may contain ritual sites. On land, not far from the tide mark, are sites containing stones, bones and shells – some at least of which are interpreted as representing metamorphized sea creatures which have become stranded on land after being washed up in an exceptional tide. At such sites in northern Australia and the Torres Strait, the various sea creatures are invoked to make them plentiful; natural conditions such as favourable winds may also be solicited.

One implication of the attribution of ancestral significance to seascapes is that the sea is in a sense conceived of as being 'owned'. In effect, of course, the territorial integrity associated with the land has now been legally extended to the sea. The *United Nations Convention on the Law of the Sea*[22] has granted island territoriality where before none formally existed leading, as Hau'ofa bemoans,[23] to the potential for division where before there was unity. It might seem that it is now underwater rather than on its surface that independent autonomy exists. As Captain Nemo, Commander of the submarine *Nautilus* in *Twenty Thousand Leagues under the Sea* (1869), remarks:

> The sea does not belong to despots. On its surface immoral rights can still be claimed, men can fight each other, devour each other, and carry out all the earth's atrocities. But thirty feet below the surface their power ceases, their influence fades, their authority disappears. Ah, sir; live, live in the heart of the sea! Independence is only possible here! Here I recognize no master! Here I am free![24]

Yet Aboriginal conception had already established a territoriality in the seas off the coasts of northern Australia – including, especially, its underwater features. The association of ancestral spirits with sea-marks is a form of 'title deed'. In indigenous terms it is to all intents and purposes 'owned' in the same way as land is 'owned'. In that sense Aboriginal people assert indigenous rights over it, notably in relation to rocks and reefs which act as tidal fish traps. In one instance, among some islanders in the Torres Strait, rights were asserted over European ships wrecked on reefs regarded as their territorial possessions.[25]

The sea will provide

Like Aboriginals, the inhabitants of Madagascar have a strong attachment to the ancestral significance of land. But, unlike Aboriginals, they do not extend these ideas into the cultural construction of the waters round their shores. Indeed, despite the maritime context of successive waves of colonization which led to the occupation of the island, very few Malagasy today make any claims to a maritime heritage. As described by Rita Astuti, the Vezo of western Madagascar (one of Madagascar's few 'maritime' peoples) must be amongst the most frustrating people for any historically inclined researcher to work amongst for they appear to live for the moment to a remarkable degree.[26] They are distinctive amongst the peoples of Madagascar in the lack of attention they seem to pay to ancestral practice and precedent. For the Vezo, speculation about the past is quite simply pointless. In relation to the origins of canoe technology, for instance, clearly some skills are inherited, for canoes need to be re-commissioned every couple of years. Yet any longer narratives about how people learnt the requisite techniques or selected the right trees to cut down to make a canoe are not deemed relevant. Astuti could find only one person who could offer any explanation and that proved a short and unremarkable account.[27] Canoe building techniques were invented once and, if knowledge of how to do it died out for some reason, it would simply be invented again. So what? And if the past is not especially an issue, then neither is the future – it too can look after itself.

This approach is in large part contingent upon the Vezo relationship to and conception of the sea. The sea provides succour on a daily basis. The Vezo see it as full of fish and assume it will always be so. All that they have to do is wade out and throw a net in the sea if they lack for a meal, or, in a more organized way, go out in canoes in the morning and return in the evening with the catch. Even so, fishing expeditions are only decided on the day, for much depends on the likely sea conditions. If something goes wrong and there is no catch it is only that the shoals have moved somewhere else temporarily; but their numbers are held to be inexhaustible so any blips in provision are only a passing inconvenience. The contrast is with agricultural practice where forethought is essential as crops have to be planted out in the right season, tended whilst they grow and only harvested after a lapse of months. They then need to be stored in a granary and new plantings put in train. There is a rhythm and cycle to agricultural practice which is lacking in the world of fishing when supplies are plentiful. If the Vezo approach to fishing has a contemporary, terrestrial equivalent it is perhaps more like shoplifting than anything else, with some of the same thrill (presumably) but without the threat of attendant legal process.[28]

The peoples of Madagascar preserve little or no account of how they came to settle the island, either when or indeed from which direction – unlike, for instance, Pacific islanders who retain detailed oral accounts of the process going back many generations. The Malagasy are almost entirely cattle pastoralists and/or rice cultivators and the Vezo are amongst the few populations in Madagascar who pursue their livelihood by exploiting the resources of the sea. Yet their cultural amnesia about the maritime past of Madagascar is already evident in the vocabulary Vezo use about the sea: they talk about something being in the sea as being 'behind one's back' (*amboho*). The reference is to the canoe as it returns to the shore.[29] The coast is conceived as a point of return more readily than as a point of departure. The emphasis is on what is brought back or harvested from the sea, on the passage home with a catch, hopefully, on board. Despite rumours which I heard of in southern Madagascar that Vezo or related peoples in the west of the island had historical contact with seagoing peoples in Mozambique, Astuti could find no confirmation of this in her work carried out a few years later. Being in the open sea is described as being 'in the middle', being surrounded by the sea with no view of the shoreline. It is not a situation Vezo welcome. Certainly their practice would seem to be to go out and come back on the same day. Offshore fishing, rather than longer-distance activities such as trade, is the main purpose of taking to the sea.

The sea is regarded as having a specific character in its own right. Whilst it is often benign, offering up its resources without question, it can also be fickle. It is like a *vazaha* (a white man), quick-tempered and irascible, given to unpredictable moods. Yet, it is as it is. Vezo do not seek to win over the sea; they do not regard it as 'ancestral' space in the way that most Malagasy regard the land. One indication of this is that it attracts relatively few taboos (*fady* or, in Vezo, *faly*). The land is pitted with places connected with the Vazimba, the first occupants of the land now unidentified and unknown, where merely walking inadvertently over an unseen grave will attract retribution in the form of illness or misfortune. Even relatively mundane activities have their more and less auspicious aspects which need to be respected. Market days and days when work should not happen are specified. These may vary from village to village and even single individuals may have predispositions which need to be rigorously observed or, if transgressed, mitigated by ritual. The taboos associated with the sea are not of the same order as those affecting work on the land. They themselves recognize that, in contrast to other Malagasy peoples, their customs are 'easy'.[30] Indeed, by comparison, they are very limited in number. The Vezo consider sea-turtles to attract *faly*, though in this case it has to do with how they are caught and cut up and who should have which parts. Otherwise it comes down to not drawing attention to unusual creatures – whales, sharks or giant octopus – by pointing at them. Taking an unusual interest in them might cause the wind and waves to get up and endanger the canoe. Neither are the seas off the coast of Madagascar regarded as the haunt of imaginary sea monsters. The most dangerous sea creature is a form of mermaid whose wiles would be displayed on the outrigger of the canoe. Her maritime origins were only perceptible in the gills which lay hidden under her armpits. A fisherman who took up with her would have the reward of exceptional catches; however, it would be a short-lived boon for inevitably he would one day look at her gills and she would disappear off again beneath the waves in a rage. Taking an undue inquisitive interest in the usual things of the sea is again inappropriate.

The Vezo approach to the sea is thus apparently much less angst-ridden than that of many other seafarers, but then they do not have to go long distances to harvest the resources of the sea, and can even do so from the beach. There is no sense that their activities will in any significant way deplete the resources of the sea – though Astuti reports a developing contemporary local concern with the impact of international trawling activity further off the coast. Yet their relaxed live-for-the-day attitude does, even so, act to forge a distinction between being at sea and being on land. 'Vezo-ness' involves practising the skills of seamanship. When other terrestrial skills are practised, someone ceases to be Vezo. When they return to take up the skills of the sea they resume 'Vezo-ness'. None of this is surprising, perhaps. For Malagasy the distinction between land and sea is as fundamental as that between the sexes. The wonder is not that the Vezo make a distinction between the forms of enskilment appropriate to the maritime and terrestrial worlds, but that they do not make more of them. We return to discuss this point in chapter Five.

A 'Great Wave' in a tranquil sea

Whether or not the seascape is endowed with ancestral significance, the idea that the sea is an extension of island or continental territoriality has widespread significance. In a British context, Robert Louis Stevenson wrote in the high Victorian era:

> The sea is our approach and bulwark; it has been the scene of our greatest triumphs and dangers; and we are accustomed in lyrical strains to claim it as our own . . . We should consider ourselves unworthy of our descent if we did not share the arrogance of our progenitors and please ourselves with the pretension that the sea is English.[31]

Of course, Stevenson himself was Scottish.

There is at present a similar ongoing debate which has developed around Korean suggestions that the Sea of Japan should be renamed the East Sea. The Japanese Ministry of Foreign Affairs has mounted a campaign with videos on the internet to prove that the name 'Sea of Japan' has been current at least since the seventeenth century and is not a product of Japanese imperial ambitions in the twentieth century. Rather like the British Isles, the Japanese sense of their national security is related to their ability to control the sea around the shores of their archipelago. Likewise, in 2010 the Iranian Transport Minister threatened to ban all aircraft from its airspace unless they used the term 'Persian Gulf' on their in-flight monitors in preference to the term Arabian Gulf.

We have seen that in the Ming Dynasty the extensive voyages of exploration and discovery by Chinese navigators through the Pacific and into the Indian Ocean were curtailed. When the Qing rulers established their sway in the mid-seventeenth century there was further retrenchment and the agenda of the Dynasty centred more on securing China's existing borders than extending them through maritime adventuring. In the early modern period the seas around Japan too were conceived in strongly territorial terms – indeed Tokugawa period

(1603–1868) maps adopt an unvarying state- or archipelago-centred perspective. Even so foundational a map as 'Dai Nihon kair'' ('Map of the Sea Routes of Great Japan'), which was published in 1842, describes and documents what were crowded seas carrying goods round the archipelago without resort to any description of passages that required a pilot to chart a course beyond the sight of land. It is essentially a topographical map of the coast focusing on notable features of the land to describe sailing routes which are little different from roads in terms of their legibility. The map also includes textual information placed at the appropriate point on the chart to identify currents or tidal runs which might otherwise impair their reliability.[32]

What, conceptually, does this cartography express? The message of the map and others of the period like it would seem to be that to all intents and purposes the oceans could be ignored. 'Sightings' were sufficient to navigate everywhere that Japanese shipping and seafarers needed to go. The Tokugawa period is conventionally portrayed as an era when Japan closed its shores to foreign influence. Whilst it may be an oversimplification to say that it shut up shop completely, this was certainly a time when external contact was strongly regulated. International trade had earlier been encouraged with up to 350 Japanese ships licensed to sail to South East Asia in the early seventeenth century. As a result, significant Japanese communities developed at trading ports in the Philippines, Thailand and Cochin. However, the Tokugawa Shogunate was to impose a ban on the building of larger ocean-going ships. Indeed, anyone voyaging beyond Japanese waters was barred from returning home. International shipping was likewise discouraged. Dutch, American and Russian ambitions to open up trade and missionary activity with Japan were effectively restricted and Deshima, a man-made island in the bay of Nagasaki, was the place where such influence was corralled and neutralized. Christian missionaries were expelled. Despite a long-standing engagement with the sea and an elaborate culinary practice in relation to the preparation of its products for human consumption, to speak of Japan as a maritime nation in this period is questionable. It would be truer to say that Japan took the deliberate decision *not* to be a maritime nation. As a result their sailing skills diminished, though the Japanese had in any case relied on Chinese or Korean navigators even before the suspension of their ocean-going ambitions. A critic of Tokugawa policy, Honda Toshiaki (1744–1821), satirized the existing level of Japanese seamanship in the late eighteenth century when faced with the difficult waters of the northern Pacific:

> Even when the weather improves, the crew are at a loss to tell in which direction to head, and the ship floats about helplessly. As a last resort they cut off their hair and make vows to Buddha and the gods. Then they take out pieces of paper on which have been written the names of the twelve directions, roll them up into balls, and put them into a basket with a hole in its lid . . . They grasp the basket in their hands and strike the lid. Then when one of the pellets jumps out, they pick it up, their eyes blinded by tears of joy, and cry that it is the direction vouchsafed by Buddha and the gods. They then set course by it, and go completely astray.[33]

What is described is a Japanese version of the Irish monks' submission to God's will in their maritime exploits, but without a supporting level of nautical know-how. A loss of sailing knowledge from these already inexpert levels was potentially irreversible because of the treacherous sea conditions around Japan itself. In winter storm conditions might take ships off across the ocean in the direction of South East Asia. In summer, typhoon winds move in the opposite direction towards Kamchatka and the Aleutian islands. And, beyond those problems, a permanent strong current runs from the Japanese archipelago eastwards into the open waters of the North Pacific. Rebuilding the experience necessary to overcome these treacherous conditions was itself a substantial challenge to subsequent expansionist policies.

As a result the seas beyond the coastal horizon were uncharted, populated with icons of the imagination – not just the threats of foreign trading or colonizing interests, but an array of real and fabled peoples said to occupy distant islands lying just beyond the fringes of the knowable world. Some of these would seem to have been versions of European mythologizing – such as the 'Long-Legs' said to inhabit the southernmost points of South America, which corresponds with a report going back to the days of Magellan of a tribe of giants said to inhabit Tierra del Fuego. These were the Patagones (or Patagonians), which means 'big feet' rather than 'long legs' – anatomically different references perhaps, but with the same underlying idea. Others derive more obviously from the Japanese imaginary, such as 'Onna no shima', an island occupied by female deities.[34] None of these beings, interestingly, are said to reside in the sea itself, which is simply an intervening no-go area effectively separating Japan from distant lands. The nearest islands of the archipelago were knowable, cultivated and civilized; the rest were mysterious and, for all practical purposes, confined in glorious isolation. As Yonemoto aptly remarks, 'Japan has always been *in* but not *of* the Pacific.'[35] The ocean, we might say, has been 'in others' rather than 'in us'.

This is not to assert that in the Tokugawa era Japan was immune to the moods of the sea, for all that Japanese of the period associated aesthetic pleasure with the land, notably the conical shape, snow-capped peak and sheer scale of Mount Fuji whose many seasonal colours and states are reflected in numerous prints.[36] As an image of eternity for the Japanese it eclipses any image of the ever-rolling sea of Christian hymnology. Contemplative scenes of tranquil waters have their place. Many of Katsushika Hokusai's images in his series *Thirty-six Views of Mount Fuji* issued and expanded over a period of years from 1830 portray calm seas or lakes mirroring the beauty of the surrounding landscape. Likewise modern images of misty tranquil seascapes by the Japanese photographer Sugimoto Hiroshi are classic reflective depictions of placid seas (illus. 4).[37] But it is, of course, the calmness of a limited area of visible sea with a hazy horizon which is characteristically pictured rather than the boundlessness or turmoil of the ocean. Where they are illustrated in nineteenth-century Japanese maps, boats are shown not in the midst of tumultuous seas but drifting quietly on calm blue waters within reach of the coastline – and thereby safe.

The most iconic of all Japanese artworks, Hokusai's *Under the Wave off Kanagawa* or simply *The Great Wave* (*c.* 1829–33) therefore stands out as a break with the pictorial practices of the past by an innovative print-maker.[38] It is not, however, unique within Hokusai's corpus of works. Hokusai was to explore the image of waves in many different contexts: as a design motif for use in architectural settings, with warriors emerging from the froth, with rabbits leaping over them, with ghosts lingering over waves where ships had foundered and with ships riding the waves – or, more often, threatened by a surge of water. What is distinctive of *The Great Wave* is that it is a rare example of an image in which the viewpoint is actually from the sea. It is almost entirely a maritime scene. We know that it is staged well out to sea

4 Sugimoto Hiroshi, *Sea of Japan, Hokkaido 1*, 1986, photograph.

because Mount Fuji – the focus of the series in which the print appears – is the only landmark in the picture and then only in the distance in the trough of the wave, small as a pimple. It is at once a reassuring landmark visible from afar and a guarantor of national and territorial integrity; yet it is at the same time portrayed in the image as itself subject to the threat of being overwhelmed. The wave is in the open sea but it appears to be rushing towards the coastline off the main island of Honshu. It moves from left to right across the picture but since Japanese is read from the right literate viewers read themselves into the wave, as it were, enhancing its menace. Viewers feel themselves participant in the fragility of the ship and the emotions of its crew and passengers, the sleek craft put to the test by a tumultuous wave capable of obliterating it with its crashing intensity (illus. 5).

It was a picture of its moment. Whilst at one level the image seems to be about the fragility of human life before the forces of nature, about Buddhist notions of transience and eternity, it is notable that the threat is one coming from outside, from across the seas. Thus, in the context of the times the threats to the exclusionist policies of Japan would seem to be another clear reference in the work. Mount Fuji stands in the distance stable and unchanging, yet threatened. What is

5 Katsushika Hokusai, *Under the Wave off Kanagawa*, 1830, colour woodblock print.

at stake at another level is Japan's territorial integrity. Concerns over the rising tide of Western influence were reaching a crescendo. What cartographic practice had sought to portray as the periphery was about to come crashing onto the shores of the Japanese islands and the seas were the medium by which such external threats were conveyed. The sea itself, therefore, came to express the intimidation from afar which was beginning to cause isolationist Tokugawa policies to creak.

Hokusai's use of maritime imagery to encapsulate Japanese fears of coming turmoil is a neat reversal of William Daniell's epic journey round the whole expanse of the coastline of Britain, first begun in 1813 and which took over a decade to complete. The result was an eight-volume documentation of the British shores, comprising over 300 illustrations, some from offshore, others on beaches and headlands (illus. 6). As the threat of the Napoleonic wars waned this compendium was also of its moment, offering – in that case – a kind of reassurance that Britain's territorial integrity was yet intact.

Ironically, Hokusai was in a sense colluding in the subtle advance of Western interests. A Dutch influence on Hokusai's work has been much discussed and certainly there were Dutch prints in circulation in Japan in the early nineteenth century which would have included marine scenes, a Dutch speciality. Direct evidence for the speculation is hard to identify, but the fact that the ships in the pictures are

6 William Daniells, *The Worm's Head in Tenby Bay*, 1814, lithograph.

Japanese rather than European does not in itself undermine the speculation. During the later period of the Tokugawa era, foreign contact was severely restricted. It would thus have been politically inept to have included a Dutch or European ship in a series devoted to the quintessential Japanese image of Mount Fuji. Even so, it is significant that the whole Mount Fuji series, of which *The Great Wave* is the best-known image, was enhanced by Hokusai's use of Prussian blue, a rich pigment itself recently imported from European sources by which sea and sky could be dramatized. The staging of the picture also benefited from another technical innovation learnt from outside sources, for *The Great Wave* is the most accomplished of Hokusai's experiments with deep perspective which he would have discovered through access to European art practices.

Alfred Gell tells an interesting story about some Umeda people from a remote inland valley in the Sepik area of Papua New Guinea, who were convicted and taken to a prison on the coast where they encountered the shores of their large island for the first time. On arrival they were lined up on the beach facing out to sea with a policeman in front of them. But the Umeda had never seen the sea before and their experience of mountainous forested landscape had not prepared them for the sight of a tranquil sea with its flat horizon and panoramic vista. They therefore at first interpreted the body of water facing them not as a horizontal surface but as a vertical, mountain-like wave about to engulf them all, including the policeman whose head was below the level of the sea from the perspective of the Umeda higher up the slope of the beach.[39] Like the unfortunate witnesses of the tsunami approaching the shores of the Indian Ocean on Boxing Day 2004, their instinct was to turn and flee. Hokusai has likewise turned the reassuring flatness of the sea and its horizon into an intimidating wall of water.

At the uttermost ends of the earth

The sea, then, is not a single conception but often has a kind of cultural geography associated with its construction. Territoriality gives one expression of this: it is state-focused: the sea as native; and, beyond the horizon, the sea as foreign. Much modern thinking has concentrated on the issues of centre and periphery with an emerging recognition that those living on peripheries regard themselves and their concerns as central. Yet in the earlier period of the Christian era the isolated islands of the north Atlantic had a somewhat different characterization. From a Christian perspective they could not be considered at the centre of the universe for that was a position already occupied by Jerusalem in sacred terms and Rome in secular ones. Rather they were if anything on the very fringes of the known world. The monastic island of Iona and other remote Christian communities are not Crete or Malta, set in a tideless Mediterranean on pilgrim routes to Jerusalem. They are located at the very ends of what for them was the known earth and, however focused its occupants were on the seas immediately around them, an awareness of their position in Christian geography must have been unavoidable. After all, the sun which rose over Jerusalem in the morning set on the horizon in the Atlantic at the end of the day. There was nowhere else for it to go; it circumscribed the known world and the Christian islands of Britain were at its periphery. The T-O maps, which were later to become familiar at least from Isidore of Seville's well-circulated writings and illustrations originally set down in the seventh century, show Jerusalem at the centre of the world with, radiating out, the continents of Asia, Africa and Europe. Land is totally encircled by a boundless, impassable and unknown ocean.[40] On this mapping, as Thomas O'Loughlin shows, Iona sits at the very far edge of the world. Beyond is the 'abyss' of Genesis (1.2), home of the Leviathan (Job 41.23), a Satanic place from which would emerge the apocalyptic beast that would ultimately bring about the destruction of mankind (Revelation 11.7; 17.8).[41] These islands then lie at the battleground between Christianity and its demons, both metaphorically and literally.

Once the Christian message had spread from Jerusalem across all Europe to these pinpricks set at the edge of a heaving firmament off the coasts of Britain, it had in effect become to all intents and purposes a 'universal faith' in terms of known geography, as St Patrick acknowledged in preaching the gospel in Ireland. O'Loughlin observes:

> So when a monk stood on Iona facing south-east he would have imagined that . . . (beyond the seas of Britain) ahead of him was a vast land-mass stretching on to Jerusalem and then out to the Asiatic coast of the same Ocean he was looking at. While to his back the Ocean stretched an equal distance: an impassable body of water heaving without interruption.[42]

In this context the voyages of St Columba, as recounted by Adomnán, are explicitly compared to Christ calming the seas, a metaphor for overcoming the great sea monsters said to reside in the oceans; of wrestling successfully, through faith, with the satanic forces at the uttermost ends both of the earth and of human experience.

What, then, must it have been like to live as a monastic settler on one of the remote islands off the coast of Britain or continental Europe – Iona, Lindisfarne, the Orkneys, the Shetlands, say, or the more distant Faroes? O'Loughlin characterizes the relationship to the sea which the followers of St Columba would have had to anticipate on Iona:

> To travel anywhere from the monastery involved the sea: in one direction lay Ireland, in another Britain, and further away the continent. The sea brought them visitors, guests, books and supplies. It was visible all round them, and its sounds and fury part of their daily lives . . . They knew ships and sailing intimately and saw the wonders of the sea around them.[43]

Being on Iona was like being on a ship surrounded by the ocean, dependent for social interaction on a limited number of people brought together on this isolated spot for a common purpose – stable perhaps by comparison with a ship, but none the less intimately and irrevocably dependent on the sea and its moods for all their needs, including spiritual ones, since their very presence in these remote places was part of a religious quest. Yet the location is significant. The *Life of St Columba* is replete with sailing and navigational detail, not merely incidental detail but essential information, for the monastery was not a single location but spread over a number of islands and in contact with the British and Irish mainlands. To go beyond this known orbit of connected monastic settlements was a kind of death. It was to go to a place from which no one returns. Clearly, however, monks did explore beyond the horizon of their island communities – and did return. They had both faith and navigational know-how. But the fundamental concept which explained all this was at root theological. The sea, its monsters and its navigators were all God's creation. Thus, if the faithful were able to traverse this unstable world, to calm its waters by prayer and establish settlements in such unlikely outposts as the rocks of Skellig Michael far out to sea, it was because it was God's will. Successful navigation and sainthood were one and the same. Only those modelled on Christ's example in stilling the waters could count on the reservoir of sanctity necessary to overcome the challenges of the oceans.

Polluting, cleansing and transforming seas

Of course to go and not come back is not just a matter of sailing physically over the horizon to an unknown fate. It is also a reference to the sea as a space of forgetting. We have cited remarks that the sea has no history in the sense that it lacks both accessible archaeological remains and historical monuments other than those in close proximity to the coastline. It can, therefore, be a convenient dumping place of inconvenient evidence. Yet at the same time it is transforming. Things immersed there change their character. Such characteristics also emerge in many cultural constructions of the significance of the sea.

Thus, for the Ancient Greeks the sea had, as Semonides described it, two faces. On the one hand it had polluting and polluted aspects; on the other it had cleansing properties. Pytheas laid out the case for the former. He imagined the sea as a kind of sewer, a coagulated miasma inhabited by teeming low-life born of its rotting substance and accompanying stench. As polluted, it was the place to dispose of corrupted substances, things which should be got rid of definitively. This included complete bronze sculptures which, if not melted down, would be cast beneath the waves and the person they depicted erased from the public memory. Such was the fate of the Athenian orator Demetrios of Phaleron, sent into exile first in Thebes then overseas in the Greek enclave of Alexandria (where, according to Strabo, he is said to have inspired the famous library) and finally to Upper Egypt. Courts might also be convened beside or even on the sea for certain kinds of crime. Thus anyone exiled for unintentional homicide who, nevertheless, was accused of further killings would be tried at a court established for the purpose on a boat moored just off the shore.[44] The purpose would seem to be to exclude them from the land as a condition of their exile. But at the same time they were associated thereby with those whose bodies were disposed of by being dumped in the depths of the sea, a group which included suicides, the victims of murder, disfigured children, unwanted passengers on a ship and enemies. The sea was regarded by the Greeks as a place where things could be made to disappear, never to be seen again.[45]

This conception of deeper waters and the seas as places of no return is one which is deployed in many different cultural contexts. The Kongo, who live around the estuary of the Congo river and adjacent to the western Atlantic, regard death as a process of passing over or under water. As the reflective surfaces of water resist seeing into their depths, so the world of the dead is inaccessible to all but those gifted with special powers of sight. Kongo art is replete with references to this separation effected by water, usually marked by the inclusion of mirrors and whitened surfaces. As with the Ancient Greek conception, it is a place from which return is not anticipated. An anecdote by the leading historian of the Kongo, Wyatt MacGaffey, draws out the extent to which reappearance is puzzling. He recalled visiting a market in what was then Zaire and overhearing Kongolese discussing the fact that he, a white man, was fluent in Kikongo. Speculation ran that he had been taken away in the trans-Atlantic slave trade and had now returned from across the water, still with his language intact, but transformed into an albino.[46] The atrocities of slavery are thereby interpreted as an extension of the idea of water as marking separation, of defining a realm of the dead, but here transferred to the inexhaustible ocean.

Of course, the Classical world had to accommodate the fact that things could and sometimes did come back despite being consigned to a watery grave – and the very fact of their unexpected return provoked uncertainty. The story told by Herodotus about the fate of Polykrates' ring illustrates the dynamics of such events. Polykrates of Samos lived a charmed life in which his annual voyages of piracy and blood-letting were consistently successful, expanding his domains and bringing him increased wealth. From his base on a small island in the eastern Aegean he was able to assemble a large fleet and subjugate the surrounding islands and even parts of the mainland. He was, however, warned by his close ally Amasis, the Egyptian pharaoh, that all this good fortune portended a disastrous fall and probably his own death. The best ploy would be to manufacture some survivable disaster, the better to stave off an actual and unpredictable level of calamity. Thus advised, he selected his most precious ring and duly consigned it to the depths, separating himself from it and incurring genuine regret. However, that evening as his cook was preparing dinner the ring reappeared in the belly of a recently caught fish. How was this shocking and unexpected return to be understood? It was at best ambiguous. Things which float to the surface and refuse to disappear are generally regarded as omens of misfortune. Amasis at this point cut off relations with his friend and thereafter their relationship seems to have been one of animosity and well-founded suspicion. However, Polykrates, for his part, might have seen it as proof of an immunity to bad luck for, as Herodotus asserts, it is only people who get things back, despite the fact that they have been thrown into the sea, who have access to an unquenchable well of good fortune.

The agency of the fish in this narrative is revealing for fish were often held to have a self-cleansing quality.[47] One aspect of the symbolism may be that the ring, to the extent that it harboured ill-fortune in the first place, had been cleansed and returned. This idea of the purifying nature of the sea – the seas that 'wash all our sins away' in the words of the hymn – is well-attested in antiquity. It contributes to the dichotomous role of the sea in Hellenistic sources. For the Greeks these two aspects of the sea – its association with contamination and with purification – may in practice reflect conceptions of two different areas of the seas, a kind of cultural geography. That which is farthest out, where the waters are fathomless, takes unto itself anything which is cast away there and puts it beyond human influence.

Things consigned there are irretrievable and unable to influence the world of humans. Shallower waters, by contrast, are rendered more suitable for votive offerings than for discarding pollutants.

In the context of spirits the strength they derive from being conceived as travelling over distant seas makes them powerful transforming entities in their own right. They partake of the transforming qualities of the sea. Ian Baucom has discussed the role of Ariel in Shakespeare's *The Tempest*, whose song he takes as a pivotal moment in literature:[48]

> Full fathom five thy father lies;
> Of his bones are coral made;
> Those are pearls that were his eyes:
> Nothing of him that doth fade
> But doth suffer a sea-change
> Into something rich and strange.

In the play Ferdinand's father, tipped into the seas of the Mediterranean, is not so much drowned as altered: in Baucom's words, he does not suffer liquidation but 'liquifaction'. 'The mutating subject merges with its new oceanic space of inhabitation ... becoming a catalogue of the things washing over it'[49] – in this case, coral and pearls. For Baucom this anticipates the contemporary world where voyages overseas – thinking particularly perhaps of the Black Atlantic – have produced multinational, multiracial societies compelling a continuing search for self-definition, a sea-change in the sense of self-identity as people move and seek to accommodate the experiences washing over them.

In the case of the islands of Zanzibar, a cosmopolitan pinprick in the western Indian Ocean, the sea is an ever-present reality to the voyaging world assembled there, a meeting place not just for people but for spirits of Malagasy, Kenyan or Ethiopian origin and beyond. They have been delivered up by the sea and their exoticism is a condition of the intense power they have to transform people. In the popular imagination sailors, too, are exotic creatures. In Madagascar spirits of exotic origin, including the spirits of French sailors, have increasing cache. It is no accident, Auden points out, that homosexuals are drawn to sailors who arrive off their ships without ties, 'the innocent god from the sea who is not bound by the law of the land and can therefore do anything without guilt.'[50]

This concept of the sea as transformative takes further the rather static cartography of inshore and offshore, of within sight and beyond the horizon. But, as Hokusai represented it, the sea is possessed of many potentialities and is itself in dynamic humour. It is, after all, not just transformative in a symbolic or allegorical sense. It is also itself in a state of permanent physical transformation.

The 'sublime' sea

Melville begins *Moby-Dick* with a meditative passage entitled 'Loomings' in which Ishmael, his narrator, reflects on the circumstances which took him to sea in the first place. He notes how on a Sunday afternoon in any East Coast American city, the piers and vantage points are crowded with 'water-gazers', posted like sentinels in their thousands 'fixed in ocean reveries'. Then come more crowds

> pacing straight for the water, and seemingly bound for a dive. Strange! Nothing will content them but the extremist limit of the land; loitering under the shady lee of yonder warehouses will not suffice. No. They must get just as nigh the water as they possibly can without falling in. And there they stand – miles of them – leagues.[51]

What he is describing is what Alain Corbin has discussed as 'The Lure of the Sea', a fascination with the seaside which in a European context he traces to the mid-eighteenth century.[52] People gather to look out to sea, but what are they looking for? In what does this allure consist?

The ambiguity we have noted in Classical ideas of the polluting and cleansing qualities of the seas re-emerge in western European attitudes in the early modern period. They came to their full expression in the eighteenth century with the identification, and ultimately the indulgence, of a kind of fretful pleasure which was held to be both uplifting and inspiring. Experience which was at once fearful and invigorating was sought out by poets, artists and what we might now consider hypochondriac temperaments alike (to the extent that these are distinct). An engagement with the sea was amongst the surest ways of inducing the condition. Its indulgence led Lord Byron to swim the

Hellespont and declare an exhausting swim in the open seas amongst the most stimulating experiences imaginable. And it also encouraged Percy Bysshe Shelley on his fateful sailing exploits round Italy. It is as evident in Turner's pictures of storms at sea as in Richard Wilson's paintings of the craggy peaks of his native Snowdonia.

In medieval times symptoms of fretfulness were conceptualized in terms of melancholia, a condition held to be associated with profound anguish over the fate of the soul. A life spent in sinful pursuits and insufficiently redeemed by evidence of true repentance held out little hope of future salvation. Depression followed in the wake of a growing apprehension about the direness of such a dim prospect. In the seventeenth century the source of the condition had been identified with 'spleen', notably through the publication of the influential writings of Robert Burton, author of *The Anatomy of Melancholy* (1621). Thus reassessed, other palliatives than the uniquely spiritual were to be recommended. Prominent amongst these was an active engagement with the environment, principally with landscape. Walks by the river were good, but so too was the bracing air of the Orkneys where the longevity of the inhabitants suggested a healthy impact. That said, bathing was better undertaken at the spas which began to be frequented by the richer classes, than in the sea itself. Better, in fact, to live inland and cultivate a pleasant garden or employ a landscape architect to produce a manicured vista than relocate to some dank seaside setting, let alone actually go sailing other than by necessity. After all, being aboard ship itself brought on less than welcome symptoms in the inexperienced. Seasickness was bad enough, but, as President de Brosses declared after a passage from Antibes to Genoa in 1739, that was the least of it. The mental torpor which accompanied it was so loathsome that he found he could no longer even think about the sea.[53] Far from curing spleen, such an experience merely escalated the suffering involved.

However, when in the 1750s Edmund Burke expounded on the characteristics of the 'sublime', changes were already becoming evident.[54] The seaside was indeed increasingly being recognized as a healthy alternative to the cities and bathing there was no longer potentially polluting but more a restorative activity. Brighton, with its southerly aspect and bracing therapeutic Channel air, was to become in effect the leading sanatorium in the world and, in its wake, other coastal towns eagerly sought to develop similar reputations.[55] Corbin accounts for the change in attitude in terms of an increasing disenchantment with the cities as healthy places to live – that and a reconfiguration of the seas as the resort of true nature when so much of the landscape was now cultivated and gardened space.[56] The sea cannot be rearranged so as to invest it with moral purpose. It, like jagged snow-covered mountain peaks, came to be the habitual repository of the Burkeian idea of the sublime, the inspiration of man's sense of the exhilarating yet threatening power of nature. It was not about scenery but access to raw nature. The moods of the sea reflected the ideals involved: tranquillity suggested beauty; a high raging sea or the ocean's immensity engendered the sublime. Whilst this was more evident in the open ocean, at the seaside you still had elements of both. You could contemplate its beauties and experience something of its qualities without necessarily inducing the horrors of violent seasickness. If the sea was thrown into violent turmoil by the winds its raw grandeur would make you shiver. On calmer days you could plunge into the waves and experience the visceral thrill of immersion – but unless careless in your choice of time and place, avoid the risks of being swept out to sea. Things were to become easier still as municipal facilities developed at seaside 'resorts'. But the sublime was neither tamed nor becalmed by such domestication for the sea itself always has another register.

Joseph Addison made the case most eloquently. 'Of all objects that I have ever seen', he remarked in 1712, 'there is none which affects my Imagination so much as the Sea or Ocean.' He continues:

> I cannot see the heavings of this prodigious Bulk of Waters, even in a Calm, without a very pleasing astonishment; but when it is worked up in a Tempest, so that the Horizon on every side is nothing but foaming billows and floating mountains, it is impossible to describe the agreeable horror that rises from such a prospect . . . I must confess, it is impossible for me to survey this world of fluid Matter, without thinking on the Hand that first poured it out, and made a proper Channel for its Reception.[57]

The language of the era – 'pleasing astonishment', 'agreeable horror' – characteristically draws pain and pleasure, apprehension and exhilaration into conjunction. The sublime is a realm of exquisite and thought-provoking wonderment, and the sea is its pre-eminent arena. The ontological implications of the ocean for Polynesian voyagers are in Addison replaced by existential, and ultimately theological, reflection.

Literary and artistic explorations of this theme are principally associated with the Romantic Movement. Coleridge had never been to sea when he wrote *The Rime of the Ancient Mariner* in 1798. Yet the image of the solitary mariner facing the challenges of voyaging in boundless oceans is less a description of actual experience than an allegory of the moral and the spiritual worlds. The Ancient Mariner bearing the killed albatross hung round his neck has been taken as an image of Adam after the Fall, or of Christ bearing the cross on his back. He tells his tale in the context of a wedding. It is as if the 'natural' man of Rousseau's *Discourse on Inequality* (1754) recounts his narrative in the company of the 'civilized' man of his *Social Contract* (1762). This raises the interesting point that the sublime is experienced most intensely on an individual basis. Indeed the experience of solitude is one of its characteristic moments. Byron experienced it when facing the seas alone on the shore at Aberdeen.

But perhaps the fullest account of the experience of the solitary mariner in such terms is from the second half of the nineteenth century in Victor Hugo's epic depiction of Gilliat in his haunting Channel Islands novel *Toilers of the Sea*. Gilliat is brought up on the island of Guernsey by a woman who may or may not have been his mother. His father is unknown. He is given no Christian name, is befriended by no one and keeps his own counsel. When walking along the road he takes the loneliest of tracks to avoid human company. Gilliat lives by the exercise of his maritime prowess. In this he is supremely self-reliant as is demonstrated by the exceptional facility with which he overcomes the most challenging of sea conditions to single-handedly salvage a wrecked steamship in what is a sustained and suspense-filled piece of writing.

Hugo, like Coleridge, deploys an idea which can be traced to the eighteenth-century concept of the sublime with more than just a descriptive sense: contemplation of the sea and the sky, he says, leads to 'the enlargement of the soul by wonder'.[58] And, as in *The Ancient Mariner*, the tale also ends with a marriage ceremony. In this case, however, it had been Gilliat's ambition himself to wed the betrothed – he in his solitariness, she as an ideal of beauty, bringing together the two elements which Burke had separated out. His salvage of the shipwreck was explicitly to win her hand. However it is not to be. The two cannot be forced into unnatural liaison. So, he returns triumphant only to discover that in his absence she has married another. The reclusive hero of the narrative seeks out a lonely rock and slips slowly beneath the rising tide to a lonely grave beneath the waves. The beautiful and the sublime are not to be brought together. They remain forever distanced.

The coming of steam

Hugo is also writing from an awareness that the terms of this finely drawn distinction are collapsing. The very language of the beautiful and the sublime was being challenged, even potentially rendered obsolete, by a new technological innovation that was radically to recast the terms of the human engagement with the sea. It is surely significant that Gilliat's heroism and seamanship is undertaken in his own *sailing* boat but in the salvage of a beleaguered *steamship* which is shown to be a defiant but ultimately futile act of heroism. Hugo describes the circumstances in which the steamship came to be introduced. The difference between being under sail, in touch with and responsive to nature, and being under steam, defiantly setting a course in spite of nature, was inevitably constructed in religious terms at the time of its invention. Where ships under sail are responsive to wind and current, those under steam are responsive to man. One represents man's concern to be in harmony with nature (or, according to conception, with God) whilst the other can readily be represented as a defiance of the natural order. Thus, when Fulton's original steamship sailed from New York to Albany on 17 August 1807 it was denounced by local Methodists on the basis that seventeen was the sum of the ten horns and the seven heads of the beast of the Apocalypse.

> Learned men had rejected the steamship as impossible; the priests for their part rejected it as impious. Science had condemned it; religion damned it. Fulton was a variant of Lucifer.[59]

Sailing on the sea in the Channel Islands it looked like the sea was on fire; and water and fire are not supposed to mix.

One reverend gentleman named Elihu called the steamship a 'licentious invention'. The sailing ship was declared orthodox. The devil's horns were clearly seen on the heads of cattle transported by the steamship.[60]

It was known as 'The Devil Boat'. After all, Hugo reflected, in a country where the Queen was criticized for giving birth with the help of chloroform it was predictable that it would be regarded as hell afloat. 'Is it right,' a local preacher thundered in a sermon, 'to let fire and water, which were divided by God, work together?' [61]

The idea that steam is an affront to nature and that the conquering of the seas came at a cost was a common literary theme into the early twentieth century. Joseph Conrad's Thomas MacWhirr, the self-righteous, unimaginative captain of the ill-fated *Nan-Shan* in his story 'Typhoon', is identified as the son of a Belfast grocer.[62] His experience of the sea is much more that of the commercial traffic of Belfast Lough than the leisure craft under sail of Strangford, as described in the last chapter. The oceans had been conquered; nature offered no impediment to any prospective voyage. Conrad's version of the challenge of the fast-running tides which contrive to keep all but the most determined of sailors within the confines of the alternative Lough nearby was the cyclone whose advance McWhirr blithely ignores in the bone-headed conviction that changing course to avert the path of the storm was a gratuitous diversion. Ships driven by vast engines and guided unerringly by compasses and charts had conquered the vagaries of nature. He needed no unnecessary lessons in caution. His divorce from the power of natural forces was complete. In Raban's words,

> The whirling cyclone that Conrad brews up to engulf the stupid captain and his crew is the ocean's revenge for the hubris of the steam turbine and the ruled line on the chart.[63]

The typhoon converts the neutral space of modern technological construction into intensity, danger and the strongly concentrated specificities of place. Nature is the victor.

Turner also evoked this transitional moment pictorially. His iconic picture of the swirling turmoil of a storm at sea was painted in 1842 just at the moment when the powers of the steamship to confront nature were being definitively asserted. Isambard Kingdom Brunel's leap into maritime engineering had just been completed when the steamship named the *Great Western* was launched in July 1837 and successfully completed its maiden transatlantic voyage to New York the following year in merely fifteen days. It was a wooden paddle steamer but its very name echoes Brunel's feat of 'terrestrial' engineering: the Great Western Railway was already in construction when its nautical extension was being conceived and built. The steam train was to run from London to the seaport of Bristol, the inaugural trip being made in 1841. A year after Turner's painting, this became even more evident when the *Great Britain* was launched at Bristol docks after four years in construction. It beached unceremoniously in Dundrum Bay in Ireland on its first outing but was to be the first iron propeller-driven ship to cross the Atlantic, which it continued to do for many years. It is as if the template of the train was being transferred directly to the sea. The train lines which took its carriages and its passengers unerringly along a predicted route were now translated into the maritime realm. You could imagine a single passage along a predetermined linear path from London to New York, all courtesy of Brunel. Ships, which before were subject to the manipulations of the wind and currents, could now steer a course through the waters impervious to the constant adjustments and antici-pation which the pilots of sailing ships had to make. It was not quite like drawing a line on a map and simply steering along it, but concep-tually it was closer to that model – the railways model – than had ever been possible before.

Turner's iconic painting has a strongly documentary feel about it which encourages us to think about it in terms of its historical context. Rather like the concern for precision in the full title of Hokusai's *Great Wave*, this is even more evident in the still longer description Turner gave his work: *Snow Storm – Steam Boat off a Harbour's Mouth making Signals in Shallow Water, and Going by the Lead. The Author was in this Storm on the Night the Ariel left Harwich* (illus. 7). The steamboat, we imagine, is in a Conradian nightmare. It has the power and the raw strength to cross the seas but nature leaves it wallowing barely outside the sanctuary of the harbour walls, frantically signalling its dilemma and adopting the time-honoured method of dropping a leaded weight over the side to check the depth of water as it desperately tries to avoid shipwreck.

But there are several oddities to this which have been the cause of much speculation amongst Turner scholars. Not only does Turner sug-gest he was himself in the storm, but he went further and said that he

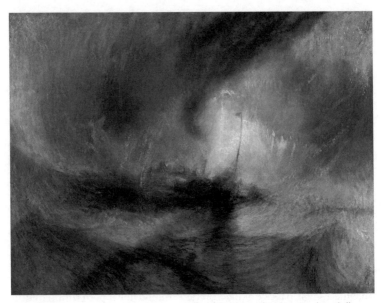

7 J.M.W. Turner, *Snow-Storm – Steam-Boat off a Harbour's Mouth making Signals in Shallow vWater, and going by the Lead. The Author was in this Storm on the Night the Ariel left Harwich,* 1842, oil on canvas.

had been lashed to the mast, sketchbook in hand, recording the event for four long hours. Indeed he records that he did not expect to escape the deluge but, since he had, he now felt a compelling obligation to record it. Certainly Turner did travel out to sea to sketch clouds and seascapes and coastal scenes from offshore on numerous occasions, following Dutch marine painting practice. A storm, however, is a different matter. If it sounds improbable that an artist could work in such circumstances, it appears that Turner was not in fact in the vicinity when the storm broke nor was there a functioning steamship route out of Harwich at the time. The claim to authenticity is not helped by the fact that the descriptive precision of the title refers to an 'author' rather than an 'artist'. We might wonder if the painting is, in fact, done after an event which he wrote about rather than sketched on the spot.

Another oddity about the picture's title is the fact that the steam-boat *Ariel* does not seem to have been listed as sailing from the East Anglian coast at the time. Rather it appears to have been operating from Dover. The fact that the *Ariel* was also the ship on which Prince Albert had arrived three years earlier to take the hand of Queen Victoria might seem to be another potential reference in the picture's title.[64]

The obsessive detail of the picture – documenting what occurred when, the scene, the place, his own presence and the ship itself – seems in the end to have been partly invention unless it actually refers to an event which had happened well before the painting was completed and shown. We are left to wonder if the *Ariel* is actually the steamboat seen dimly through the storm – or is Turner himself Ariel, inheritor of the mantle of the magical trickster dreamed up by Shakespeare in his 'tempest'?

The storm painting has been described as 'the supreme example in all his [Turner's] art of that sublime realism which accurately records a natural event as perceived by a profoundly receptive mind.'[65] The painting itself focuses on the power of natural forces suggesting the subject – the steamer struggling against a sudden conflict with an overwhelming force of nature – but dwelling rather on the funnel of dark cloud moving in on the beleaguered paddle steamer. It is hard not to see the picture as an allegory of the confrontation with nature which is central to the idea of the sublime – of which Turner in his seascapes as much as his landscapes was the acknowledged master of his era.

The synaesthetic experience of the sea which is characteristic of sail ships was, arguably, coming to an end in this moment. The 'devil boat' was to revolutionize human engagement with the sea, to render being at sea like being on one of the piers which began to be projected out into the sea as viewing platforms rather than for the protection of shipping. Conrad was to describe the steam tug, for all of its utility, in derogatory terms. He too was in the grip of late Romanticism about the sea: as the tug turned for the land after seeing the *Narcissus* in the story of the same name safely into open water, she resembled, he remarked

> an enormous and aquatic black beetle, surprised by the light, overwhelmed by the sunshine, trying to escape with ineffectual effort into the distant gloom of the land. She left a lingering smudge of smoke in the sky, and two vanishing trails of foam on the water. On the place where she had stopped a round black patch of soot remained, undulating on the swell – an unclean mark of the creature's rest.[66]

The profound sensory engagement with the seas, to which we turn next in discussing navigational techniques, was becoming unfamiliar.

It was still to be many years before steam finally overtook sail. By 1860 there was only somewhat above 400,000 registered tons of steamships in comparison with four million tons of sailing ships.[67] Conrad could still experience the disjunction at the end of the century. But, in Europe at least, it is to the early Victorian era that the conceptual sea change which led to the definitive reconfiguration of our thinking about the maritime world in terrestrial terms – the one we are seeking to critique here – can be ascribed.

The steam ship was to be reconceived in political terms as a vehicle of release from restraint, a liberating technology which ultimately promised less restricted movement across the oceans. Thackeray was to write in the 1860s:

> We are of the age of steam. We have stepped out of the old world on to 'Brunel's' vast deck, and across the waters *ingens patet tellus* [an enormous land stands open]. Towards what new continent are we wending? to what new laws, new manners, new politics, vast new expanses of liberties unknown as yet, or only surmised?[68]

And there is an inevitability about 'progress'. Thackeray continues:

> They have raised those railroad embankments up, and shut off the old world that was behind them. Climb up that bank on which the irons are laid, and look to the other side—it is gone. There IS no other side.[69]

Hugo, Conrad and even Turner can be seen in the light of this conceptual reconfiguration as expressing a conservative diktat which regretted innovation and feared its implications of unfettered individualism. Steam and democracy threatened to rock the boat.[70]

three

Navigation and the Arts of Performance

The sea, in conjunction with the wind, is a composite of mechanisms. The sea's forces are mechanisms of infinite power; the ship's mechanisms are forces of limited power. Between these two organisms, one inexhaustible, the other intelligent, takes place the combat that is called navigation.
VICTOR HUGO, *The Toilers of the Sea* (1866)[1]

In the Marshall Islands in Micronesia navigators learn their skills by creating what have been called 'stick charts'. These illustrate wave patterns and swells using splints of curved cane and they represent islands with shells. They are clearly a significant adjunct to way-finding at sea; yet, when an actual ocean voyage is undertaken, they are deliberately left behind and not taken on board.[2] Elsewhere in the Pacific successive anthropological studies have remarked that despite the availability of compasses and accurate sea charts, mariners trained in indigenous observational methods of navigation show little interest in using them when at sea. In the Indian Ocean medieval period navigational texts make little or no reference to either charts or compasses, despite the fact that both were known and were in all probability carried as a standard item of technical equipment on ships involved in the extensive Indian Ocean trade. Similarly, in the Mediterranean a text originally attributed to the thirteenth-century writer Brunetto Latini asserts of the use of the compass:

> No master mariner dares to use it, lest he should fall under the supposition of being a magician; nor would even the sailors venture themselves to sea under his command if he took with him an instrument which carries so great an appearance of being constructed under the influence of some infernal spirit.[3]

The text was subsequently discovered to have been written at the turn of the nineteenth century by someone else. But that is almost more interesting, for, given the advances in navigational techniques in the intervening centuries, it expresses even better the suspicion with which a device working according to what for many was an unexplained and mysterious property like magnetism, might be viewed. Although the combat of which Victor Hugo speaks in characterizing navigational skills may be the same for all mariners, the rules of engagement are clearly variable. Traversing the sea with chart and compass or, as in much of the Pacific, sailing with literally no manufactured navigational equipment at all, are not just different strategies; they also seem to be incompatible ones.

To explore this theme we turn to elaborate on the implications of the experience of two navigators from very different maritime traditions, one a fifteenth-century Arab, the other an eighteenth-century Polynesian. They are linked by one common accident of history: each was amongst the first from their respective oceans to encounter European mariners, their sailing methods and practices. Each was also regarded as an exemplar of his own maritime tradition and was primarily engaged in the encounter between different traditions of practice. Ibn Mājid, with whom we begin, is by tradition the person who is said to have instructed Vasco da Gama on the best way to cross the Indian Ocean from Malindi on the coast of what is now Kenya to the west coast of India in the summer of 1498. An Arab navigator certainly did assist the Portuguese, though whether it was actually Ibn Mājid is perhaps doubtful.[4] He was, however, the foremost navigator of his time, expert in the traditional navigational techniques from which the Portuguese were to benefit, and he was also the author of a foundational text on Arab navigation. It was inevitable that later commentators would associate him with the act of conducting the Portuguese to India. Tupaia, a Polynesian navigator, was taken on board Captain Cook's ships in 1769 during his first voyage and is identified as the author of a renowned chart showing islands in the Pacific which had yet to be 'discovered' by European explorers. His knowledge of Polynesia was so comprehensive that it seems to have encompassed the whole of the vast area from Fiji in the west to the Marquesas Islands in the east, a distance equivalent to the width of the Atlantic, and to have included all the larger island groups with the exceptions only of New Zealand and Hawaii.[5] The skills exemplified by each navigator attracted surprised comment (Ibn Mājid perhaps by proxy) both for their sophistication and for the seeming indifference of each to Western achievements in maritime technologies at these different periods.

'The Lion of the Sea in Fury'.

Ibn Mājid (otherwise Aḥmad b. Mājid al-Najdī) is best known to the western world from the work of the Arabic scholar G. R. Tibbetts, who in 1971 published *Arab Navigation in the Indian Ocean before the Coming of the Portuguese*.[6] The focus of this book is a translation with commentary of the *Kitāb al-Fawā'id fī uṣūl al-baḥr wa'l-qawā'id*, otherwise often referred to as 'The Book of Profitable Things' or, more completely, 'The Book of Profitable Things Concerning the First Principles and Rules of Navigation'. The original is dated 1490.[7]

The *Fawā'id* is a kind of nautical encyclopaedia, a synthesis of a life of study and practical knowledge which is thorough in its observations and stands as the single most important source of information on maritime practice in the Red Sea and the Indian Ocean in the late fifteenth century. This is the very moment at which Portuguese intrusion into the region began to link in to local patterns of trade and exchange and to globalize its connections to include the Atlantic and beyond – though in truth the Chinese fleets of Zheng He had already explored the western Indian Ocean in the first part of the century. Indeed the Indian Ocean was itself already an integrated trading system by then, even if many goods tended to be moved by ships in shorter hops rather than on single voyages right across the ocean and on into the South China Seas. As we will see both events – the advent of the Chinese and of the Portuguese – are evident in Ibn Mājid's writing which incorporates knowledge of Taiwan and the coasts of China as well as, for the first time, an account of south-eastern Africa as far as the Cape of Good Hope and the so-called 'Seas of Darkness' beyond; that is, the Atlantic, conceived by Indian Ocean mariners as a barren ocean with no opportunities for trade or exploitation.

The text is written largely in prose, though it incorporates a significant amount of verse; and much of Ibn Mājid's other extant work is also written in poetic form. He was undoubtedly proud of his literary abilities and saw himself as writing 'literature' rather than just an instructional manual for would-be navigators. One of the questions to be tackled here is why – beyond being an exercise in literary skill – it should have seemed appropriate to write such a work partly in verse. He was not, after all, the only Arab writer on navigation to do so. And, tied to that, it remains distinctly odd that there is so little reference made in his work to the compass or other navigational devices, that there are no charts or drawings to illustrate the very detailed information he incorporates. We know that compasses existed. Indeed, the first written reference in Arabic to the compass seems to date from 1282.[8] Ibn Mājid even claims in the *Fawā'id* to have been responsible for mounting the compass needle in a case and to have perfected the method of magnetizing a metal needle with a lodestone. He also refers to the first use of the lodestone being when David threw a rock of lodestone with unerring accuracy to kill Goliath as if responsive to magnetic force. He goes further and associates the invention of the arts of navigation with Noah.[9] We may assume, therefore, that Ibn Mājid, like his fellow master navigators, was entirely familiar with the compass. So why are bearings and the details of its use not described? Is it enough to say, as Tibbetts does, that its use was actually so well known that fuller elaboration was unnecessary?

Though he came to occupy a pivotal position in Arab navigational lore of the Indian Ocean and the Red Sea, in truth we know little about Ibn Mājid's life beyond his writings.[10] These certainly drew on extensive first-hand experience but are not recounted in any autobiographical or chronological sequence. His interests were both in the practice of navigation and in its theoretical basis, for which he regarded a knowledge of geography and especially astronomy as essential. From the wealth of reference in his work and his recommendations of readings appropriate to budding mariners we know he was well read in relevant texts and conversant with ancient Arabic poetry and literature as well as the most immediately relevant writings. All of this led him to assert his primacy as a practical exponent of navigational way-finding in the Indian Ocean and as a leading Arabic literary figure.

Ibn Mājid saw himself, as he famously remarked, as 'The Fourth after Three', 'The Successor of the Lions' or again as 'The Lion of the Sea in Fury'.[11] He is referring to the three most prominent medieval writers on Arab navigation systems whom he considered himself to have succeeded. Indeed, although fulsome in acknowledging their achievements, he did regard them more as mechanical compilers than as original authors; and he was critical of his own contemporaries in similar terms. History has treated him well on that account. The Turkish navigator Sidi Çelibi acquired copies of his writings in Basra in the second half of the sixteenth century and recommended them as the essential source in navigating the Indian Ocean;[12] and many still regard his observations as accurate and ground-breaking, especially for the areas he knew best – the Red Sea, of course, and the routes between eastern Africa, the Arabian coast and the western coast of India. His reputation was still evident into the nineteenth century. For example, in *First Footsteps in East Africa* (1856) Richard Burton talks of sailors repeating a prayer honouring Sheik Mājid before they venture out into the open seas.[13] This was over 300 years later and, although Burton identifies Ibn Mājid as a Syrian saint, modern critics suggest he is probably the same person as the author of 'The Book of Profitable Things'.[14]

The *Fawā'id* begins with a preface which is in itself interesting. From the beginning, Ibn Mājid suggests that his work is not just about navigation and way-finding – it also has an underlying sacred context which is far from incidental. His opening words are:

> Verily I have seen sciences in this world more worthy of glory, more exalted in rank and more meritorious, for did not the Prophet say, "All of the other prophets enjoined people to seek after knowledge" and so on till, "not any evil knowledge, for ignorance is the most evil of all." Then how can this be, for this is a science without which one cannot measure the Qibla of Islam accurately, and everything that I say and do will show just how accurate we can be.[15]

In other words, the same knowledge and practice which serves the purposes of navigation coincides with that which can be used to find *Qibla* accurately – the direction of Mecca towards which the faithful offer prayer – no matter how far the follower of the Prophet is removed in latitude or longitude from Mecca. The many tables that characterize Indian Ocean sailing directions often include not just information on how to calculate the direction of Mecca, but such details as the times for prayer at the Grand Mosque in Damascus (and how to calculate them at different places); and this overlap of information allows the faithful to fulfil their daily obligations of prayer when travelling at sea without access to mosque architecture with its directional and devotional frameworks.

The bulk of the long text is taken up with technical information on such subjects as the 28 lunar mansions, and the stars associated with the rhumbs of the compass (the system here being by stars not, as in the Mediterranean, by winds), the times and dates when sailing can be most expeditiously conducted given the monsoonal system, the appropriate sea routes across the Indian Ocean including the latitude of the major ports and harbours, and so forth. Of all of this detail, perhaps the most 'profitable' thing is giving the latitudes of important destinations, for the most secure way of successful wayfinding was that of latitude sailing. This is especially so in the Indian Ocean where journeys between the African coastline and Arabia could be directly east or west, taking advantage of monsoonal winds (running north–west/south–east, or the reverse) and the lack of restrictions in the form of shoals, atolls or islands to sailing across that long stretch of water. With the surety of an open ocean, this meant that the navigator could simply sail northwards or southwards to reach a latitude line and then sail along it towards a distant harbour. Without intervening restrictions, this was a potentially infallible method of finding port when under clear night skies.

The detailed latitude coordinates which Ibn Mājid gives are in the form of altitude readings of the Polar Star (or Polaris). This has the unique characteristic in northern skies of remaining in the same general position regardless of the observer's changes of longitude or the seasons of the year. Such variation as there is in the position of Polaris could be allowed for by taking readings when the stars nearby – the so-called Guards – were in particular alignments. Apart from giving a more or less reliable indication of north, this characteristic allows latitude to be determined by estimating the height of the star above the horizon. This remains constant for places of similar degrees of latitude to the north of the equator and throughout the year. Its altitude was estimated by Arab navigators using a disarmingly simple instrument known as a *kamal*. This was essentially little more than a cord with a number of knots along its length, each appropriate to the latitude of a port. At one end the cord was attached to a rectangular block of wood no more than a few inches square. To use it, the length of the appropriate knot was held to the eye or gripped with the teeth and the wood plaque stretched out so the cord was taut. It was then aligned with the lower edge on the horizon and the upper edge on Polaris. If the star appeared exactly on the upper edge the ship was sailing at the correct latitude to reach a particular port. If it was above the plaque the position was to the north of the required latitude and if the plaque covered the Pole Star the position was too far south. Though more complicated, solar altitude could similarly be assessed for daytime readings.

This is the navigational device which it is assumed Vasco da Gama learnt to use through his encounter with Arab navigators. He may have been familiar with its general principles through its similarity to the cross-staff (or so-called Jacob's staff) of European navigators. Likewise Portuguese instrumentation may not have been a surprise to Indian Ocean navigators. The astrolabe was already well known to Arab astronomers.[16] It was in fact one of the recognized instruments by which *qibla* could be accurately determined. In the tenth century its many uses had been described by al-Sufi, a Persian astronomer. Little wonder then that when the Portuguese showed Ibn Mājid (assuming it was him) their astrolabes, he was to their surprise reportedly unimpressed.[17] All of this makes it especially intriguing that Ibn Mājid refrains from discussing technical equipment of more sophisticated forms in the *Fawā'id*. If he mentioned compass rhumbs, it was only to situate a knowledge based on astronomical observation, which in his account was the most amenable source of navigational knowledge. Indeed Ibn Mājid's description is notable for his emphasis on being on the open ocean and without elaborate instrumentation. He is dismissive of those who ply their trade close to coasts, whom he did not regard as true mariners. As Daniel Defoe was to remark of the Phoenicians, the Genoese and even the Portuguese of Ibn Mājid's period, they were fair-weather seamen:

> The chief of their Navigation was Coasting; and if they were driven out of their knowledge, had work enough to find their way home, and sometimes never found it at all: but one Sea convey'd them directly into the last Ocean, from whence no Navigation cou'd return them.[18]

Ibn Mājid is equally disparaging of the skills required for travelling in proximity to land – though in practice it is actually much more dangerous, involving 'wearing' (as opposed to tacking which was not possible on Arab dhows) and knowledge of the characteristics of the sea and in particular the tide, which in the open seas is of no consequence from the point of view of the mariner. However, the 'authentic' life at sea in Ibn Mājid's account requires the umbilical cord which links sea to land to be extended to the point where finding a distant port placed the emphasis exclusively on the wits, knowledge and attentiveness of the navigator at the expense of technology or ready sight of land.

So, in addition to latitude sailing with the aid of a string and block of wood, how did Arab navigators find their way across apparently featureless stretches of ocean with sufficient accuracy to reliably make port? A whole series of other indications are described in the *Fawā'id*. The greatest risk at sea is drowsiness or inattention. The *mu'allim* needs to be alert at all times. He is not just looking for the stars by night and the altitude of the sun by day, but also a whole series of other phenomena – cloud formations, winds and currents, different patterns of colour and disturbance on the sea, the movement and assembling of seabirds. As sea snakes come up for air they lie stretched out on the surface. They are rarely seen on the open ocean, but they congregate in large numbers on continental shelves off the coast of India, indicating the approach of as yet unseen land. Soundings taken of the bottom will also give a reliable indication of general location in relation to unseen coastlines.[19]

Thus one emerging answer as to why the wonders of Western navigational technology did not make an immediate impact amongst Indian Ocean mariners – why indeed description of more complex technologies is largely absent in Ibn Mājid's work – concerns the *self*-reliance implicit in indigenous methods. It cannot surely be mere oversight on Ibn Mājid's part that he focuses on the observation of the maritime environment in place of secondary instrumentation. The combination of altitude readings and direct observation of nature is arguably a complete system which, once mastered, requires no artificial technologies to perfect it in an ocean whose characteristics were already entirely familiar to the experienced *mu'allim*. A modern navigational writer, Commander W. E. May RN, reminds his readers that the first moon landing was effected by the captain taking the controls of the satellite to determine the best place to set down.[20] Navigation, he asserts, is art as well as science. The engagement of the experienced navigator with the sensory world of nature was potentially infallible; it did not need fixing.

What, then, can be said about his literary style? This too might be construed as an aspect of an overall injunction towards self-reliance. In a text intended as an encyclopaedic assembling of navigational and geographic knowledge it looks distinctly odd to modern Western eyes to indulge a taste for verse; and in fact the *Fawā'id* is a mix of poetry and of prose which is also written in a distinctive and individualistic way. The presence of poetry, though, is perhaps not as surprising as it might seem. His father, as we have noted, also wrote navigational works in verse and, in addition to his navigational poetry, Ibn Mājid himself also wrote reflective poetry on the human condition in general. As it happens, apart from other Arab writers on navigation using verse, the Chinese did the same. The anonymous author of *Shun Fêng Hsiang Sung* ('Fair Winds for Escort'), written in 1430, uses verses for the azimuth rising points of the sun and moon and corresponding lengths of day and night at different latitudes, on weather signs, notably lightning, and other features.[21]

Song is also a device for recalling navigational information. Among the Bajau Laut of the archipelagos of South East Asia sea journeys are mostly to known fishing grounds which, though they may be some miles out to sea, are not usually out of sight of land. Yet, whilst regularly visited fishing grounds may be most easily located more distant ones are challenging. To recall all the permutations of wayfinding a series of traditional sailing songs (*kalangan tebba*) are sung to the rhythm of the oars fixing the visual coordinates of different sea locations in the memory.[22] Likewise, a Norse handbook for mariners – *Konungs skuggsja* ('King's Mirror'), which was written by an unknown author about AD 1250 – also uses language and narrative that is highly coloured. As with Ibn Mājid, there is no mention of navigational technologies. None the less a great deal of information is conveyed. The format is that of a father explaining to his son the significance at sea of different natural phenomena.[23] Narrative form, poetic verse, personification – all are regular aspects of such navigational instructional manuals, paralleling in language the sensory engagement with the nautical environment.

Ibn Mājid regarded his poems on general navigation as his really notable literary contribution. It is, of course, hard to judge the quality of poetic works in translation where it is not just vocabulary but literary traditions and conventions which need to be rendered for readers unfamiliar with their nuances and reference. Frankly, in Tibbetts's translation, and whatever its other virtues, it is hard to find much poetic merit. Thus, for example, on the ending of the sailing season, Ibn Mājid states that '[E]very decision is important when dealing with sailing dates' and he emphasizes the point in verse:

> Whenever Ghurāb shines in the dawn, the heavier ships
> In Yemen are prevented from crossing to India.
> And for some time after the winds are full of rain,
> But it is possible for them to reach Shiḥr with much trouble;
> But 'tis a gamble. Thus is the Tīrmāh and after that;
> 'Tis not good for one to gamble, oh Hasan.
> And when Simāk rises at Mandab
> Take Zaila ' but avoid Siyāra and al-Ḥazn.[24]

It continues in the same vein. All sound advice, no doubt – even if, in the available translation, Ibn Mājid's works read rather more like McGonagall than Masefield. That, however, need not delay us here. The point is not to assess the veracity of his claims to literary merit but rather to explore why it was significant that he should seek to write in a distinctive way.

In his chapter on the lunar mansions, Ibn Mājid quotes with approval the poet al-Baḥrī:

> Whenever I compose poetry, the stars recite it
> Who has ever seen Sirius reciting another,
> I am not one whose standing is based on my poetry alone.
> My standing is based on my poetry and Sirius together.[25]

At one level this would seem to be a straightforward evocation of the arts of navigation, of the navigator as a sentient being in tune with language and with the disposition of the heavens. And indeed being 'attuned' is one of the qualities that all descriptions of navigational practice insist on. Navigation is the exercise of apparently intuitive knowledge, whether it be the Irish monks (the *peregrine*) who occupied the Faroe Islands 150 years before the Norsemen,[26] mariners from the Gilbert Islands in the mid-twentieth century,[27] or contemporary Icelandic fishermen.[28] These, of course, are external views of how navigation is effected as it seems to modern observers. The sense that it works by intuition is enhanced by the fact that, unlike any situation the modern Western navigator faces, the kinds of way-finding being described here are unaided by sophisticated instrumentation. Nor is it a mechanical process whereby one set of actual circumstances confronting the mariner is formally compared to a previous experience of similar conditions and a course thereby established and followed. It is not a case of referring to a set of rules and applying them. To that extent a manuscript like the *Fawāʾid*, for all that it has the appearance of a guide book, is not intended as a book of rules, a kind of Highway Code for navigators. Apart from the practical difficulties of carrying manuscripts at sea – and reading them in adverse conditions, worst of all at night – there are no injunctions in the text that this is how it is to be treated. The purpose is to describe navigational practice in such a way that the background tenets or 'rules' to be followed are so completely internalized that their application can seem entirely personal to the navigator, like well-prepared students drawing on their range of knowledge to answer in their own particular way an unseen question in exam conditions. The navigator, indeed, is not so much *following* rules as *making* them in the practical conditions of actual navigational practice. There is a sense in which the conditions confronted from moment to moment require a continuous creative engagement between navigator and the conditions of nature encountered at sea.

The insistence on attentiveness in Ibn Mājid's work is one pre-condition of successful navigation; another is the absorption of its distilled observations such that any intellectual or analytical application becomes imperceptible. Navigation in this sense is not a self-conscious act. Mariners talk of navigating by the 'feel' of the conditions of sea and sky. Ernest Hemingway's old man of the sea 'did not need a compass to tell him where south west was. He only needed the feel of the trade wind and the drawing of the sail.'[29] Mark Twain talks of Mississippi river pilots steering by their sense of the shape of the sky – that is, not by pointing unwaveringly at a dot of light in the distance but by taking their course from the larger configuration of the heavens. And Thomas Gladwin remarks that 'Puluwatans steer by the feel of waves under the canoe, not visually.'[30] Navigational skill of this kind is an embodied faculty which it is difficult and indeed perhaps inappropriate to articulate in any actual situation. It is almost as if the successful mariner no longer knows how he finds his way – he simply does it. There is no complete technological analogy for the process.

He is in one sense navigating as if on 'automatic pilot', but he cannot simply sit back and let some version of instrumentation take him from A to B; he, as navigator, is completely engaged in the process as an absolute precondition of its success. It is his sentience that makes it happen.

Arguably, the process of internalization is assisted by this mnemonic function of his verse and the reportedly euphonic style of Ibn Mājid's prose in Arabic. Like the process in medieval scriptoria of reading aloud, the purpose is less to document as to assist with the process of memory.[31] His text is meant to be memorable, and as such it can be recalled and thereby 'personalized' by the reader, himself potentially a navigational novice. The aim is to get to an agile engagement with the rules. In Tim Ingold's words the novice becomes skilled not by acquiring and abiding by rules 'but at the point where he or she is able to dispense with them'.[32]

Mental maps?

Yet where does this leave the intellectual aspects of navigation? Sea charts, cartography and the discussion of so-called 'mental maps' all tend to privilege the activities of the mind over those of the body. The act of locating a position on a map converts space into place. Yet arguably way-finding is about a fluid process, not the fixity of a picture of objective geography. It is about the sensory experience of movement, the movement of the maritime environment and the movement of a vessel within that environment. Are we right, therefore, to think of some of the seeming navigational strategies of indigenous mariners in cartographic terms?

We started this chapter by noting that Marshall Islanders make diagrams of islands and wave patterns but when venturing out to sea they leave them behind on land. These so-called 'charts' are clearly intended as mnemonics not as maps (illus. 8). Three different types have been identified and are distinguished linguistically. The first, the *mattang*, is essentially instructional in nature representing the characteristics of the sea rather than the position of islands and is regarded by some as the 'authentic' indigenous device.[33] It differs from other versions in being less a 'picture' of the sea and islands and is much more individualized in what it chooses to represent. The second, *meddo*,

8 Stick and shell navigational device (*rebbilib*). Marshall Islands, Micronesia, late 19th century.

shows swell patterns in relation to certain chosen islands, whilst the third type, *rebbilib*, purports to show the whole of an archipelago and is focused more on the position of islands than on swells and wave patterns. In so far as it approximates most completely to the Western idea of a 'map' as a description of objective space, the last is regarded as most influenced by European ideas. It may even have been a type of representation produced specifically for sale to visitors rather than for local use. Indeed, one reason why foreigners have been so intrigued by Marshall Island stick charts must surely be precisely that they appear to anticipate in rudimentary form the representational imagery of charts. Their inclusion in a major exhibition of the British Museum's collection in Japan in 2004 attracted as much attention from visitors and reviewers as did major works from Greece or Egypt. Yet the initial reason for their popularity was almost certainly due to misapprehension, for clearly they are focused less on land or seamarks than on the characteristics of the sea itself. In that sense they might be regarded as truly maritime. Where charts mark the characteristics of the seabed and of the land, Marshall Islanders are much more interested in the detailed description of what happens on the surface of the water – the effects of wave and current.

Certainly the fact that indigenous 'stick charts' are made by individuals for their own use suggests that they are intended to be entirely personalized devices, just as the wave patterns that any navigator chooses to see as diagnostic in way-finding is entirely a matter of individual perception. David Lewis quotes a remark by Captain Winkler suggesting that 'even an entirely competent navigator cannot under any circumstance read the deliverances of a chart which he himself has not made'.[34] The distinction from a 'map' as it is conventionally understood is clear: a map in the usual sense is seen as an objective representation in which, by definition, features occupy an absolute and fixed position in relation to each other. The point would seem to be that stick charts are less representations of space as representations of the *experience* of space. We are back to navigation as the 'feel' of the combined conditions of sea, sky and wind, to navigational devices as more aide memoire than documentary instruments of objective conditions.

This knowledge of the sea and coastlines is often configured by commentators in terms of so-called 'mental maps', thereby employing a physical graphic system with its own particular historical context to describe a form of geographical knowledge which is not otherwise externalized. It is a means by which a cartographic culture seeks to understand the thinking and skills of a non-cartographic one. However, a basic confusion arises in Western perceptions of navigation because of what we might see as the influence of Braudelian habits of generalizing from the experience of the Mediterranean. In the Mediterranean, of course, most journeys take place within sight of land or at least in sufficient proximity to the coast for sightings to be reasonably frequent. The idea of mental maps as an adjunct to navigation is thus not an unusual metaphor since such maps are about coastlines rather than seas or stars. And, for reasons already outlined, voyaging in the Mediterranean is more about coasting than about long-distance sailing across the open ocean. But where journeys take place largely out of sight of land, the idea of a mental map seems more or less redundant. This is very different from the experience of the seas which Barry Cunliffe outlines in *Facing the Ocean*. There, for instance, he describes a typical journey in the medieval period:

> For regular trips of whatever length, the master would have
> built up a familiarity with the environment through which

he travelled, able to assess the movement of his craft in relation to the sea and the winds, to interpret the signs of land
still out of sight, and to recognize the shape of land once it
came close enough to be visible. What was required was a
mental map of the voyage incorporating knowledge gained
from all the senses. A Bristol ship's captain bound for Lisbon
in the thirteenth century would be familiar with the Scillies,
Ushant, and Cape Finisterre but may have known little of
the coasts between – his mental map needed only to identify
the landmarks and to know how to progress from one to
another.[35]

There is no problem at all with much of this. Clearly mariners
have some – even some very precise – idea of where they are going
before they set out. Shame, indeed, if they did not! They know landmarks and are looking out for them as coasts come into view. But
would we be justified in generalizing this experience? Mental maps,
or even physical ones, were only of use on approaching landfall and
then almost entirely for pilotage rather than navigation – you needed to know what Rio or Cape Town looked like when you got there
so you knew you had arrived in the right place. But both are very distinctive anyway: the typography of Rio was conventionally figured as
a man lying on his back looking at the sky, and Cape Town, of course,
as a table. However, beyond that what you really needed to know was
how to get safely into harbour.

For the open seas a different set of skills were required. It is
important to remember that it is only in more recent historical times
that navigation by increasingly sophisticated technological means was
to become a matter of plotting a course on a chart and following it,
aware night and day from sensing equipment of deviations from
planned courses or impending hazards and obstructions. For the rest
of human history way-finding has been a matter of observing and
adapting, keeping a compass when it became available only, perhaps,
as an insurance policy if direct observation should be impaired by
weather and cloud. There were no charts to be followed. Indeed, it
can be argued that translating indigenous practice into graphic form
is potentially flawed for the experience of the sea is not fundamentally
about the measurement of objective space but the sense of movement
within it.

Tupaia's 'chart'

A second example of the skills of a named indigenous mariner highlights the differences between conceptions of space based on cartography and on movement. If there is uncertainty about how, and even
if, Ibn Mājid contributed to Vasco da Gama's understanding of the
Indian Ocean system, there can be no doubt about the involvement
of an experienced Polynesian navigator with Captain Cook's Pacific
voyaging. We know of him as a collaborator aboard the *Endeavour* –
and specifically from the interest Joseph Banks took in him, hedged
as it is in the Enlightenment language of collecting interesting speci-
mens for study and intellectual stimulation and all the more startling
for being applied to a person. Banks wrote: 'Thank heaven I have a
sufficiency and I do not know why I may not keep him as a curiosity,
as well as some of my neighbours do lions and tygers.'[36] He is referring to Tupaia, someone variously described as a dispossessed high
chief and navigator from Raiatea, or, less floridly, as a 'priest and
chiefly advisor',[37] who joined Cook's first voyage in 1769. Like Ibn
Mājid, Tupaia was from a family of navigators and was deeply imbued
with the lore of the sea. He seems to have been born around 1725,
within a few years of Cook himself. At the time Cook and his illustrious companions encountered him he was living, probably in exile, in
Tahiti. There, it is speculated by some, he was free to divulge navigational knowledge to an extent that would not have been possible given
prevailing rules of secrecy in his home territory. However that may be,
it seems beyond doubt that his knowledge of over 70 islands – many
of them as yet unlocated and unknown to Europeans – so impressed
the learned men of the *Endeavour* that, partly at Banks's insistence and
partly at his own wish, he was enabled to join them on their voyaging
when they set out from Tahiti.

Tupaia was to be with the vessel until his death eighteenth
months later in Batavia, by which time he had shared the experiences
of Cook's ship's company on the *Endeavour* in their extensive explorations of the Pacific and New Zealand. Various written reports of the
impression he made on his fellow-voyagers survive together with a
few fascinating scraps of archival documentation by or after his own
hand. Banks sets the scene: the quotation above is preceded by the
explanation that

[H]e is certainly a most proper man, well born, chief *Tahowa* or priest of this Island, consequently skilld in the mysteries of their religion: but what makes him more than anything else desirable is his experience in the navigion of these people and knowledge of the Islands in these seas . . .[38]

Cook's views of Tupaia were somewhat more muted and he had needed persuasion to take him on in the first place. Part of Cook's mission was to identify and plot a possible southern continent, so the fact that Tupaia 'hardly [had] any Idea of any land larger than *Otaheite*'[39] was a disappointment. But, that said, Cook still found him to be 'a very intelligent person and to know more of the Geography of the Islands situated in these seas, their produce and religion laws and customs of their inhabitants then [*sic*] any one we had met.'[40] When Tupaia passed away Cook reflected '[H]e was a Shrewd, Sensible, Ingenious Man but proud and obstinate which often made his situation on board both disagreeable to himself and those about him.'[41] Not a ringing endorsement perhaps, but then Tupaia enjoyed Banks's support and patronage and Banks and Cook themselves were to have a strained relationship. Furthermore, Cook and Tupaia were from two alternative systems of navigational practice and knowledge. The ambiguity here attributed to the Polynesian's character might also be read as a response to the professional disjunctions between the two mariners, the one schooled in the more abstract scientific procedures of eighteenth-century voyaging and mapping, the other conversant with an entirely practical approach to navigating which was responsive to actual situations.

Such disjunction is harder to detect than it might otherwise be because of the existence of a number of illustrative drawings and a famous map associated with Tupaia. We have already seen that maps in the European cartographic sense are not a part of Oceanic tradition; nor yet are illustrations. Yet Tupaia is associated with both aspects of Western graphic representation. In a way it is not surprising. Tupaia was, after all, embarked on a voyage with both naval surveyors and the expedition artist Sydney Parkinson with whom he had every opportunity to exchange ideas and observe their working methods. Yet sketching everyday scenes in a representational visual idiom is certainly a radical departure from Polynesian traditions of representational art. These were largely sculptural and focused on the representation of

9 Tupaia, *A Scene in Tahiti*, 1769, pencil and watercolour..

deities rather than people, let alone everyday scenes. Their purpose was
not to reflect the everyday but to visualize sources of power and embellish prestige. Indeed, Tupaia's home island was the focus of an emergent
religious cult in the eighteenth century associated with the deity 'Oro,
whose development may have been amongst the reasons for his departure to Tahiti. The extant objects of the 'Oro cult are non-representational priestly staffs.[42] As with the emergence of descriptive practices of drawing and illustration in many places outside of the Eurasian
tradition, it is contact with outsiders which initiated a graphic tradition
of representing everyday life. Thomas enumerates a series of sketches
identified with Tupaia's hand.[43] They include musicians, a young
woman dancing, canoes with a building and vegetation behind (illus. 9),
a chief mourner and two views of a *marae* (a Maori meeting house). The
figures in the canoe image, interestingly, though humans, are drawn in
the style of sculptures of deities from Tupaia's home islands. The pictures seem to have been executed both in Tahiti and in New Zealand
and all must date to a period between July 1769 and November 1770.
A famous illustration showing Joseph Banks offering a piece of cloth
or paper to a Maori wearing a flax cloak, who offers a large red lobster
in exchange, can now be added to that list. A letter from Banks himself
identifies the depiction and reflects:

> Tupia [*sic*] the Indian who came with me from Otaheite
> Lernd to draw in a way not Quite Unintelligible. The genius

for Caricature which all wild people Possess Led him to
Caricature me . . .[44]

We find Banks engaged in endorsing the natural aptitudes of the
Noble Savage.[45]

However, it is from the production of a chart of the islands of the
Pacific that Tupaia's renown principally derives. It was purportedly
produced aboard ship and was subsequently published as an illustration to Johann Reinhold Forster's account of the voyages, though
Forster in fact never met Tupaia himself. The map is best described as
after a map or diagram by Tupaia – or even a rendering of information
he was able to provide – for we have no record of the original (illus.
10). However, the fact of such a diagrammatic representation itself
raises interesting questions. If Tupaia could learn to draw representational imagery in a style appropriate to European expectation, why not
a chart? Lewis surmises that it was 'drawn for Cook under Tupaia's
direction'.[46] In other words, although Tupaia had shown himself more
than capable of drawing and graphic illustration, map-making was
another story. This is not, perhaps, how Thomas sees it. For his part
he regards the map as a remarkable, if largely unrecognized, document. It is, he suggests, 'the exception that proves the rule', noting
that more usually 'European and indigenous imaginings – of history
and place – have intersected, not merged'.[47] This, in David Turnbull's
assessment, misrepresents the situation: 'perhaps the answer lies',
Turnbull reflects, 'in the overly representationalist perspective he
[Thomas] and many others have adopted to knowledge and intellectual exchange.'[48] Or, more precisely, perhaps it is that the expectation
has sometimes been that the representations used in European navigational practice are assumed to provide a universally appropriate
description.

One issue which some commentators have raised is that the map
– *qua* map – is not in fact based on information that was strictly accurate; and this has been seen as an understandable defect in what is,
as Thomas suggests, a foundational exercise. A nineteenth-century
source, Horatio Hale, makes the interesting observation that as printed
the chart is in fact upside down. He surmises that:

> Knowing that *toerau* in Tahitian signified the north (or north-
> west) wind, and *toa* the south, they concluded naturally that

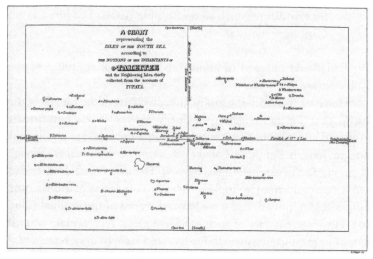

10 'A Chart representing the Isles of the South Sea, according to the notions of the inhabitants of O-Taheitee and the neighbouring Isles, chiefly collected from the accounts of Tupaya', published in Johann Reinhold Forster, *Observations Made during a Voyage round the World* (London, 1778).

> *apatoerau* and *apatoa* were names applied to the corresponding points of the compass; whereas *apatoerau* signifies, in fact, the point towards which the north wind blows, – i.e. the south, and *apatoa*, for the same reason, the north.[49]

And this is confirmed by the observation that those islands known to Cook and his crew are in fact represented in the reverse orientation to those known only to Tupaia.

We have suggested that navigation throughout much of human history is not a matter of portolan, or point-to-point, sailing in many of the world's seas. This suggests that a further divergence of Tupaia's 'chart' from an accurate mariner's map in the European mode – which it purports to be – is because it is not a replication of objective geography but of how islands stand in relation to each other given known vicissitudes of wind and current. How, then, do Pacific mariners navigate without access to compasses, themselves only of any use when associated with an accompanying map of sailing directions? Much voyaging in the Pacific, after all, takes place between distant isolated islands that may be little more than the smallest of specks on the ocean and days sailing time away. Fortunately, there are a number

of authoritative ethnographic accounts of Pacific navigational knowledge and practice which can be summarized for present purposes.

There is no single navigational method that is used on its own.
However astronomical observation, as elsewhere, is the most sophisticated method practised. Throughout the Pacific the most important
stars are those on the horizon, which, depending on the direction
being sailed, are either those which have just risen (in the east) or
those which are setting (in the west). These are chosen because they
are known to lie in the direction of an island towards which the navigator is travelling. However, whilst stars always rise in the same place
at the same latitude, once up they arc off to either side so the period
of their utility is limited. Thus an overnight sailing potentially involves
observation of a whole succession of rising stars in order to maintain
direction with allowance being made for the increasingly inaccurate
trajectory of a guiding star if another does not appear at once. The
observation of up to ten stars may be needed successfully to chart a
complete night's course (though confusingly to European minds they
are often known by the name of the first star to appear even if they
are all successive).

Let us take an example quoted by Lewis to gauge what might be
involved even on a clear night. The passage being made was 100 miles
from the Reef Islands to Vanikoro with one of Lewis's most informed
navigators, Tevake, in charge.[50] Just over halfway was a small intervening island with a dangerous surrounding reef that would be difficult to
navigate in the dark. The relevant stars for the journey were two in
number, Canopus and the Southern Cross, and neither was easy to use
as a guide as both moved to the right once risen and, though not high
in the sky, still had to have their movement estimated off the desired
sailing direction over time. Lewis continues:

> But, as if this were not difficult enough, there was an added
> complication in that the navigator deduced by the shape of
> the waves that a strong current had set in and was running
> to the eastward of north. He therefore altered course $1\frac{1}{2}$–2
> points ($17°$–$22°30$) to the right of the proper star course.
> That he was successful in maintaining this course between
> $175°$–$180°$ with the sole aid of the mobile Canopus was
> proved when the Southern Cross topped the horizon at the
> correct position on the port bow an hour before midnight.[51]

Further confirmation was provided when the intervening island was approached in the middle of the night on a course avoiding the dangerous reefs.

A more complex version of this is a star or sidereal compass, as used for instance in the Caroline Islands, in which the stars indicate a panorama of points around the night horizon rather than the bearing of any single island.[52] This enables complex navigational journeys to be worked out from any number of starting points to any destination. None the less their usage follows similar principles; and, as a result, even where magnetic compasses are available many are carried not as a primary source of information but, again, as back-up in case of thick cloud.

Yet, whilst all this is a possible feat of navigation on a clear night, it is much more difficult when the sky is partly or largely obscured by cloud. In those instances the stars that are visible have to be used, checking the accuracy of the estimate of direction as and when desired guide stars can be glimpsed. What this requires is knowledge of the complete sky at different phases of the night. It may be necessary to steer not by stars in front of the helmsman but off the stern, or at unaccustomed angles. The relative position of stars in relationship to the rigging may provide another check. Some routes, of course, may not be in straight lines but would require changes of course requiring estimates of distance and time travelled, themselves a function of an assessment of the influence of wind and current on the ship's progress.

Apart from the indicative characteristics of the stars, a vast array of other checks also come into play, depending on such factors as whether the sky is fully visible, the time of day, the season of the year and the location of the canoe in relation to land. None is straightforward to assess in actual situations. Thus wind direction, whilst it is fundamental to the operation of sailed boats, is a changeable and thereby unreliable guide to direction, even in the open ocean where the mariner is spared the variability that arises in proximity to land. Winds throw up waves but these may have been generated far from the actual location at which they are observed. Indeed, a complex of waves generated at different places is contributory to the actual conditions encountered in any given location at sea. The ability to identify the significant swell amongst a whole series of contrary wave patterns is not something that can be learnt on land. Yet it may be critical. Many Pacific navigators are reported as giving precedence to the feel of the waves over other indicators. The most important in influencing the course to be sailed may be those set up by distant and more permanent weather systems such as the trade winds. Yet the process of their detection is not a swift one since it requires a great deal of watchfulness to distinguish what are often slight and intermittent effects: it involves assessing a complex of characteristics involving wave direction, size, steepness, regularity, and so forth. The mariner already mentioned, Tevake, told Lewis that his practice was to go and lie down in the small shelter on the canoe's outrigger and to concentrate on analysing the motions of the waves looking to identify the feel of small and perhaps more intermittent swells which represent the underlying structure of currents amongst larger and more locally generated waves.

Close to land the wave patterns take on a different character again. As the waves hit a landmass so the backwash sets up interference to the normal wave pattern in open sea which can be detected at a considerable distance offshore. For an experienced navigator the effects are detectable up to fifteen or twenty miles offshore as the bow rises first and then the stern – 'I feel the sea hit the canoe, – shake him like move him go back' as one navigator, Rafe from Tikopia, remarked to Lewis.[53] This is easiest to identify as turbulence in the approach to a single isolated island. However, with a complex of islands the wave patterning becomes distinctly scrambled and interpreting the complexity of wave disruption may be no easy matter. In complex situations of contradictory wave patterning the swell is detectable only by the feel of the vessel as it pitches and rolls even slightly in encountering waves at different angles.

Clearly interpreting these sensory perceptions operates as effectively at night as in the daytime, for it does not rely on sight. However, Lewis goes on to quote a veteran island skipper, one Captain Ward:

> I have heard from several sources that the most sensitive balance was a man's testicles, and when at night or when the horizon was obscured, or inside the cabin this was the method used to find the focus of the swells off an island.[54]

The testicles, it seems, may sometimes act as a kind of plumb line. But all the possible sensory organs are called into play as required. For instance, the source of currents may even be associated with the taste of different streams of water in the ocean. Thus the account of a blind mariner from the Pacific who navigated with the assistance of his sighted son endorses the fundamentally sensory nature of navigation; we read:

> Kaho is said to have dipped his hand into the sea, tasted the spray and bade his son tell him the directions of certain stars. He then averred that the water was Fijian and the waves from the Lau group where they duly arrived the next day.[55]

In reality the navigator does not have to pinpoint a distant island precisely by the balance of these various navigational methods. He only needs to get within a radius of 30 miles or so of an island to be sure to achieve landfall. At that range, even if land is low-lying and remains out of sight, its presence can be detected. This effectively expands significantly the target and provides a significant safety net or 'screen'.[56] And, of course, if two islands lie within 60 miles of each other they form a block from a navigational point of view which includes the distance between them and 30 miles to either side making a total target of 120 miles wide. The techniques allow the navigator to refine his sailing directions with increasing precision when within range of still-invisible islands.

One sure sign is the observation of birds, principally terns and noddies, which roost at night on islands but spend the day out at sea. Their radius of flight around an island is primarily what sets the limit of the indications of the unseen presence of an island at between twenty and 30 miles. In the morning they fly out, taking a more or less straight line from an island and in the evening they return again. All the mariner has to do is follow their line of flight. So sure is their habit that seafarers will often heave-to during the night or day and wait until dawn or dusk when the birds are in flight to find their route. Like sailors elsewhere, Pacific mariners would also sometimes take captive birds on voyages and release them in the hope that they will fly in the direction of land.

The lore surrounding clouds as an indicator of land is extremely subtle. Experienced navigators can tell the configuration of the seascape from the minor variations of coloration on the underside of a distant cloud. A greenish colour might indicate lagoon islands; lighter coloration would suggest areas of white sand or surf; darker hues could indicate a green island.[57] Yet, considerable study is required to read the signs with confidence. In overcast conditions it is still possible to derive appropriate clues. A consistent thickening and darkening of cloud cover observed in one place over a period of time would suggest the influence of an underlying landmass. Even where there is no cloud cover at all some navigators are able to deduce a subtly different lightness indicating the presence of land, especially towards noon when the sun is evenly distributed across the horizon.

Finally, a kind of luminosity is reported as a directional sign in parts of the Pacific.[58] This is said to flash out from the direction of islands under the surface of the water or flicker in the bearing of land as a phosphorescence. It is, in fact, detectable at very large distances of up to 80 or 100 miles offshore. On dark nights it may sometimes be used to replace stars as an alternative navigational device. However, it is not uniquely generated around islands but also by reefs and can be a hazard as much as a help if it draws the unwary towards its source.

The navigator, then, might be described as reminiscent of a virtuoso conductor surrounded by a complete orchestra and with a known musical score to negotiate. But despite the existence of scripted music there are subtleties to each successive performance. Different instruments need to be brought into play in sequence, their arrival anticipated, adjustments made and a constant state of alertness maintained. Different concert halls have different acoustic properties. It is not just a matter of casual observation but of a complete sensory engagement for, just as two successive performances of a piece of music are different, so no two sea passages between islands are ever the same. Navigation is a complete, embodied, synaesthetic activity. The navigator has at his disposal all the information needed for innumerable successful acts of way-finding at sea. He needs no additional technologies or knowledge or ways of representing what he already knows. His navigational skills are in all respects 'fit for purpose'. In Gladwin's words, the system works 'and if at any time it does not work it is not the fault of the system'.[59]

Tupaia was heir to such traditions of navigational practice. That he should be able to draw a map is not perhaps in itself difficult to conceive as he otherwise showed every ability to pick up graphic skills even if cartography was not, for all that, his milieu. Hipour, an experienced mariner who sailed with both Lewis and Gladwin, is quoted as being constantly puzzled about how islands came to be on charts in the first place; yet, though unable to read or write, he had no trouble at all in interpreting a chart. However, given the character of Polynesian experience of the sea, a map none the less seems an enigma, a concretization in the form of European cartographic practice of forms of knowledge which are performed rather than prefigured. There are differences between thinking about way-finding in a maritime context and thinking about it in a terrestrial one. Clearly, whilst there are seaways and sailing directions known to mariners, it is not like walking down a forest path or along a road. The sea has no routes inscribed on its surface – which is not to say that skills like latitude sailing are not in some ways comparable to terrestrial travel, but it is to recognize the extent to which maritime travel is a much more intense sensory experience, especially on the open ocean. The information to be gained from soundings was undoubtedly extensive and many accounts from the earliest times make detailed mention of the findings in different seas. But in terms of maps of course, until the depths of the ocean had been surveyed, maritime maps were mostly maps of coastlines – indeed, being charted mostly from the sea, such maps tended to mark promontories and landmarks with the gaps in between drawn in rather than accurately represented.

Sailing by staying still

One of the glories of the National Geographical Society of Egypt in Cairo, founded by Khedive Ismail in 1875, is a reconstruction of a journey along the Suez Canal which had been opened up to shipping just six years earlier. It is still functioning today. The visitor is seated as though in a cinema – or rather as on the prow of a ship – whilst a painted landscape gradually unfurls on large spindles, unrolling the scenery in front and down either side of the seating. Thus the landscape can be seen to left and right as it would be on an actual trip along the whole length of the canal. The visitor remains stationary whilst the scenery itself is moving.

In parts of the Pacific a similar conceit is instilled in novice navigators in the very process of their training. In some places stone boats are constructed on land facing the night sky in the direction of particular voyages to be undertaken. The sequence of the stars rising on the horizon, their interrelation with other stars and their movements across the heavens are all learnt by direct observation. It is an indigenous version of a driving simulator. At sea this approach is manifest in the much-discussed *etak* system of navigation.[60] This is a version of dead-reckoning which relies on the fiction that an imaginary island just beyond the horizon is moving whilst the boat being sailed is stationary. The destination advances towards the boat whilst the starting point recedes.

Likewise we might argue that the distinctiveness of maritime navigational practice before sophisticated instrumentation is due to its person-centred character. Ingold draws a distinction between the activities of navigation on the one hand, and way-finding on the other.[61] Navigation, he suggests, relies on having a complete representation of the territory to be traversed laid out in front of you on which a course can be charted in anticipation of a journey. The crossing of the territory, whether land or sea, can be planned in advance such that when it is undertaken for real it merely replicates the predetermined routes through the movements of the travellers. Wayfaring, by comparison, is characterized as a process of following a path rather than predetermining a route in its entirety within a total territorial context. The path may be one which others have trodden before but it is only on arrival at the desired destination that the traveller has found his or her way. The first conception of journeying, in fact, requires the intermediation of an artefact – a map or a chart. The second is based on experience. Both Pacific and western Indian Ocean or Arabian Sea mariners are unequivocally identified as 'navigators', as in the very titles of the books outlining their practice. Yet it would seem hard to resist the conclusion that the kinds of navigational feats achieved without sea-charts or compasses are actually wayfaring.

This framework of navigation places the navigator himself and his engagement with the maritime environment at the centre of the acts by which way-finding at sea happens. An account by a contemporary writer on maritime experience, Jonathan Raban, makes the point well. He writes:

> The egotism of a man by himself in a boat is bolstered by everything he can see. Out on the water, you *are* the centrifugal point of the world through which you move, carrying the great disc of your horizon with you as you go. The first lessons in navigation entail an almost-scientific proof

of the magnificent fallacy that the universe has been
constructed for your convenience alone.[62]

What we have here is the exact inverse of the principles of chart-
making. In one islands occupy a fixed and immutable position; in
the other they are configured as mobile. But, even if the mobility of
mariners is asserted over the mobility of the seascape, there is still
a fundamental distinction between a static representation of space
as opposed to the performative nature of indigenous navigational
practice. All this gives those moments when two systems come into
contact particular evidential importance. Cook does not appear to
have asked Tupaia how he found his way between islands or what
indigenous skills he had at his command. The process was one way.
Rendered in the form of a nautical chart it excited no further curiosity. It could be judged according to its accuracy in strictly objective
cartographic terms, critiqued for any deviations from physical realities as established by scientific calculation, but in its already translated
state it invited no further inquiry. Yet the system of knowledge which
it appeared to codify was of another order. The arts required of the
Pacific or Indian Ocean mariners are less those of mapping than of
memory.

The 'aesthetics' of sailing

In this chapter we have invoked the notion of aesthetics, or synaes-
thetics, to describe aspects of the experience of being under sail. We
do so not in any ill-considered or loose way. It emerges as readily in
the training of mariners as it does in the practice of being under sail.
Thus, another way to configure the poetics of Ibn Mājid's navigational writing is to see it as contributory to the artistry of way-finding
with its emphasis on the evocative power of words. The sensory characteristics of learning parallels the sensory experience of way-finding,
just as in the Pacific anticipating the sequential rising of the stars and
their arcing movements in the night sky from a stationary boat on
land rehearses the actual experience of way-finding on voyages in the
open sea. Indeed, the burden of the discussion here is to suggest that
the emphasis in phrases such as 'mental' maps on intellectual activity is
at odds with what might better be described as the 'sensory mapping'

which is arguably more characteristic of the pre-modern experience of being at sea. Here it is the attentive response to the fluid and constantly changing effects of wind and swell which are critical, not acts of 'mental' prefiguring. Poetics, aesthetics and sensory experience are interrelated aspects of the habitation of the sea which mind/body distinctions fail to register adequately.

But if 'aesthetics' is an appropriate idiom for speaking of being under sail, Richard Dana gives a more detached, conventional view of it. He writes:

> Notwithstanding all that has been said about the beauty of a ship under full sail, there are very few who have ever seen a ship literally under all her sail. A ship coming in or going out of port, with her ordinary sails, and perhaps two or three studding sails, is commonly said to be under full sail; but a ship never has all her sail upon her, except when she has a light, steady breeze, very nearly, but not quite, dead aft, and so regular that it can be trusted, and is likely to last for some time. Then, with all her sails, light and heavy, and studding-sails, on each side, alow and aloft, she is the most glorious moving object in the world.[63]

He goes on to talk of the billowing sails as 'sculptured marble'. For Dana this is largely a visual experience. Indeed, he suggests that it requires an objective perspective to fully appreciate the beauty of the sight. There is rarely an opportunity to achieve this. Climbing the rigging and looking down on the ship from on high is one of the only positions which affords the mariner a view of his vessel as a separate entity. In the right circumstances the view is all-engrossing; it induces a loss of a sense of self. This is the aesthetics of the many marine paintings which portray ships from a distant viewpoint under sail and moving efficiently through the waves.

However, the vocabulary of the aesthetic takes this a stage further and into less obvious areas of experience. If way-finding at sea may be described as an activity that engages all the senses, its purpose is to bring them together into a cathartic conjunction, a moment which some of our sources describe more simply in terms of the 'thrill' of sailing. Writing in *Three Men in a Boat (To Say Nothing of the Dog)* (1889), in a spirit of eulogy rare for a book otherwise distinguished by its unforeseen twists and turns, Jerome K. Jerome reflects on the joys of being under sail:

> There is no more thrilling sensation I know of than sailing. It comes as near to flying as man has got to yet – except in dreams. The wings of the rushing wind seem to be bearing you onward, you know not where. You are no longer the slow, plodding, puny thing of clay, creeping tortuously upon the ground; you are a part of nature! Your heart is throbbing against hers. Her glorious arms are around you, raising you up against her heart! Your spirit is at one with hers; your limbs grow light! The voices of the air are singing to you. The earth seems far away and little: and the clouds above your head are brothers, and you stretch your arms to them.[64]

Inevitably, given the humorous chaos that daily overtakes Jerome's three would-be sailors, immediately after this hymn to the joys of sailing the boat whose unrestricted progress induces these reflections ploughs into a punt containing three elderly fishermen, knocking them from their quiet contemplation of the river and turning them into an angry cursing tangle.

For Conrad the enthralment of sailing is an adjunct of mutual self-reliance. He talks of sailing as a form of 'elemental moral beauty',[65] by which he means two things. One is the distance it creates from the concerns of the land and especially from complex forms of interaction. To be at sea, he remarks elsewhere, is to occupy a simpler space of moral clarity and discipline.

> The true peace of God begins at any spot a thousand miles from the nearest land; and when He sends there the messengers of His might it is not in terrible wrath against crime, presumption, and folly, but paternally, to chasten simple hearts – ignorant hearts that know nothing of life, that beat undisturbed by envy or greed.[66]

A second implication is the fact that on merchant ships such as those on which he served, progress and safety required the combined actions of a complete crew. This is the aesthetics of working in combination. For the ship to sail effortlessly through the waters everything has to work together in a perfect harmony of forces. It is this which leads us to talk of navigation as an art of performance. By extension sailing itself might be described in such terms. The purpose of complete sensory engagement is to achieve an ideal calibration of the potential of the ship, the effort of its crew to make all the relevant adjustments moment to moment in the constantly changing conditions of the maritime environment. The ship, as the three men in a boat experienced, moves as if in flight. Dana describes this state of efficient interdependence:

> Here things are done 'with a will', everyone is like a cat aloft: sails are loosed in an instant; each one lays out his strength on his handspike, and the windlass goes briskly round with the loud cry of "Yo heave ho! Heave and paw! Heave hearty ho!"[67]

Sailing might be described as an embodied experience. It is to this proposition that we now turn.

four

Ships as Societies

*A dozen men are shut up together in a little
bark, upon the wide, wide sea, and for months
and months see no forms and hear no voices but
their own, and one is taken suddenly from among
them, and they miss him at every turn. It is like
losing a limb.*

RICHARD HENRY DANA, JR,
Two Years before the Mast (1840)[1]

*No man will be a sailor who has contrivance enough to
get him into jail: for being in a ship is being in a jail,
with the chance of being drowned . . . a man in jail has
more room, better food and commonly better company.*

DR JOHNSON IN JAMES BOSWELL,
The Life of Samuel Johnson (1791)[2]

As a certain genre of detective story thrives on the study of crime
in small, self-contained villages or committed at weekend parties in
isolated country houses, so anthropology cut its teeth on the study
of small-scale societies. Before the emergence of urban anthropology, this used to be one of the distinctions commonly advanced to
describe the disciplinary difference between anthropology and sociology. Yet it was not really a difference of scholarly discipline but only
of scale and the coherence of its subject. Anthropology was seen as
something pursued amongst bounded groups of people – or so it
was often portrayed – usually living in foreign fields or amongst
outlying communities of Western societies in timeless insularity.
Sociology was an equivalent discipline but, typically, focused on
much larger, more diffuse, urban, mostly Western populations. For
all that they share a common set of founding fathers and overlapping interests, scale emerged as an initial defining distinction between
the two.

Ships and their crews, therefore, would seem an ideal subject of traditional anthropological concern: a vessel of interaction in the context of the deployment of learnt skills as part of an integrated approach to sailing. Michel Foucault remarked 'the boat is a floating piece of space, a place without a place, that exists by itself, that is closed in on itself and at the same time is given over to the infinity of the sea.'[3] In such spaces success, livelihood – and even life itself – depend on coordinated acts of seamanship. Richard Dana's evocation of the sense of mutual dependency aboard ship is preceded by a heartfelt passage. He writes:

> A man dies on shore – you follow his body to the grave, and a stone marks the spot . . . A man is shot down by your side in battle, and the mangled body remains an object, and a real evidence; but at sea, the man is near you – at your side – you hear his voice, and in an instant he is gone, and nothing but a vacancy shows his loss. Then, too, at sea – to use a homely but expressive phrase – you miss a man so much.[4]

Dr Johnson's sense of the advantages of the jail over the ship misses the active engaged sense of mutual self-reliance which actual experience of the sea engenders. Losing a fellow crew member at sea is indeed like losing a part of oneself.

Yet anthropologists have rarely exposed themselves to the 'culture shock' of being on ships at sea or considered them as social units. Indeed, had they done so they would have discovered, as Redmond O'Hanlon did,[5] that as social entities ships, if they are not modern cruise liners (and sometimes even if they are), are quite distinctive kinds of societies from those that an older generation of anthropologists characteristically studied. One major distinguishing feature is that, far from being uniform communities, ships' crews, other perhaps than when constituted as 'national' navies, have often been very diverse in their composition. Arguably ships are the first truly cosmopolitan spaces. Their crews might be of different ages and experience, often recruited amongst those with differing first languages and cultures, and often brought together to work as a unit on ships of unfamiliar design. Indeed the one common feature of ship's crews is that they are very largely male, a situation made even more evident in the fact that ships themselves in different cultures and contexts are sometimes explicitly regarded as female. This sets ships and their crews apart and raises a leading question for this chapter. How does such a diverse community as that brought together for specific voyages come to form a community of skill and discipline? If we have just looked at how a ship becomes an embodied technological space, here we discuss ships as embodied social spaces.

The making of a Jack Tar

Given the lack of conventional anthropological accounts – and what there is mostly focused on the Pacific – we return to one of the best 'ethnographies' of this experience of the sea and of life aboard deep-sea ships in Richard Dana Jr's autobiographical account of the life of a merchant seaman. Dana's lengthy account of life as a common seaman 'before the mast' was regarded in its day as an objective picture of maritime life from the point of view of the merchant seaman. A large part of the success of his subsequent narrative lies in the simplicity and immediacy of his style of writing and the elevation of the experience of the ordinary seaman with all its trials and pleasures to a subject of general interest. Dana opens his book by quoting a verse from Coleridge's *Wallenstein* which contains the line: 'Housed on the wild sea with wild usages'. His book, however, is no unashamedly romantic essay on the sublime. In this he implicitly refuted the idealized Byronesque glamour of a life on the ocean wave.

Dana's immediate reason for taking to the sea at the age of nineteen was the hope of recovering his failing sight brought on by the bookish regime of university life at Harvard with its attendant risks of eyestrain. But, despite his background and upbringing he joined not as an officer but as a common seaman. Indeed he draws a distinction early in his narrative between the naval officer who goes to sea 'with his gloves on' and the life of the ordinary sailor. He, by contrast with the social status which he was leaving behind, had become a 'hand', who received and followed orders rather than gave them out. Gloves 'on' or gloves 'off'[6] encapsulates two completely different states and Dana was to experience profound culture shock in switching from one to the other. Even when he was habituated to the new social order which he had entered, it held its ironies. Thus on the return journey which lasted many months, his ship, the *Alert*, carried a passenger who was virtually never seen by the ordinary seamen. He turned out, however, to have been a New England professor who was well known to Dana, yet such was the separation of roles aboard ship that they only spoke briefly · once – and even that was in contravention of the rules of the ship.[7]

Dana was being reclassified in his role as a common sailor and in the process entering another world:

> However much I was affected by the beauty of the sea, the bright stars, and the clouds driven swiftly over them, I could not but remember that I was separating myself from all the social and intellectual enjoyments of Life. Yet, strange as it may seem, I did then and afterwards take pleasure in these reflections, hoping by them to prevent my becoming insensible to the value of what I was leaving.[8]

That the separation which he was on the verge of entertaining was a form of embodiment is already implied in his description: he was, he said, anxious at the start that he would become 'a sailor' in every conceivable respect. As he sets sail he dreads changing his character and his humanity. Later he imagines what might become of him if he is obliged to spend even longer at sea than he had imagined:

> Three or four years would make me a sailor in every respect, mind and habits, as well as body – nolens volens; and would put all my companions so far ahead of me that college and a profession would be in vain to think of; and I made up my mind that, feel as I might, a sailor I must be, and to be the master of a vessel, must be the height of my ambition.[9]

Like an ethnographer his purpose is to suspend disbelief; but – like many an ethnographer – he is on the brink of going native. Indeed, a taste for swearing, copious quantities of rum and a succession of liaisons with native women encountered on the coast of California (which never made it into his final published account) suggest he made a good fist of it.

What, then, does it mean to become a sailor 'in body'? As he gets on ship for the first time Dana imagines himself to be every inch a Jack Tar in terms of his external appearance; yet he quickly realizes his error:

it is impossible to deceive the practised eye in these matters;
and while I supposed myself to be looking as salt as Neptune
himself, I was, no doubt, known for a landsman by every one
on board as soon as I hove in sight. A sailor has a peculiar
cut to his clothes, and a way of wearing them which a green
hand can never get.[10]

Dana's experience paralleled that of seamen on many European
sailing ships of the period. Sailors developed their own way of walking
which was subsequently to be mimicked in the music halls. Their
swinging gait is generally identified as the result of seeking to retain
balance on a deck which typically rolls with the passing waves. An early
eighteenth-century commentator, Ned Ward, remarked that sailors
'swing their Corps like a Pendulum, and believe it the most upright,
steady Motion'.[11] New initiates into sailing in even moderate seas all
recount the difficulties and dangers of walking in straight lines across
a pitching walkway; and of course virtually all dwell on the equally
defining experience of having to overcome seasickness. It is no accident that colloquial English puts the two together: overcoming bouts
of sickness is talked of as 'finding your sea legs'. But if these are already
linked in maritime speech, the emphasis is on walking – and therefore
the gait: the permanent visible change of bodily condition rather than
the passing sensitivities of the stomach.

In terms of clothing, the distinctive wear of seamen in the Americas
in Dana's day also replicates that of their European brethren. In
Britain in the seventeenth and eighteenth centuries there were
specialist clothiers who supplied the requisite kit to sailors, such as
Joseph Haycock's in London whose stock ran to over 1,000 items.[12]
These included clothing made of cotton or ticking which were not
otherwise in general use and thus distinctive of seafarers. Jackets
and breeches were often tarred to add an element of waterproofing
(hence the common name for a sailor) and each had a particular cut,
breeches being typically baggy and knee-length. These would be worn
with an outer garment of thicker wool for bad weather. Colourful
neck-cloths, then as now, were another mark of the typical seaman,
all topped off with one of several types of headgear – whether a flat
round 'Monmouth' cap or one supplied with ear flaps. Apart from
that, a wrinkled face was a giveaway, as was the habit of investing in
the requisite tattoo.

When Dana returned to the harbour in Boston from which he had set out two years earlier the first person to come aboard the *Alert*, the ship on which he had returned, was the junior partner of the firm to which his ship belonged. He turned out to have been a former student colleague at Harvard. Dana reports the meeting:

> The last time I had seen him, I was in the uniform of an under-graduate of Harvard College, and now, to his aston-ishment, there came down from aloft a 'rough alley' fellow, with duck trowsers and red shirt, long hair, and face burnt as black as an Indian's.[13]

Motley crews

Throughout history, ships' crews have proved just as often to be mercenaries as disciplined patriots loyal to the flag under which they sailed. Many were groups of men (and boys) assembled for a particu-lar task with obligations to each other only for as long as the immediate voyage lasted. Once the passage was complete they dispersed to find other employment; or, on shore midway through a long voyage, drunk-enness and its consequences might quickly replace the more disciplined behaviour expected of a crew aboard ship. The very term 'a motley crew' suggests a diversity of character, ethnicity and background. Yet, thrown together in the appallingly cramped living conditions of a wooden hull far out to sea (or even a modern iron one) their own mutual safety, as much as that of their ship or cargo, depends critically upon their submission to a common purpose. Some differences might be expected between navies assembled for national purposes, merchant crews involved in particular trading activities, and privateers licensed in times of war to attack foreign shipping and reap the benefits; not to mention pirates, that other category of seamen who stalk the pages of maritime histories from accounts of Indonesia to the West Indies, to (in modern times) the waters off the coasts of Somalia. Likewise those seamen involved in short-haul coasting may have a different experi-ence of crewing to those engaged on deep-sea voyaging involving months or even years to complete a round trip with only limited con-tact with the land. None the less, the differences may be of kind rather than substance since many seamen are dedicated to many of the same purposes – principal of them being, from the ordinary seaman's point of view, to get to the other end of any passage safely and to be able to collect your remuneration, which was not always guaranteed on either account.

Again, everyday English is layered with expressions reflective of maritime experience – to be 'all in the same boat' is to have found oneself in the same situation as others, at the behest of a common destiny. There are a series of questions that arise about the acquisition and interrelatedness of transferable seafaring skills, about the maintenance of order and discipline amongst crews assembled in these often haphazard ways and about the extent to which the concentrated purpose of managing a complex instrument like a ship overcomes (or not) the kinds of cultural difference which on land would mitigate against commonality of practice. If the ship provides an operational context for the working through of such issues, the implications are most evident in situations where polyglot crews are recruited for longer distance voyages.

Both history and literature are replete with examples of such cosmopolitan crews. Dana embarked on the *Pilgrim* sharing his ordinary seaman's quarters with various Americans, one 'Black', a German, a Swede and an Englishman. He remarks:

> It is to be remembered that more than three fourths of the seamen in our merchant vessels are foreigners. They are from all parts of the world. A great many from the north of Europe, beside Frenchmen, Spaniards, Portuguese, Italians, men from all parts of the Mediterranean, together with Lascars, negroes, and, perhaps worst of all, the off-casts of British men-of-war, and men from our own country who have gone to sea because they could not be permitted to live on land.[14]

A preponderance of single nationalities was the exception. Magellan's crews, for example, were only partly Spanish in origin. At least 90 of the 265 men employed were from elsewhere in Europe including Portuguese, Italians, Greeks, Belgians and Dutch, Germans, French, Irish and English. So numerous were the foreigners employed that Magellan had to swear a notary to the effect that – try as he might – he had been unable to raise an adequate crew amongst Spanish seamen. Cabot had an even higher percentage of international seamen in his recruitment of a crew for his expedition in search of the source of the fabled riches of the Queen of Sheba; this approached half of all those engaged. The disposition of foreign nationals on such ships clearly favoured those more aligned with Spanish interests – which effectively reduced the presence of French and English, representatives of hostile states in the sixteenth century.[15] Yet even these statistics may be flawed, for the very regional diversity of Spain itself made for confusion. Castilian Spanish was little known to those from the Basque country, Galicia or Catalonia. French, Italians and Portuguese could easily be passed off by a ship's master as natives whilst to a Castilian the category 'Basques' might include anyone from the eastern Mediterranean or elsewhere so long as they otherwise conformed to the composite image of a mariner as possessing 'middling stature, a sound body, and a black beard'.[16] Given the difficulties of emigrating across the Atlantic at that period, taking passage on a Spanish galleon and then jumping ship was the most efficient way for a foreigner to enjoy the freedoms of the Indies.

Once routes round the Cape of Good Hope or Cape Horn were opened up, so the cosmopolitanism of ship's crews developed exponentially. This was partly to take advantage of local know-how in the Indian and Pacific Oceans as we saw in the last chapter, but also to replenish crews that may have fallen foul of the scourges of scurvy and other pestilence on long trips without access to fresh supplies. Up to a half of the crews on some Portuguese ships sailing to the east were lost to such privations and the Dutch too recorded large losses of their own nationals to such causes. Thus the Portuguese, despite a history of antagonism towards Islam, were obliged to rely on Muslim crews mustered at Indian Ocean ports to support their commercial voyaging right up to Japan. Spanish and Dutch galleons off the coasts of South East Asia also needed to call on the services of locally recruited seamen, the so-called 'manila-men', an overall term for the mix of Chinese, Malays and Pacific islanders who moved from ship to ship, back and forth round the shipping routes familiar to European merchant shipping. The Spanish also used the term 'Indios' for this wide mix of origins. A whole series of such terms became current identifying the international element in these crews, but without much ethnic precision. Thus Indian Ocean sailors were grouped together under the term 'lascars'; 'kanakas' were Oceanic mariners, a generic term used by whites of all South Sea Islanders, which in fact derives from Hawaiian where it simply means 'person';[17] West Africans – especially those from Liberia – were known as 'Kru', the term itself derived from the word 'crew' and still an ethnic term in that part of West Africa.[18] As they sailed round the waters beyond the Atlantic they were gradually redistributed to distant ports, many Indios reaching Mexico on Spanish ships, others of various nationalities ending up in major 'sailor towns' in places like Singapore, Foochow, Hong Kong, Shanghai, Yokohama, Manila, Rangoon, around the coasts of Australia and New Zealand, or on the American coast in ports such as Valparaíso, Panama, Acapulco or along the Californian coast.[19]

In Britain long-haul merchant shipping was the most international in the composition of its crews. N.A.M. Rodger in his history of the Royal Navy makes virtually no mention of foreigners, though clearly some did occasionally find their way onto British naval vessels.[20] The merchant service, however, was different. In the seventeenth and eighteenth centuries a quota was placed on the number of foreigners allowed in their crews which, by law, should not exceed one quarter. The limits may well have been exceeded, as there is a remarkable similarity in the disposition of crews engaged in the East Indies trade which in the 1730s were routinely declaring 75 British crew members and 24 foreigners.[21] In times of war, however, regardless of measures taken by masters and shipowners to protect their peacetime crews from being pressed into naval service, the available pool of labour shrank. As a result the regulations were relaxed and the percentage of non-nationals could legitimately mount to as high as three-quarters. There were disparities in the extent to which different ports and shipowners took advantage of this relaxation in the rules; and for those heading for the Indian Ocean no doubt the local recruitment of 'Manila-men', out of sight of the authorities at home, may have further diluted the percentage of British crew members. Into the nineteenth century the practice continued in the merchant navy where it has been estimated that as few as 54 per cent of merchant seamen on British ships were British.[22]

In a literary context we have many reflections of the international composition of deep-sea sailing crews, especially from later periods. Perhaps the most complete literary portrait of the life of a cosmopolitan crew is that given by Melville in *Moby-Dick*, an account which, although it has profound observations to make on human experience, is also, of course, rooted in first-hand experience, like Dana's more explicitly autobiographical writing which was one of Melville's inspirations. *Moby-Dick* deploys a familiar literary device, that of taking a specific set of skills and experience, that of the whale-fisherman, and turning it into a parable of the life of everyman. As on any ship the crew are so involved in each others' activities and so dependent on each others' skills for the successful completion of their quest that the ship becomes an enclosed social world, a microcosm of wider social situations.

Melville's whaler, the *Pequod*, as has often been pointed out, has a thoroughly mixed crew. Apart from Captain Ahab himself, the four non-white pagan races are represented in the role of the harpooners: Queequeg (a South Sea islander, and a cannibal), Tashtego (a native American from Massachusetts), Daggoo (a massive African) and Fedallah (a South Asian); and the crew of Ahab's whaleboat are otherwise composed of 'manila-men'. All are described in positive terms as skilful, physically impressive and of notable character. As David Chappell points out, this 'challenges the triumphalist tale of European seafarers globalising the world and offers us instead an image of interdependency with alien "others"'.[23] Melville has chosen deliberately to construct Ahab's crew on a representative basis reminiscent of Noah – except without the prospect of redemption. His crew are all what Melville terms '*isolatos*', individuals assembled from separate backgrounds for a common purpose. In fact Melville remarked that in the fishing industries and navy of his time (like the army, and the engineering and labour work forces assembled to build the canals and railroads) barely one or two in every thousand employed were Americans.[24] It was characteristic that they were assembled from all parts of the globe. Of the crew of his own fictional ship he says:

> Yet now, federated along one keel, what a set these Isolatos were! An Anacharsis Clootz deputation from all the isles of the sea, and all the ends of the earth, accompanying old Ahab in the Pequod to lay the world's grievances before the bar from which not very many of them ever come back.[25]

The reference to Anacharsis Clootz is to an eighteenth-century Prussian nobleman who espoused the revolutionary idea of uniting humanity into a Universal Republic.[26] The ship itself has become a vessel of modernity, a reflection of the increasingly international character of labour forces, both at sea and on land. And of course for them to be

assembled on land they must first have got there principally by travelling in the first instance by sea.

Conrad, too, has many a portrait of the functioning of an international crew. His own experience at sea covered all the relevant roles. In
the twenty years from 1874, as Józef Teodor Konrad Korzeniowski, he
served on eighteen different ships moving from an ordinary seaman to
third, second and first mate, before finally spending fourteen months
as captain. Conrad's story 'The Nigger of the "Narcissus"', published in
1897, takes as its name that of a ship on which Conrad sailed from
Bombay to Dunkirk in 1884. True, his narrative is fictionalized. The
'foreign' element of the story's crew consists of a Russian Finn, two
Scandinavians and the 'nigger', James Wait. In reality the ship on which
Conrad sailed had eleven non-British out of 24 crew members, including, of course, Conrad himself at that point. But actual numbers are
perhaps less the point. Despite the reduction in percentages from the
reality, the story is no less effective for the questions it raises about
the coherence of a cosmopolitan crew voyaging together out of contact
with land for many months, with all the tensions and conflicts that arise.

In Conrad's story the 'nigger', Wait, feigns illness but only to con-
ceal (from himself) the truth that he is, in fact, terminally ill. His
self-regard is narcissistic; but it triggers a series of situations which act
to undermine the coherence of the ship's crew. What the presence and
condition of a sick black seaman, already on the fringes of the society
of crew members, exposes are moral fissures in what Cynthia Fansler
Behrman calls the 'Victorian myth' of the English seaman.[27] In the figure
of Donkin Conrad pictures a xenophobic response to the diversity of
background of the crew. It is made all the more pointed by Donkin's
assertion of his quintessential Englishness: 'I ham a Henglishman, I
ham', he says.[28] Donkin not only hastens Wait's demise by anticipating
it, he also seeks to subvert the already fragile authority of the ship's
hierarchy. He whinges his way through the story, a stark contrast to the
silent values invested in the old sea dog Singleton. He was of a different generation, the one in whom Victorian myth had taken root.
Conrad's narration continues:

> They had been strong as those are strong who know neither
> doubts nor hopes. They had been impatient and enduring,
> turbulent and devoted, unruly and faithful. Well-meaning
> people had tried to represent those men as whining over

every mouthful of their food; as going about their work in fear of their lives. But in truth they had been men who knew toil, privation, violence, debauchery – but knew not fear, and had no desire of spite in their hearts. Men hard to manage, but easy to inspire . . .[29]

Their successors, the Donkins of the world, were 'the grown up children of a discontented earth' – 'less naughty, but less innocent; less profane, but perhaps also less believing; and if they have learned how to speak they also learnt how to whine.'[30] Moaning, complaining disagreeably at every turn, Donkin seeks to undermine the very sense of fellowship on which the mariner's confrontation with the forces of nature depends. Solidarity of purpose, a shared collective identity as crew members, disciplined determination – all critical factors on a successfully managed ship – are constantly thwarted.

This is very different to the functioning of a cosmopolitan crew envisaged by Melville. On the *Pequod* commonality of purpose is gloriously achieved in terms of seamanship, even if Captain Ahab's underlying motives are gravely flawed.

They were one man, not thirty. For as the one ship that held them all; though it was put together of all contrasting things – oak, and maple, and pine wood; iron, and pitch, and hemp – yet all these ran into each other in the one concrete hull, which shot on its way, both balanced and directed by the long central keel; even so, all the individualities of the crew, this man's valour, that man's fear; guilt and guiltiness, all varieties were welded into oneness, and were all directed to that fatal goal which Ahab their one lord and keel did point to.[31]

In Melville's description, the captains of New England whaling vessels in the nineteenth century inspired respect, despite the fact that they were engaged in some of the longest voyages sailed ships ever undertook. On Nantucket ships, he says,

you will see the skipper parading his quarter-deck with an elated grandeur not surpassed in any military navy; nay, extorting almost as much outward homage as if he wore the imperial purple, and not the shabbiest of pilot-cloth.[32]

147

This is loyalty inspired not by patriotism or submission to some established form of naval discipline, but by a common understanding of the role of captaincy.

Clearly, however, the creation of the social and professional cohesion on ships crewed by mariners of different backgrounds, religion and ethnicity, and speaking different languages, required more than the inspirational character of a good captain; and, no doubt, there were many, if not more, captains modelled on Captain Allistoun of the *Narcissus* struggling to motivate his crew, than Captain Ahabs capable of welding disparate experience and cultural expectation into uniformity. The ships that they handled were also often complex vessels. The 'Indios' who were recruited to sail on Spanish galleons would have been confronted with the successors of what Pablo Pérez-Mallaína has called 'the most complex machine of the epoch' (the Spanish ships of the sixteenth century),[33] a challenge to technical skills and health and safety considerations alike. Such ships were a Byzantine confection of capstans, levers and pulleys all operated within a forest of rigging and cables supporting multiple masts, spits and sails. For the ship to work efficiently there were many arduous tasks to be carried out, often in harsh conditions; all had to be calibrated and that calibration was in the hands of crew whose experience was in vessels as diverse as outrigger canoes, Chinese or South East Asian junks or Arab dhows. A larger ship of the period might include up to three miles of rope to hold the mast in place and a further eight miles of rope to manipulate the complex systems of sheets, pulleys and other equipment. Many of these mariners showed abilities to adapt to different sailing methods which amazed their European employers and fellow crew members. One Spaniard is quoted as remarking,

> [t]here is hardly an Indian who has sailed the seas who does not understand the mariner's compass, and therefore to this trade route there are some very skilful and dextrous helmsmen.[34]

However, even with the familiarity of later centuries and the development of shipping technologies, the potential for disaster remained; and the manila-men as a group were treated very poorly which hardly encouraged solidarity of purpose.

How then were successful international crews mustered and maintained? In cosmopolitan crews, often recruited 'on spec', language would seem to be an immediate difficulty. Yet it is surprising that very few of the historical sources mention it at all. Indeed, to the extent that the issue of language arises in the literature, it is only by way of dismissing it as any particular problem. In areas with considerable and regular contact between different nationalities, pidgin languages developed amongst seafarers and coastal populations alike through which to conduct transactions – such as the Mediterranean, where a 'lingua franca' was in common use. Otherwise, even the least educated rapidly acquired a smattering of language which seems to have allowed them to get by. Peter Earle cites one Nicholas Lawrence sent to sea on a merchant ship sometime between the mid-seventeenth and eighteenth centuries who, 'tho' he could never read a word in a book, has been so much abroad as to be able to speak French, Spanish, Italian, Portuguese etc'.[35] Likewise a foremastman on HMS *Newcastle* was able to operate effectively in Spanish and Italian and could 'speake as much of each as relates to buying and selling'. There is some evidence, in fact, that the ordinary sailor on the lower deck may have had more linguistic skills than his officers on the quarter deck. Two privateering brothers, the Bicknells, who served on the *Swallowe* had reported competence across a range of European languages – 'Latin', French, Dutch and some Spanish and Portuguese – and were called on to interpret on occasion for their captain whose linguistic abilities did not extend beyond 'good West or Devonshire' English.[36] Likewise those foreigners recruited onto British merchant ships under the quota system seem to have got by in broken English perfectly well. Earle remarks that the increase in the percentage of foreigners working in the merchant service in wartime made virtually no difference to the discipline or effectiveness of seamanship. Indeed, he suggests, 'the historian would be hard-pressed to know that wartime crews were any different from those employed in peacetime.'[37] On land, in proximity to harbours English was also usually understood. Stan Hugill remarks that versions of English were commonly understood along seafronts from Calcutta to Buenos Aires. 'It was better to stay in the waterfront area where "English was spoked" than to go "rovin" up town where it weren't.'[38]

Captaincy

Seamanship has a way of overcoming the rights of ownership. Far away from Nantucket and the 'owners' of his vessel, Captain Ahab is airily dismissive of their entitlements when the first mate Starbuck (the inspiration for the famous Seattle-based coffee company) raises the question of their interests in the welfare of the ship. 'Owners, owners?', Ahab responds, 'Thou art always prating to me, Starbuck, about those miserly owners, as if owners were my conscience. But look ye, the only real owner of anything is its commander . . .'[39]

The position of ship's captain, however defined, is a critical one. There are many models for this. In a European context, the command of a merchant ship was in the hands of the master. In most cases this would be the captain, though on sixteenth-century Spanish ships that was a more or less honorific title and the 'captain' had few official roles assigned to him other than organizing the ship's defence in cases of attack. The pilot was responsible for navigational matters, leaving the master as the person with the kinds of responsibility which involve the management of the crew as a whole and the safe passage of the ship and its cargo. On fishing boats, whilst there was always a ship-owner and a captain (often the same person), a more egalitarian set of relationships could develop in part due to a system of sharing in the proceeds of the catch which transformed the crew from wage-earners into participants in the commercial aspects of an enterprise.[40] This could, at best, be described as an uncertain life, but mutual benefit incentivized cooperation. Gladwin talks of the traditional methods of organization at Puluwat atoll in Micronesia, where the captain/navigator is alert to the suggestions of those travelling with him, despite his superior experience.[41] He makes the final decision but it has the air of a collective judgement. Similar practice is reported on Anutan, a Polynesian island in the Melanesian Solomon Islands group.[42] There is a difference between these perceptions of the role of captain as participant and as the 'enforcer' of rules and disciplines. Here, indeed, the best captains seem not to issue instructions at all but occupy the wheelhouse without fuss and almost without their presence influencing the rhythm of heavy work otherwise involved in trawler fishing in particular. The skipper of the fishing trawler on which Redmond O'Hanlon embarked in Scotland is of that kind: 'Jason' is unobtrusive, trusting in the competence of his crew, notwithstanding the heavy financial burdens which the whole enterprise places exclusively on his shoulders.

Yet larger crews and ships required – and require – more formalized processes. The writings of Abu'l-Fadl 'Allam give us insight into how responsibilities were allocated on fifteenth-century dhows plying their trade on the Indian Ocean routes on the eve of European incursions into established Arab mercantile sea lanes. He identifies twelve roles, not all necessarily the responsibility of a single person: the crew of a larger medieval Arab ship may well have extended significantly beyond that number.[43] Firstly, the roles of the owner and of the captain/navigator seem to have been distinguished as categories. The *nākhod* (the owner) might, as now, have seen to the preparations of the ship, though another important source, Ibn Mājid, writing in the late fifteenth/early sixteenth century, does indicate that the roles of the *mu'allim* go well beyond that of pilotage and start whilst the ship is still on land. Thus the owner would establish the ports to be visited in the light of the commercial opportunities he was looking to exploit but it was up to the *mu'allim*, the elite fraternity within the Arab maritime enterprise, to take charge of the process in their capacities as captains and navigators of the ships. *Mu'allim* were contracted for particular voyages and would over the course of a career work on a large number of ships. Interestingly when Sindbad wanted to travel overseas he first bought a ship and then contracted a captain/navigator to sail it for him. Other roles typical of ocean-going dhows encompass those of the lead sailor, the helmsman (who works directly to the *mu'allim*), the storemaster, the steward responsible for the passengers and for the cargo, the keeper of the ship's accounts (who also distributed water), the lookout, the sailor responsible for bailing out leaks, the gunner and the common seaman. The balance of roles would seem to have altered since Ibn Mājid's day as more recent commentators credit the *nākhod* with a more central role and relegate the *mu'allim* to the secondary role of pilot/navigator.[44]

A third term, *rubbān*, also seems to have been in use, though possibly for the captains of coastal ships rather than for ocean-going dhows.[45] In the fifteenth century, however, the responsibilities of the *mu'allim* were all-encompassing. For instance, in addition to the practice of navigation, Ibn Mājid, whose account is the fullest and most wide-ranging, offers the following advice to would-be navigators:

Look thoroughly at all the passengers and the crew and assess
them carefully then you will recognise any evil in them and
be prepared for it. Listen to everything they say, accepting
anything good and rejecting the bad. Be firm and strong when
speaking to them but pleasant. Do not fraternise with the man
who disobeys you over any affair of yours. In distress you will
not find any companion except secrets kept. Be courageous and
a possessor of bravery, do not be neglectful and show great
zeal, and great patience and forbearing. Be God-fearing and
pure. Do not wrong one man for another.[46]

This is not advice on how to find your way at sea, but a lesson in
good administration and team-building. The role described is that of
the captain of a ship. The idea would seem to be to size up the qualities
of everyone on board so that the *mu'allim* can anticipate how they will
respond when he is otherwise preoccupied in stormy sea conditions.
Handling the conduct of the merchants, with their direct financial
interests in any proposed voyage, will have been a particular issue.
Whether the *mu'allim* had the formal right to order the merchants
around is not clear though something of the kind is implied. Ibn Mājid's
principal recommendation is firm diplomacy in dealing with merchants
aboard ship. Beyond that, his writing draws particular attention to
the responsibilities of the captain/navigator for the performance of all
the equipment aboard ship. This starts before the ship ever sets sail and
continues whilst at sea. Particular attention is paid to the rigging and
the rudder but there is also advice on setting up a burgee, a small wind
sock, and a compass (though in his discussion of navigational practice,
as we have seen, he devotes little further attention to its use, preferring
instead to discuss direct observational methods).

The widening of the role of the specialist navigator to include
the welfare of the ship, crew and passengers is found in other societies.
On Anutan for example Richard Feinberg discusses the role of the *tau
tai mau kaavenga* (literally, 'expert at finding guide stars'), the specialist
navigator. Discussion amongst the crew is the usual way in which deci-
sions are made about all matters when at sea with the views of the
person with the greatest experience given greatest weight. When a
specialist navigator is aboard, however, his role is paramount. To achieve
this status a navigator must have a superior knowledge of the lore relating to the stars. This is not just about familiarity with single guide stars

but with the whole night sky so that, if some of the critical stars that might be known to a competent mariner are obscured, others that might be visible to port or starboard may be used to maintain the right course. The skills extend to calculating the effects of wind, current and the drag of the canoe's outrigger. However, his authority is endorsed by social and leadership qualities. He must be calm in emergencies, able to remain composed even where others make mistakes in difficult weather. Having expert knowledge allied to a tendency to become irascible compromises that authority. 'Anutan seamen', Feinberg concludes, 'value social skills almost as highly as they do one's technical abilities.'[47] This idea of an expert at way-finding who also possesses personal qualities that instil confidence in others is sufficiently well-founded to be used metaphorically in other contexts. Dom Henrique, or Prince Henry, presided over the great expansion of Portuguese influence, much of it the result of maritime voyages of discovery. However, he had very limited personal experience of being at sea – just a few trips around the coasts of Iberia and to Morocco. His patronage of navigators is well known; but at sea he would have had to admit to the superior seamanship of others. None the less, history knows him as Henry the Navigator.

There is in the French archives an illustration in a thirteenth-century Arab document of a dhow under sail with activity taking place above and below deck (illus. 11).[48] It is interesting to maritime historians as a unique representation of an early medieval Arab dhow. But it is also interesting sociologically for the separation of roles that it portrays. George Hourani, who included it in his book *Arab Seafaring*, may be right that the artist was no seaman – there are indeed errors.[49] But, seen as a kind of visual organogram rather than a mimetic representation of such a ship, it is certainly instructive. The vessel is running before the wind. The dominant figure seated at the helm is clearly in control of 'his' ship, even if he is neither the owner nor appears to be the helmsman as he is not holding the rudder. He would seem to occupy the position of the *mu'allim*. Illustrated on a larger scale than the other seamen, he is seen to adjust the sail from his seat of authority with the assistance of a number of sailors on deck beyond. A look-out boy sits in a version of a crow's nest whilst on the lowest deck sailors are portrayed bailing out what is clearly a very leaky ship, as many such – with their sewn planking and caulked hulls – would have been.

All this coheres with the general disposition of responsibilities on such a vessel, even if all the roles identified by Abu'l-Fadl 'Allam are

11 Illustration of an Arab ship, from a 13th-century manuscript.

not portrayed. What has attracted most attention, however, are two
additional features. One concerns the apparent racial distinction
between the crew and the merchants. The archaeologist Mark Horton
has suggested that the blackness of the crew reflects an African, probably Swahili, element in the sailing of 'Arab' dhows.[50] There is certainly
evidence of Swahili communities distributed around the Indian Ocean,
though whether their dispersal from the coastal region of eastern
Africa is the result of trading or of seafaring activity is less clear. The
second point relates to the separation between all the earnest and
focused activity of seamanship undertaken by whomsoever the crew
might be and the Arab merchants or passengers staring out of the portholes of their cabins, where, it is assumed, they have been confined
whilst the real business of sailing the ship is carried on above. They are
portrayed as inactive, looking at the sea outside whilst the real action

takes place above. Like the protocols in place on Dana's ships an inalienable distinction is effected between those engaged in professional seafaring and other interests. Whether the *nākhod*, as owner of the ship, would have been amongst those excluded from the company of the *muʿallim* and his crew at that period is an interesting question. Certainly, at least in the case of this one image, the separation of the merchant passengers is definitive.

In terms of the maintenance of maritime discipline Ibn Mājid's advice veers more towards the carrot rather than the stick. His only words about disciplining his crew are reserved for the helmsman. The helmsman needed to be constantly vigilant. There was, Ibn Mājid insisted, no point in having a dozy man at the rudder; all the finesse of measurement and judgement exercised by the navigator in setting directions was rendered useless if the helmsman was not fully attentive to the resulting details of the course to be set. The *muʿallim* needed to be constantly on his case, hounding and harrying him to maintain alertness despite any onset of fatigue – giving him rest when tiredness threatened to overcome him, certainly, but not too much. His regime should match that of the *muʿallim* himself, constantly struggling to remain watchfulness despite advancing exhaustion. For the rest, though, Ibn Mājid's theorizing around the governance of the sea-going dhow was based more on the ability of the captain accurately to assess the character of all those on ship and to draw them together through the exercise of clear and consistent leadership. In that he was not so different from the various British naval dignitaries who sought to articulate the principles of good captaincy in the wake of a series of jolts administered to national pride by the mutinies in 1797 firstly at Spithead and subsequently at the Nore, the gateway to the River Thames.

Discipline and mutiny

Richard Dana remarked of his experience at sea that '[T]here are no fancies about equality on board ship', 'nor wish that the power of captains be diminished one iota'. 'It is', he remarks 'absolutely necessary that there should be one head, one voice, to control everything, and be responsible for everything'.[51] The fact of hierarchy and the need to administer punishment as occasion demanded was not in itself an issue amongst most seamen. The acceptance of discipline as an essential aspect of the maritime life is demonstrated by the nature of the demands made by the mutineers of 1797 and by their own behaviour during the period of their rebellion against the naval authorities. Their demands were not, as might have been expected, against the rough treatment which had traditionally been meted out for failures to follow established procedures. The lash itself was not the cause of mutiny. The procedures for punishment were laid down in the Articles of War and the Regulations and Instructions. Floggings were an expected and understood part of naval routine. They were to be administered with an air of inevitability for their purpose was not retribution but the making of an example. They were clean and definitive leaving no moral scar, just the physical one on the back of the miscreant. The person administering the punishment should do so with detachment, rather than in reprisal, and the person receiving it should come out of the experience without stain on his character.[52] It would be recorded in the ship's log but it was not like a prison record and any lasting sense of guilt was not its intended outcome. Flogging and its corollaries drew a line under deviations from accepted behaviour so the routine of the ship could be maintained. To that extent, in eighteenth-century naval contexts, punishment was not retributive but restorative.

The participants in the 1797 mutinies had a different set of grievances. Theirs concerned issues of differentials in pay, the quantity and quality of food served to them aboard ship, the nature of medical support and a general sense of being taken for granted – seemingly confirmed by the Admiralty's failure to respond to their petitions with any sense of urgency. As mutineers, their own sense of *self*-discipline was, indeed, very notable. At Spithead, there was no violence, officers' belongings were largely left undisturbed, and when the Grand Duke of Württemberg came on a prearranged state visit with the dignitaries of the Admiralty all the protocols were meticulously observed. At the Nore, the mutineers gave vent to no quarrel with naval discipline in relation to the perennial naval issues of punishing drunkenness or the process of impressment. Indeed the mutineers themselves flogged any fellow-mutineers who gave way to excessive drinking. As frustration grew, the North Atlantic fleet off the coast at Yarmouth sailed to the Nore to blockade the Thames estuary. Even so, the mutineers still fired a full gun salute in honour of the king's birthday and to celebrate the anniversary of Charles II's restoration. Nelson, though far away from the scene off Cadiz, remarked 'for a *mutiny* . . . it has been the most manly that I ever heard of, and does the British sailor infinite honour.'[53] Reflecting on the events nearly 100 years later in the novel *Billy Budd, Foretopman* (1891) Melville remarked that he regarded the Nore Mutiny, the Great Mutiny, as 'analogous to the distempering irruption of contagious fever in a frame constitutionally sound, and which anon throws it off'.[54]

Perhaps the fullest account of what might appear to be the ambiguities of maritime discipline in this period is that by Greg Dening in his account of the background to the mutiny on the *Bounty*. Dening argues that discipline was an accepted part of the routine of a ship at sea. Indeed Captain Bligh's fatal error was not any descent into violence and tyranny, as it has often been portrayed – he was in fact one of the least inclined of naval captains to turn to the lash or any more horrendous forms of punishments to deal with lapses in discipline. Bligh on the *Providence*, the ship on which he sailed subsequent to the *Bounty*, had less than one in ten of his crew flogged. Captain Vancouver, by comparison, had the lash administered to approaching half of his crew of the *Discovery* on his voyage through the Pacific to the north-west coast of America.[55] Bligh's failing was rather that of a misunderstanding of the role of captaincy itself, which involved administering appropriate levels of punishment, but much else besides in terms of fair-dealing. When things turned to mutiny it was, arguably, less that the functions of the captain were being subverted than that they were being supplanted. That may well be because they were not being exercised justly or effectively in the eyes of the crew. Others saw they could do better and seized the moment. To lead a successful mutiny implied having the confidence of fellow-seamen, given that involvement with an unsuccessful one would inevitably lead to a one-way trip to the gallows. Indeed even a successful one could lead to the mutineers being hunted down, even if there seemed objectively to be some justification for their actions. The attributes of inspiring loyalty and unstinting cooperation were supposed to be those exercised by the occupants of the quarter deck. Mutiny, as Admiral Lord Collingwood remarked, was caused by captains, not by sailors.[56]

Writing in June 1797, in the midst of the year of mutiny, Collingwood's reflections have a touch of pragmatism about them. Just complaints needed to be addressed with alacrity. Delay implied denial. Because they were not responded to expeditiously, sailors were obliged to continue the search for adequate redress and in the process were learning the strength they represented as a concerted labour force. In not acceding to just grievance, other grumbles, perhaps advanced with less justification, would proliferate – or so he feared. However, a year later his thoughts had moved on and turned to the principles on which a well-run ship should function. He wrote:

> It has always been a maxim with me to engage and occupy my men, and to take such care for them that they should have nothing to think of for themselves beyond the current business of the day.[57]

His approach was strongly paternalistic. His officers should always act courteously to his men and call them by their personal names. He encouraged reserved but appropriate behaviour between officers and crew, rather than either over-familiarity or, still worse, abusive and dismissive attitudes. He had before him Bligh's example of a decade earlier, if he cared to reflect on the events that had happened in the South Pacific. Though Bligh's version of events clouded a clear under-standing of what occurred, it must have been obvious that courtesy was not a technique that came naturally to him. His approach to captaincy (though in fact he was only a lieutenant at the time) was of another order. Arguably, the roots of the insurrection aboard the *Bounty* lay in the inappropriateness of his actions in relation to the whole of the ship's company, including those through whom the good order of a ship would otherwise be maintained, notably his protégé Fletcher Christian. It was less a question of 'us' and 'them' and more a question of 'me' (Bligh) and 'them'. As Vancouver was to do with the 'gentlemen' officers who came with him on the *Discovery*, Bligh expended much energy in diminishing those around him as much by the lash of his tongue as by the lash of the 'cat'. His 'bad language' – hardly a matter of much moment amongst sailors in most circumstances – rebounded on his men indiscriminately. Bligh, by his actions, isolated himself and enforced a tyrannical regime on all, not by inflicting physical punish-ment but by his random victimization of those around him; in the process he forfeited the respect of his crew, to the extent that he had earned it in the first place.

Dening's description of the circumstances of the mutiny on the *Bounty* revolves around character, expectations of appropriate behaviour and the niceties of good captaincy as conceived at the time. Thrown together on a ship such things, often small and otherwise without moment in themselves, undoubtedly matter. Take, for instance, the descriptions of mealtime etiquette aboard the *Pequod*. The usage of the times was for the captain and mates to live aft of the mast and for the ordinary seamen to live forward of it. Captain Ahab eats in company with the officers – the first, second and third mates: Starbuck, Stubb and Flask. The harpooners, because of their specialist skills, are also admitted though in practice they only enter the captain's cabin to eat. This in itself, we are told, is a residue of the days when what subsequently became known as the chief harpooner ('specksynder' in Dutch, 'specksioneer' in English – literally 'fat-cutter') shared the control of the ship with the captain. The one was responsible for everything to do with hunting whales, the other with navigational and administrative matters.[58] 'Federated along one keel' they may have been, yet Ahab's table is a social disaster. The crew are described at their work in terms which suggest qualities of easy interdependence. They all know what to do, have a seemingly unconscious awareness of their mutual roles in any situation and a disciplined sense of mutual self-reliance – born in part, no doubt, of the knowledge that their wages are only to be paid in the form of their portion of the catch. Off-duty, they rub along with few complications. However, at the captain's table there is none of this relaxed familiarity. Ahab's glowering, tormented presence casts a pall over proceedings. The three officers are called to table and enter in order, they eat in awful unrelieved silence and then retreat from the captain's cabin and presence in the reverse order to that in which they had taken their places. As table guests they enter 'as a street-door enters a house; turning inwards for a moment, only to be turned out the next.'[59] In the cabin itself

> was no companionship; socially, Ahab was inaccessible. Though nominally included in the census of Christendom, he was still an alien to it. He lived in the world, as the last of the grisly Bears lived and settled in Missouri.[60]

Ahab's role as captain is asserted in his ability to deny sociability, not in his capacity to engender it. Like Bligh he is isolated, victim of an obsessive nature which brooks no camaraderie.

To the extent that anything like untroubled informality is found in the Captain's cabin it is in the behaviour of the 'barbarian' harpooners who tuck into their meals with noisy relish in a spirit of 'care-free licence and ease'.[61] Queequeg has the filed teeth of a 'cannibal': he eats with 'a mortal, barbaric smack of the lip'. Tashtego jokes with the Steward that if he cares to present himself his bones too might be 'picked'. Daggoo, the African, is obliged to sit on the floor for his size is at odds with the low cabin ceiling. The contrast is stark. Ahab eats differently from everyone else, he sleeps differently, lacks congeniality and is overwhelmed by the isolating confines of his office. He lives, as he himself admits towards the end of the book, within 'the masoned, walled-town of a Captain's exclusiveness', a 'Guinea-coast slavery of solitary command'.[62] And, in practice, in terms of the matter of sailing the ship he is effectively supernumerary. The ship sails by the efforts and efficiency of the ship's company, not by his authoritative command. His knowledge of charts and navigation is comprehensive; but he deploys it not for the commonly understood purposes of the voyage but for his own monomaniac pursuit of revenging himself on the great white whale which has taken his leg on a previous whaling expedition and fractured his life.

This highlights one of the most notable distinctions on many ships between captain and crew. Captain Ahab's isolation is part of the job. In *Trawler*, Redmond O'Hanlon almost exclusively reports on his interactions with the other crew members rather than the captain. The skipper is in the wheelhouse most of the time. He has privacy; his crew, on the whole, do not. They live together, eat together and work together. Bunks replace individual cabins. In smaller boats the lack of privacy is even more marked. The so-called Sea Gypsies of South East Asia, who we have encountered in chapter Two, live on boats whose dimensions rarely exceed ten feet in length by five feet in width (3 × 1.5 metres) with a height of barely four feet (120 cm). In such restricted circumstances personal intimacy is constrained and boats are generally limited in occupancy to the nuclear family. If a husband and wife have more than two or three children then they may place them with relatives who have fewer offspring and once someone is married it is expected that they will very soon acquire their own boat. Likewise because space is limited, sea-peoples' possessions, like those of crew members on the ships we have been describing, are few in number. When someone dies the limited number of personal items they possessed are buried with them, with only small items such as jewellery being inherited. On sea voyages in other parts of the Pacific some measure of privacy is provided by a small shelter that may be erected on the outrigger. This is designed for the use of any women travelling with the party. Since their presence aboard ship is regarded as abhorrent they are regarded as polluting when at sea, as in many parts of the world. Their ablutions and other activities must be undertaken separately from the hull of the canoe which is exclusively for men.[63]

Women and ships

Such domestic arrangements aboard ships are the exception. Until this chapter we have not had occasion to mention even a single woman aboard ship, and encounter no roles which they fulfil. N.A.M. Rodger's review of the history of the Royal Navy makes scant mention of the presence of women on ships and Earle's equivalent history of the merchant navy has even less to say on the topic. Ibn Mājid, writing about Arab shipping in the Indian Ocean as the fifteenth century became the sixteenth, also characterizes ships as male spaces. Contemporary North Sea trawlermen not only bar women from their ships but will not go to sea if a woman has even touched the guardrail of their boat.[64] To the extent that women voyaged on ships at all it was as passengers or very occasionally as companions of sailors. Another aspect of Dr Johnson's comparison between ships and jails is that both are sexually segregated societies. That was to change only with modern times and the introduction of large cruise ships which function more like floating hotels with the attendant requirements for domestic staff. Prior to that women's presence at sea was largely transgressive.

Clearly, though, there were significant numbers of women aboard ships in the eighteenth and nineteenth centuries.[65] The difficulty is that they were only there on sufferance, so they do not appear in official records.[66] Those who did attract attention were those occasional women who managed to get employment on ships by disguising themselves as men – or rather as boys since their disguise was effective only because of the presence aboard ships of adolescent boys wearing the loose fitting clothes of a young apprentice and often with longer hair. Perhaps the most successful of these was 'William' Brown, a black woman who sustained the guise of a Royal Navy seaman for eleven or twelve years during which she worked in one of the most challenging of all tasks aboard ship – that of a topman, required to climb to the highest points of the rigging in all weathers to attend to the topmost sails. She appears to have been unmasked around 1815, but was subsequently re-employed even so.[67] Their biographies made popular tales, but that in itself is a mark of their rarity – and there were inevitably a significant number of fictionalized accounts of female seafarers which were published as accurate accounts especially in the early nineteenth century.[68] When one Captain Charles Johnson (otherwise sometimes thought to be a pseudonym of Daniel Defoe) published the biographies of twenty pirates in his *A General History of the Robberies and Murders of the most Notorious Pyrates* (1724),[69] he included illustrations of four pirates: two infamous male figures, Blackbeard and Bartholomew Roberts, and two female pirates, Mary Read and Anne Bonny. Both achieved notoriety, became the subject of seafaring songs and are to this day celebrated in pub names and the like in coastal areas of Britain. However they are in fact the only two female pirates recorded amongst perhaps 2,000 to 3,000 who were operating in the West Indies at the time they came to public attention by being put on trial.

Otherwise it was largely the wives, mistresses or daughters of officers who occasionally sailed on ships. In that role they were anomalous. In *Nostromo* Conrad has Captain Mitchell remark: 'I was never married myself. A sailor should exercise self-denial.'[70] Conrad, whose own life culminated in a late marriage once he had given up the life of a seaman, is sensitive to the inappropriateness of women at sea. In a short story, 'The Secret Shearer' (1909),[71] the young chief mate Leggatt's deepest love is for the sea but the master of the *Sephora* is portrayed as having committed a kind of maritime infidelity in bringing his wife aboard the vessel. The presence of a woman aboard is presaged in the narrative by an association with the catastrophes that strike the ship. The captain of the *Sephora*, recounting his troubled outward passage, runs together his account of the weather with his wife's presence – 'He had had terrible weather on the passage out – terrible – terrible – wife aboard, too.'[72] And again the conjunction is evident when he alludes to the murder aboard ship which has cast a shadow over his career as a skipper:

> 'I have been at sea now, man and boy, for seven-and-thirty years, and I've never heard of such a thing happening in an English ship. And that it should be my ship. Wife on board, too.'[73]

What has happened is that the chief mate has killed one of the crew. For the captain these events are made worse by having his wife aboard; for the crew there is an implication these events happen *because* he had his wife aboard. In a recent context similar ideas prevail. There is a story told about a Rolls-Royce engine which blew up on a modern destroyer when, exceptionally, a female computer technician had spent the night aboard ship. The tragedy would have happened anyway because of an engineering fault, but why had it happened then?[74] Women were only allowed to come aboard ship when they were in port, and then only until the Blue Peter flag was hoisted and the time for the ship's departure announced.

Linked to this is the absolute intolerance of acts of homosexuality aboard ship, and in particular sodomy. Recorded cases are in any event rare, but when they did occur they were treated harshly. The Dutch East India Company was perhaps the least tolerant: when homosexual acts were uncovered the partners were tied together back to back and thrown overboard.[75] Hanging, however, was a known punishment in the British Navy under the 29th Article of War which potentially classified sodomy alongside mutiny and desertion as one of the 'unnatural offences'.[76]

Ships were 'manned'; but ships themselves, of course, were almost always explicitly understood to be female – the appropriate pronouns in English are 'she' or 'her' rather than 'it' (or even, in most contexts, 'the'). The image of a ship in Western maritime tradition – and to an extent beyond – is of a fictive woman, despite the fact that it may have a male as well as a female figurehead and that other gendered terminology intervenes: 'East Indiamen' or 'men-of-war', for instance.[77] The ship may be socially a male space, as we have described, but it is within a female vessel which is named and conceptualized as if animate. It is a significant question why sexuality should be so harshly and 'superstitiously' regarded. After all, drunkenness was common enough at sea and more likely to lead to undisciplined activities imperilling the safety of ship and crew. At one level the inappropriateness of sexual acts of any sort – or their possibility – on conventional ships at sea might be related as much to this symbolic security of the ship as female. It is a protective vessel offering security in a changing and challenging environment. To transgress it is to invoke retribution. The ship of redemption – the Ark – rapidly transforms into the Ship of Fools, the offshore quarantining of madmen. But such a layered symbolism has a wider context. It is not just a question of gendering but of the whole set of inverse symbolic relationships which are asserted between being at sea and being on land – and of the liminal role played in these relationships by the beach and by ports.

five

Beaches

> This wet stretch between land and sea is the true beach, the
> true in-between space. Among the peoples of Oceania about
> whom I write — the 'maohi' of Tahiti, the 'enata' of the
> Marquesas, the 'kamaiana' of Hawai'i — it is a sacred,
> a 'tapu' space, an unresolved space where things can happen,
> where things can be made to happen. It is a space of trans-
> formation. It is a space of crossing.
> GREG DENING, *Beach Crossings* (2004)[1]

Having refocused on the sea as a knowable, navigable domain and on
ships as social and working spaces, beaches and ports come to the forefront as the points of interaction between the maritime and the
terrestrial. The beach is an ambiguous place, an in-between place. It is
a place where for much of the time nothing much seemingly happens:
the tide comes and goes; people arrive to pass time in leisure activities;
occasional ships anchor there. But at the same time, the beach is a place
where everything transformational in the cultures of coastal peoples
begins and ends. The tides create a shifting boundary between sea and
land. Their effect is to emphasize the liminality of the beach as parts of
it are successively revealed and then swamped by tidal action. The
boundary between sea and land alters on a daily basis. It is a neutral
space, neither properly terrestrial nor yet thoroughly maritime, await-
ing a metamorphic role. Ports can be construed as a transgressive
extension of the land. They are the scene of behaviours which are dis-
tinctively different either from those aboard ship or further inland.

Those who arrive from the sea, whether castaway, shipwrecked or
simply looking for supplies of whatever sort, are likewise liminal
characters. They have become disconnected from the set of rules which
sustained them in the world they have left behind; yet they are not of
the world on whose fringes they have been washed up. Licentious and
wayward activities are tolerated at ports even if they are at odds with
the disciplined behaviours which, in principle, are the ideal to be

achieved aboard ship. Boats and their crews come from over the horizon, a space which, as we have seen, may be conceptualized in many different ways. They dress differently, possibly share no common language with the coastal peoples into whose world they have erupted, and they may be without their own resources, culturally or materially, on which to draw. Their presence on land is often transitory. They may be uninvited, possibly unexplained, sometimes threatening.

The landings of castaways, madmen and gods

In Daniel Defoe's *Robinson Crusoe* (1719) the beach and all that happens there is centre stage. It is here that the goods which initially sustain Crusoe are washed up from the shipwreck that dumped him on his un-populated island in the first place. He arrives destitute: all he has when struggling ashore are a knife, a pipe and a tobacco box. Abandoned goods are deposited by the tides or rescued from the waves and put back into service to his benefit. Castaways rapidly become beach-combers. Thus the pickings from the wreck become the means by which Crusoe sets about taming and occupying the island. Salvage is his initial strategy of survival. As Vanessa Smith points out, Crusoe is not a trained technician of any sort – 'Being the third Son of the Family' he is 'not bred to any Trade'; before setting out on his ill-fated voyage, he had already passed the age when apprenticeship was a possibility for him.[2] To make do with the goods and limited tools he has at his disposal he is obliged to improvise and in the process gradu-ally recreates the practices of weaving, pottery-making, baking, tailoring, carpentry and masonry, cultivation, milling and animal husbandry. The beach and the wreck just offshore provide at once a bricoleur's toolbox and the source of sodden, rusted remnants in whose re-assemblage and reconfiguration utility is restored and the resources of the island exploited to his benefit. Usefulness, Defoe reminds his readers, has the highest value in such circumstances, not conventional marks of wealth. A drawer of diamonds has no value for Crusoe because it has no practical utility. What the tides deliver on the beach is strictly assessed according to its functional potential.

The beach is also potentially a place of deliverance. Crusoe needs to know what is going on there for many different reasons, but most importantly he recognizes it as a site of potential rescue. He chooses carefully where to build his first shelter, settling on a location that, amongst other attributes, will facilitate

> [A]View to the Sea, that if God sent any Ship in Sight, I might not lose any Advantage for my Deliverance, of which I was not willing to banish all my Expectation yet.[3]

The beach is construed, as indeed it ultimately turns out to be, as the site of his redemption.

Yet the beach is also, of course, a place of unwanted and threatening intrusion. It is here that, after fifteen years of isolation, Crusoe spies the footprint which on comparison with the size of his own foot confirms that he is not, after all, alone in the world. Two years on and he is confronted with a confusion of skulls and other human remains left along the shoreline together with the remnants of a cooking fire. He jumps to the terrible conclusion that – unremarked by him until that moment – the beach is the site of occasional cannibal feasting. He is, however, comforted by the thought that the isolation of the beach and of his island is the sole reason for it being visited. The 'savages' are not intent upon colonization but on finding a remote and, as they believe, uninhabited spot at which these 'horrendous' ritual acts can be conducted in secrecy. His personal safety could be guaranteed if he kept the evidence of his presence inland secret. As Crusoe reflects:

> To milk my She-goats, and manage my little Flock, in the Wood; which is quite on the other Part of the Island, was quite out of Danger; for certain it is, that these Savage People who sometimes haunted this Island, never came with any Thoughts of finding any Thing here, and consequently never wandered off from the Coast . . .[4]

Crusoe of course arrived on a deserted beach on a deserted island and his is at once a narration of colonization and an allegory of the rise of civilization. If Defoe's cannibals are only interested in the island because of the remoteness which affords them a place to carry out their guilty practices unseen by fellow 'primitives', it is also (so the conceit runs) intended to be unseen by the prying eyes of eighteenth-century opprobrium. Published in 1719, the real anticipation of the

Enlightenment idea of the 'noble savage' is Crusoe himself, reduced in circumstance and resource maybe, but able to recreate the circumstances of sustainable human life in isolation through self-reliance. In that sense he is the pioneer recreating in his colonization of the island the conditions through which human kind have passed to cultivate 'civilized' behaviours and practice – which later in the century was to be a major source of intellectual curiosity.

Whilst the figure of Robinson Crusoe is widely thought to be drawn on the life of a real castaway, Alexander Selkirk, the idea of the isolated island, unoccupied and unexplored by anyone else, is an enduring but largely fictional construct.[5] Most shipwrecks and castaways are obliged to deal with other people into whose lives they intrude uninvited and unexpected. Ford Madox Ford, in a book on the Cinque Ports, tells the arresting story of a shipwreck which occurred near the lighthouse at Dungeness in Kent in the late nineteenth century, all the more poignant for being true.[6] The ship was a merchant vessel with a German crew. As the ship foundered on the rocks one of the seamen took to the waters and being a reasonable swimmer was carried by the currents to a distant shore which turned out to be Romney Marsh. Here on a wintry night he crawled ashore having lost everything, hungry and penniless. As day broke he began to look for help, knocking on the doors of the few cottages around. However, he could not make himself understood and was treated with fear as either an escaped lunatic or some kind of supernatural visitation. Doors were locked against him and windows firmly secured; and as the men of the marsh came to know of his presence they chased him away whenever they saw him. Having been washed up he knew not where, unable to read any road signs or village names and unable to communicate, he wandered around destitute. At night people barricaded themselves in. Like Mary Shelley's monster Frankenstein, the German-speaking castaway was forced to make do as he could without human contact or help. He came to be known as 'Mad Jack'. This situation continued for several weeks until at last the police got to hear of it and came looking for him. When they found him he was living in a pigsty with his tattered shirt hanging from his neck and an old shoe in his hand in which he kept his food – a mouldy crust and the raw wing of a chicken – to protect it from the other occupants of the sty. During this wretched period he had been wandering around in the marshes repelled by all he encountered but moving within a radius of barely nine miles.

Mad Jack's emergence from the sea is without explanation – and he has no means to offer one. If beaches and coasts are places of trans-action, of negotiation between the realms of the sea and the land, there needs to be some means of reconciliation between them. Without it, the local population resorts to the usual speculation in such circum-stances: he is either psychologically deranged or he is some form of spectral jetsam washed up from the marine depths. Though Ford's account leaves it there, the fact that the castaway was nicknamed 'Jack' suggests that his maritime background was also part of the scenario rehearsed in seeking to understand how he came to be there. Yet sailors would not normally land at a place whose immediate hinterland is a marsh. This one arrived in just such a remote place without any belongings or means of support. Mad Jack could have been starved or died of cold through being shunned and chased away. Arguably what was more significant was the lack of a common language than of the material goods or currency through which any transaction might be initiated. Without a language of discourse misunderstanding and misrepresentation are unavoidable.

If Robinson Crusoe and Mad Jack are towards one end of the spec-trum of mariners who passed across beaches, Captain Cook is at the other. There are parts of the world where 'white-faced' gods are said to arrive from over the sea with uncertain but possibly benign motives. The Edo people of the Benin kingdom in southern Nigeria have such a tradition of the arrival of a divinity from the sea. The dead and the unborn are held to journey over the sea in their transitions between the material and the spiritual worlds. They move between the domains of the Benin ruler (the Oba) and that of his counterpart in the spiritual world, Olokun, and vice versa. In trance states initiates into the cult of Olokun are possessed by the divinity from the sea. Olokun is config-ured as having a light-coloured visage and his shrine includes a mix of colours but white chalk is prominent amongst the characteristic con-fection of objects and earthen sculptures. [7] It represents the positive side of Olokun's character, his association with calmness and beneficial outcomes. When, then, a British Punitive Expedition lead by white-faced outsiders was dispatched to enact retribution for an attack on British diplomats, their arrival and purpose was unclear in Benin itself. And when they carried the Oba into colonial exile, this catastrophic event had a local context. The Oba could be conceived as journeying across the sea to be in the domain of the god of good fortune.

The Hawaiians had a similar idea in 1779. Captain Cook arrived in the wrong place at the wrong time. His death was the product of circumstances that he did not realize he had sailed into and went beyond what, to those of his crew who witnessed it, appeared to be the immediate cause. Yet Cook's welcome in Hawaii could hardly have seemed more generous.[8] Ten thousand people were said to have been assembled, many more than habitually lived in Kealakekua Bay where he made landfall. They were in celebratory mood, reverential in behaviour and all unarmed. Many swam out to Cook's ships or came in canoes bringing gifts. Once on land Cook himself was led to the temple which happened to be just by the beach to which his boats delivered him, and there he was wrapped in red *tapa* cloth by one of the priests. As he processed he was greeted with cries of 'O, Lono'. People prostrated themselves before him. Things seemed to be going well.

However, Cook had strayed into the middle of the Hawaiian *makahiki* ritual cycle, a form of the New Year festival. Had he but known that 'Lono' was the name given to persons with divine attributes – to chiefs and sometimes priests as living embodiments of divinities – he might have seen the deferential behaviour shown towards him differently.[9] He was the focus of the ritual; the sacrifice of pigs was for him in the guise of a living god, a new incarnation of Lono appropriate to the annual event. A more worrying feature was that the king was not present at any of these events. He deferred to Lono during this period of the god's ascendancy. When he did appear the gift-giving was ostentatious. Cook sought to respond in kind as best he could. However, as Nicholas Thomas notes, gifts offered to the king by the priesthood were not reciprocated.[10] An alternation of powers was about to occur and Cook in the guise of Lono was on the wane. When one of Cook's seamen died the king insisted he should be buried on land. But a Christian burial began to turn into a version of a sacrificial one as the grave was showered with offerings of pigs and plantains when it was being filled in.

It was time to begin surveying the other islands in the Hawaiian group. Cook took his leave. However, several days later his ships ran into a heavy storm and were obliged to return to moorings in Kealakekua to undertake necessary repairs. Their welcome this time was distinctly muted. It was not perhaps so much that Cook had returned but that he returned too soon. By coming back not a year later at the appropriate moment in the ritual cycle but within days, Cook/Lono was unwittingly challenging the authority of the king. Gifts and reverence were replaced by coolness and distance. Things which had not happened before began to occur: Cook himself was now mocked; thefts from Cook's ships and supplies became numerous – and it was one of the more serious of these which was the immediate cause of Cook's demise. In the night the large cutter from the *Discovery* which had been anchored in the bay was stolen. Cook's response was to arrange a show of superior force, which throughout his voyages had been his tactic in dealing with unwelcome attention. Initially he intended to take canoes and hold them against the return of his own boat. In the event, though, he seems to have decided instead to take the king himself as a hostage pending the return of the cutter. Given the alternation of power which had happened between his visits to the bay this was to prove a fatal decision. Although the king himself seemed willing to come, one of his wives threw herself at his feet, weeping, and he sat down on the beach and refused to go any further; meanwhile muddled news came of a Hawaiian having been shot elsewhere, leading to anger and confusion. A man threatened Cook with a long dagger, ironically one of those which had been traded by Cook's expedition, and then took up a stone. Cook shot at him but the man was protected by his traditional battle matting. Others took up the cause and began to stone Cook's party. Cook himself was stabbed, stoned and drowned. He had wound up in the wrong place at the wrong time – and then taken the wrong action.

Crusoe's beleaguered circumstances led to a Herculean effort of self-reliance. Mad Jack's situation was one of complete helplessness. Cook, by contrast, was well provisioned, fearing theft rather than destitution, able to engage in lavish procedures of reciprocal gift-giving. Crusoe was alone; Mad Jack was attributed lunatic status; Cook divinity. Yet things did not end up as might have been expected. One spent long years sequestered in Adamic isolation; another was duly rescued by the constabulary; Cook, seeking to exercise an authority he no longer possessed, was killed. He, like Mad Jack, was involved in provocative acts: both had transgressed the boundary between the sea and the land. They had, in Dening's construction of it, crossed the beach. But where Mad Jack's traversing of the beach was uninvited and unanticipated, Cook was expected to cross – only he had not understood the circumstances.

Crusoe's actions are a truer reconciliation of sea and land. He maintains a watchfulness on the beach and the horizon beyond whilst yet cultivating the land and domesticating its wild stock. He explores the coastline as far as he can, takes advantage of anything the sea offers up and otherwise sets about developing the skills to turn terrestrial resources to his advantage. He is at once sailor, farmer and beach-comber, moving freely between these different realms, traversing the beach without transgressing it. It is only when others violate the privacy of *his* beach, leaving their prints on its pristine surface, that a separation takes place between sea and land, land and sea.

Beach living

It is at the coastline that the maritime world 'touches' the terrestrial, but even if the hinterland is rich in natural resources that does not necessar-ily mean that seaborne voyagers seek to exploit them. If someone else is engaged in growing crops, manufacturing goods, mining for ores then a maritime culture will have resort there. Likewise things which arrive from the sea have value and utility to shore-based peoples. From that develops the more extensive mechanisms of exploitation which see a developing relationship between maritime and terrestrial arenas of inter-est. However, one large island, Madagascar, remained unoccupied for a long time after much more remote ones had already been colonized. It has been argued that this is because it was only known to maritime cultures with no concern for colonizing the land.[11] The metaphor of the Indian Ocean as a trading wheel is apposite. It is like two cogs in a care-fully calibrated watch mechanism, one focused on the land, the other on the sea. They intersect with each other in a precisely controlled way, each spinning off into their own separate orbits once they have made contact and only interacting again when the time for their return is come. Madagascar had no inland trade and without that there was no cog with which to intersect. When eventually Madagascar was colonized, trade became a possibility. However, the first ports were small, fortified estab-lishments with their fortifications anticipating attack from the land, not the sea.[12] Such sites were a maritime foothold on the coastline rather than a terrestrial defence against maritime aggression. This is the reverse of what happens elsewhere. When the maritime world comes into con-tact with the land their interactions are sometimes corralled into a limited, designated space as the Japanese did with European traders at islands in the bays of Kobe and especially Nagasaki. The comparison of trading practices in different places is instructive.

An evocative account of the beach as a trading place occurs in Richard Henry Dana Jr's nineteenth-century narrative. Dana exchanges his life on ship for a four-month period in early summer 1835 on shore at San Diego, then a small harbour. It is here that sailors treat cattle hides prior to their enshipment. In order for these to be best stowed aboard they must first be prepared so they will neither rot nor take up unnecessary space in the cargo holds. The process involves collecting them, tanning and drying them, scraping off any meat or fat attaching to them and removing their 'flippers', that is, the ears – an interesting use of a maritime term for a terrestrial animal.[13] However, although this is life on land, their habitat is almost exclusively the beach relieved only by occasional excursions to the nearby town with its mission station and *presidios* (the Spanish term for garrisoned forts of which four were set up along the Californian coast), and trips into the bush to collect firewood and hunt with the dogs.

The business of tanning, however, took place on the beach itself. 'I was transformed', Dana comments, 'from a sailor to a "beachcomber" and a hide-curer.'[14] As with Crusoe, a constant watch is kept on the horizon for the sails of ships. Dana gives a thorough sketch of life on the beach.[15] He lives in the hide house itself where a corner is given over to accommodation and cooking equipment. Here the white sailors of European and American extraction live. Further along the beach is a large bread-oven, originally built by a Russian ship which laid up there and now home to up to eight natives from the Sandwich (that is, Hawaiian) Islands, referred to collectively as *kanakas*. There was also a large population of dogs on the beach (Dana estimates about 40) which were of use both in hunting and as guard dogs, since incursions at night would set off a 'general alarm'. In addition to the dogs were 'hogs' and chickens. There were also around a dozen horses allowed to roam in the nearby hills and, although individually owned, kept as common property.[16] The routine of the beach involved all the sailors who effectively set up their own separate community there.

This, then, is not a colonizing process at all. The community remains a seafaring one, with their focus, literally, on the sea. When, occasionally, other ships came into the bay their crews might set up tents also on the beach and temporarily swell the community by their presence to form a truly multinational, multilingual society. Dana enumerates the nationalities during one ship's stopover:

> Two Englishmen, three Yankees, two Scotchmen, two
> Welshmen, one Irishman, three Frenchmen (two of whom
> were Normans, and the third from Gascony), one Dutchman,
> one Austrian, two or three Spaniards (from old Spain),
> half a dozen Spanish-Americans and half-breeds, two native
> Indians from Chili and the island of Chiloe, one negro,
> one mulatto, about twenty Italians, from all parts of Italy,
> as many more Sandwich Islanders, one Otaheitan, and one
> Kanaka from the Marquesas islands.[17]

As on ships, they somehow manage to rub along together despite differences of language, ethnicity or nationality. Indeed, so self-regulating was the beach community that, Dana suggests, some found it preferable to landing at ports. It was, for instance, one of the sole resorts of some ships otherwise obliged to remain at sea for long periods as they engaged in illegal trade or sought to avoid having to pay taxes. These unlicensed ships 'frequently remain on the coast for years, without making port, except at islands for wood and water, and an occasional visit to Oahu for a new outfit'.[18]

We have other descriptions of how the transitory life on beaches operated. In 'The Beach at Falesá' (1892) – one of the essays in his collection published as *South Sea Tales* – Robert Louis Stevenson makes extensive use of the concept of the 'beach', adopting it emblematically in his very title.[19] The island in question was a mix of peoples, like many Stevenson knew from the voyages he made criss-crossing the Pacific between 1888 and 1890 when he decided to set up permanent home in Samoa (and where indeed he died four years later). There were native Polynesians, 'Kanakas', some of whom were indigenous to the island in question and others, like Uma – the native woman the narrator Wiltshire marries – were displaced by circumstances from other islands. There is also a mobile community of whites speaking different European languages and variously engaged in trade and missionary activities. It is this latter to whom the term 'beach' refers. They not only lived on or by the beach, they themselves as a group were known as 'the beach'. By extension, the lingua franca which developed amongst them came to be known also as 'Beach de mar' or 'Beach-la-mar', which comes to mean the speech of the beach, the medium by which Europeans communicate with each other and with Pacific islanders. This is a corruption of the term *bêche-de-mer*, French for a sea cucumber, one of the items traded on the islands. Stevenson saw it as becoming the language of the Pacific, a common pidgin. In practice, though, it was more or less limited to Melanesia where it is the basis of Bislama, a pidgin language spoken in Vanuatu.

Ports had similar linguistic characteristics. The languages spoken here were often not simply translocations of the language seamen develop amongst themselves on ships, and which we have referred to in the last chapter. That did indeed occur at particular ports where historically seamen have gathered, changed ships or simply laid up whilst repairs are made or fresh supplies taken on board. Seafarers were readily identifiable in such places by their dress, their gait, their weathered features, their tattoos – but also by their language. In nineteenth-century Boulogne, for example, the maritime quarter used a special *patois des marins*.[20] In the same vein those parts of London where the shifting multi-ethnic, seagoing populations congregated retained their own maritime language. Marcus Rediker quotes Sir John Fielding, writing in 1776:

> The seamen here are a generation differing from all the world. When one goes into Rotherhithe and Wapping, which places are chiefly inhabited by sailors, but that some-what of the same language is spoken, a man could be apt to suspect himself in another country. The manner of living, speaking, acting, dressing, and behaving are so very peculiar to themselves. Yet with all they are perhaps the bravest and boldest fellows in the world.[21]

Thomas, who also cites this quotation, goes on to remark that they were 'fish out of water'.[22]

In San Diego in the 1830s the beach community that Dana joined had virtually no direct contact with those they traded with. Native Americans would bring their hides to the nearby cliff face and simply throw them over onto the shore beneath. Sometimes they lingered and looked over the top. It is the indigenous population who are spying on the activities of the interlopers on the beach rather than the other way round. A system of brokerage operated at the nearby settlement allowing the two worlds to interact, but beyond that mutual curiosity was unrequited by actual contact. The beach was not crossed.

Systems of brokerage

The idea of coastal peoples with no experience of international trading communities beyond their own, such as Defoe imagined and Cook
experienced, are hardly the rule. Dana witnessed a system which was
already in place and which was to change radically in a short space of
time; when he returned in older life to California he found San Diego
a booming town – the beach had become a port; brokers had become
agents with developing international clienteles. Similarly when the
Portuguese first arrived on the western coast of India there was already
a long-established system for reconciling maritime and terrestrial
interests in place. Foreign agents had already settled in many Indian
ports where they often had their own quarter, managed their own
affairs and were frequently married to local women with whom they
had children.[23] These children of mixed race, able to interact with
two different societies, were powerful interlocutors in the trading relationships between maritime and terrestrial interests. They came to
represent the interests of far-flung kinsmen who might derive from
ports right round the rim of the Indian Ocean. Such compatriots were
able to offer to act as go-betweens with a full network of local contacts
in place. A new arrival could simply plug in to an already operating
trading system.

When the Portuguese arrived in Calicut in the opening decade of
the sixteenth century they found there were enough foreign competi-
tors in place for their appearance on the scene not to be an unwelcome intrusion. None the less the existence of an established system
of brokerage allowed the Portuguese to make initial inroads into the
local Indian markets. Calicut was under the influence of both Hindu
rulers and Muslim traders with sea-based interests. It is said that at
the start of the sixteenth century there were 4,000 Muslim households in Calicut alone, whose occupants were from places as distant
as Egypt, the Red Sea, Persia, Gujarat and the Deccan.[24] With so
many 'foreigners' permanently resident, systems were in place to cope
with exotic visitors. Sufficiently confident were the participants in
the system that we learn that Cabral's second Portuguese expedition
to Calicut was welcomed, initially at least, and his representative was
accommodated in a Gujarati-owned house whose Muslim owner took
on the task of instructing him in the practices of the local market
system – effectively encouraging a potentially rival brokerage.

In such circumstances linguistic accommodations will already have been substantially made and even if a plethora of languages were in use, means of communication were established including both the development of pidgin languages and multilingualism. But it was not totally so, it seems. Herodotus talked of the practice of 'silent trade' in the ancient world. A sixteenth-century European traveller, Ludovico di Varthema, gives a fascinating example of such a negotiation conducted by a broker in Calicut where there appears to have been no form of common language in place to effect the transaction. The silent bargain was arranged thus:

> When the purchaser and the seller make an agreement, they all stand in a circle, and the Cortor (broker) takes a cloth and holds it there openly with one hand, and with the other he takes the right hand of the seller, that is, the two fingers next to the thumb, And then he covers with the said cloth his hand and that of the seller, and touching each other with these two fingers, they count from one ducat up to one hundred thousand secretly, without saying 'I will have so much', or 'so much'. But in merely touching the joint of the fingers they understand the price and say: 'Yes' or 'No'. And the Cortor answers 'No' or 'Yes'. And when the Cortor has understood the will of the seller, he goes to the buyer with the said cloth, and takes his hand in the manner above mentioned, and by the said touching he tells him he wants so much. The buyer takes the finger of the Cortor and by the said touches says to him: 'I will give him so much'. And in this manner they fix a price.[25]

Clearly the broker as agent in these relationships has a critical role to play. Such methods imply a common understanding of the process and the purpose of the negotiation. As beach communities developed their own linguistic accommodations, sustained trading relationships required an evolution in language whether through secondary translation, multilingualism or the development of a common pidgin language. The British East India Company sought to have its employees develop fluency in Indian dialects but with limited success. By then, however, the Portuguese were already conducting their affairs in 'Negro Portuguese', a luso-pidgin language which was widely used in Indian ports.[26] Likewise, in the Channel Islands a smugglers' language is said to have developed – 'related to Spanish as Levantine is to Italian'.[27]

However, beyond that, there are also languages which have a wider currency along the littorals of various seas and oceans. Kiswahili is an interesting example. The word 'Swahili' itself derives from an Arabic term for a border or coastline. The people and the language occupy a long section of the shores of the western Indian Ocean stretching almost 3,000 kilometres from northern Mozambique northwards to the Kenyan coastal border with Somalia. Swahili is also the first language of many offshore islands, notably Lamu, Zanzibar and the Comoros. The fact that versions of it are also spoken in the African hinterland and across into the Democratic Republic of Congo is the result of nineteenth-century exploitation of the interior by Arab slave and ivory traders (or their agents) and latterly by British colonial expansion. In origin, however, it is a coastal language, the language of traders, merchants and seamen who worked the East African coast and beyond. To search for a stable Swahili identity which is ethnically precise is as impossible as it would be to try and associate the Hanseatic League of north-western European with any single national or ethnic identity. Participation in a mercantile trading system with its systems of seafaring trading and brokerage, and above all fluency in the lingua franca of the western Indian Ocean shores is as close to a definition of Swahili identity as is practicable.[28]

Fishermen and farmers

Rabelais in his classic sixteenth-century comic novel has Pantagruel express a strong preference for the terrestrial over the maritime. He wrote of a great storm at sea:

> Tempests and squalls, whirlwinds and hurricanes were lighted up all around us by thunderbolts, flashes, forked lightening, and other manifestations. Our looks expressed horror and dismay, as the hideous tempests whipped the mountainous waves of the sea. Believe me, we felt that ancient Chaos had come again; that fire, earth, sea, air, and all the elements were in rebellious confusion . . . How blessed, blessed, and four

times blessed are those men who plant cabbages in solid earth. Why, O fates, did you not spin me a cabbage-planter's lot? Few and signalled blessed are those whom Jupiter has destined to be cabbage-planters. For they've always one foot on the ground and the other not far from it.[29]

The idea of 'beach crossing' implies a maritime culture becoming reconciled to a terrestrial one and for the purposes of the argument being developed here the distinction between the two is, as Rabelais construed it, sharply drawn. Analytically, however, it remains an issue as to how far it is advisable to dissociate the understanding of what happens at sea from what happens on land. Brokerage provides one system of intersection; but in practice there are many societies in which people pursue a livelihood that is in reality a mixed economy of activities, being fishermen for part of the year and farmers for the rest. This pattern characterized many of the fishing communities of northern Europe until very recent times, and to some extent it still does in remoter parts of the Celtic seaboard. Similarly, as we have seen, the Faroe Islands in the north-west Atlantic were known to the earliest sources as the Islands of Sheep, occupied it seems by monks who travelled there to explore the inner self in the solitude of these isolated places. They were mariners, they were clerics and they also tended livestock, transhipped there in currachs for the purpose. No doubt they also took full advantage of what the sea which surrounded them had to offer. The regime of fishing and of living off the sea along the North Atlantic coasts involves harvesting the resources of the sea when the migrations of fish stock and weather conditions are most favourable and of small-scale agriculture at other times. It is only the kind of accounting reminiscent of the census forms which obliges a choice between the two. For those pursuing such a mixed economy their way of life is not simply to be described as one or the other; it is both: they are fishermen and they are farmers.

Yet the skills required for each are specific and anthropological accounts of other parts of the world than the Atlantic seaboard suggest that this distinction is recognized culturally. For example, the Vezo peoples of Madagascar are described as 'People of the Sea' in the title of the most insightful anthropological monograph on their livelihood and the complexities of their sense of social identity.[30] True, they live beside the Mozambique Channel and sail off in search of fish in their outrigger canoes on a daily basis. As discussed in chapter Three, 'Vezo-ness' is not unequivocally a matter of ethnic affiliation or descent but a quality which can be acquired even by those who are not by birth Vezo. Equally it can be foregone by those who, though brought up in one of the Vezo villages along the south-western coast of the island, move away and no longer participate on a regular basis in its practice. Even people of Vezo descent who make a blunder at sea and display incompetence in seamanship or fishing may temporarily be reclassified as Masikoro, the term for groups of agriculturalists and cattle keepers who live inland.[31] People can move in and out of being Vezo because it is not a fixed ethnic identity; indeed, it is better thought of as a body of knowledge and skill. Certainly this needs to be acquired over time and is not just a matter of current residence; but, more than that, it needs to be practised. It is by doing the things of the Vezo that people become Vezo.

This sharp division between sea-people and land-people is found elsewhere also. Thus in scattered areas of Burma, Malaysia, Indonesia and the Philippines a fundamental indigenous distinction is made between people whose livelihood centres entirely on boats and on harvesting the products of the sea and those who live in permanent communities on land. In the past they were also instrumental in complex networks of international trade linking up with Chinese and Malay traders in exchanging goods on an inter-regional basis. Nowadays their seagoing activity is very largely limited to fishing and supplying marine products to land-based peoples. However, their maritime links are comprehensive. The situation is little different from that originally described in 1667 by Francisco Combés:

> They (the sea-people of the Philippines) are of this nature,
> that they know no other home than their boats . . . [and]
> are such enemies of the land, that it does not get from them
> the slightest labour or industry, nor the profit of any fruits.
> All of their work is in fishing and by this they barter for what
> they need . . . And as they have put down very few roots,
> they move easily to other parts, having no fixed dwelling
> but the sea.[32]

Although the sea-people of the region follow (or followed) similar livelihoods, 'true' Bajau Laut will only eat fish and crustaceans, foregoing all meat deriving from land-based animals. Rice, vegetables, fruit and drinking water are all they require from inland sources. Amongst the Bajau Laut community their fear of the sea – to the extent that it exists – is limited to only one or two places where strong currents are known to run or deep holes in the reefs cause dangerous undertows. In practice only one boat has ever been lost at sea in living memory – and that over 50 years previously.[33] More to the point, Bajau Laut are preyed on by pirates who look to take their catch of fish and, in reality, constitute the greatest threat to their livelihood.

Yet the predominant language of advocacy is not on their side. To settled, land-based peoples they are *pala'au* – 'that which is spat or vomited out'. They have come to be described colloquially as 'outcasts' or 'sea gypsies', a colonial-period nomenclature indicating that they do not share conventional terrestrial ideas of home and hearth.[34] An origin myth current in a number of variations among land-people sets the seal on their status. They are said to have insulted the Prophet, denying him fish and cooking dog instead. As a result one of his followers, Prophet Ibrahim, uttered some special verses from the Koran which caused the land of the fishermen to sink into the sea, leaving them clinging in the waters to logs like so much flotsam. This would be their condition until the verses of the Holy Koran should disappear and be repeated no more. In other words, their punishment was to be eternal.[35]

The implication of this cursing of the fishermen is that they were expelled from the land (rather than 'preferring' to live on the sea, as they themselves might construe it), condemned forever to live outside the Islamic – or any – faith. They are people without land, with limited possessions and 'without religion'. To this conceptual and theological stigma are added demographic and political factors. Their life on the sea and the shores places them physically and politically at the margins. In the hierarchical structure of the Sulu kingdom of which they were part, they occupy the lowest rank on the fringes of a polity with a strong Muslim base. Though some myths relate circumstances of intermarriage between beautiful Bajau Laut women and rich land-based husbands, their relationships with the Sulu state and its merchants was very largely a mediated one. In practice, an appointed patron effectively negotiated the relationship between the boat-people moored in their anchorages and their trading partners on the shore. Living on the sea, they escape the conventional archiving of historical experience and

miss the opportunity of any form of organized self-assertion. A practice of endogamous marriage has maintained their distinctiveness.

One argument, then, is that the patron-client relationship is
critical to preserving the sea-peoples' way of life. Their specialism in
fishing allows them to barter for goods that they do not have access
to by their own toil. To that extent their engagement in trade through
patrons is actually a form of subsistence, not a development beyond
it. They could not preserve the exclusiveness of their way of life
without the system of intermediation, for they would otherwise be
obliged to take up farming or to trade on their own behalf.

The totality of this engagement with the sea is evident in other
ways. Their knowledge of fish stock in the maze of islands they inhabit
is all-embracing – over 200 varieties of fish are identified and eaten;
added to that are 40 different named shellfish. Different skills are
required for catching different kinds of fish – whether by line, net, spear
or harpoon – and Bajau themselves specialize individually in one or
other of these techniques.[36] In terms of the language used of directions
the Bajau Laut again situate themselves in the sea. The principal directions used in everyday conversation are those given by familiar sailing
directions, even if the reference is to a land-based orientation – the relative positions of houses within a coastal village, for instance. They talk
of objects, persons and events as happening or being located to the 'seaward' or the 'landward' of each other. Seaward is the direction a person
sails when going out on a fishing expedition; landward is the opposite,
the direction they sail when returning to their moorings.[37]

Since the mid-twentieth century this system has broken down
somewhat as the idea of the boat as a permanent home has been supplanted by the development of villages raised on poles in the waters
which formerly provided anchorage. None the less such dwellings are
still 'halfway houses', built above, if not literally on, salt water. Villages
considered part of the same coastal/maritime complex are those which,
though on rivers, are still within the tidal range. Villages built on fresh
water would often be considered to be occupied by 'land-people',
though riverine and readily connecting to peoples living on estuaries.
Towards the end of the century the numbers of those who could be
regarded as entirely boat-dwelling was down to as few as 5,000. They
have become increasingly shore-people who may well continue to live
by fishing and trading their catches and retain a distinction between
themselves and agriculturalists living inland.

The similarities and contrasts between Bajau Laut and the Vezo are interesting. Both live principally from fishing and regard aptitude in maritime techniques and technologies as ethnically defining. 'Authentic' members of each have, by definition, an association with the sea which overrides any association with the land. The role of patron who moves between sea-people and land-people in the maritime world of the Philippines is taken in Vezo society by women who take the fish caught by their sons and husbands to market and negotiate for any other goods needed to sustain their communities. However, where Bajau Laut situate themselves in the sea to express ideas of direction the Vezo point of reference, as we have seen, is solely the homeward journey, not the contrast between the outward and return voyages. The open sea, by contrast, is a place surrounded by water where it is not possible to have it 'behind' you – in other words it is a place where you are lost and unable to return to your village.[38] 'Authentic' Bajau Laut live on boats or in houses on platforms perched above salt water; Vezo live on the coast regarding the interior as the place of non-Vezo, a place to bury their dead, but not a place Vezo otherwise want to visit without being prepared to take the risk of compromising their ethnicity. For both Bajau Laut and Vezo the coastline is a boundary.

Breaching the beach

However, in myth there is also some expression of the interdependence of sea-based and land-based peoples and some anticipation of a more complete integration than is evidenced in current categorization. The Bajau provided various services to the developing terrestrial sultanate of Sulu, undertaking useful tasks of provisioning and supplying luxury goods: they dived for mother-of-pearl, collected *bêche-de-mer*, and fished for shark fin, all valued products, and they also provided dried fish. Those who had foregone the sea-nomadic life none the less continued to give the sultanate a maritime edge as inter-island traders and maritime raiders who brought back slaves as well as more conventional products of the sea. Yet, in myth, it is envisaged that they might provide another valuable resource. It is recounted in a tradition from Sabah that the ruler of Johore, one of the Bajau centres, had a beautiful daughter whom both the sultans of Brunei and of Sulu wanted to marry. The daughter herself preferred the suitor from Brunei, but her father insisted that the marriage should be with the prince from Sulu; and he duly sent her to him by ship under escort. On the way, however, the forces of Brunei attacked the Johore ships and took the princess. Thereafter, myth records, the people of Johore were so ashamed that the arrangement with the Sulu aristocracy had not been fulfilled that they feared they would be punished. They determined to remain at sea, moving from mooring to mooring as their descendants now do. In other versions the Bajau princess simply disappears at sea.[39]

This story is one of the expulsion of sea-people from the land, or at least (since they were already conceived of as having a maritime context) relocation somewhat further offshore. However, here it is portrayed as a self-inflicted penalty. No matter that the marriage did not occur, nor that it is envisaged as having happened in mythical times: to those narrating the story the implications would be clear. The Bajau rules of endogamy have been broken, and the lowly status of the Bajau in relation to the aristocratic Sulu sultanate breached; in contemporary terms, it would be equivalent to a Muslim marrying a person 'without religion'. The boundary-crossing is more than a transition from sea to land. In short, a person of the sea would come to have high status on the land and potentially bear the children of the ruling aristocracy. The potential marriage remains unconsummated with the Sulu not because it has seemed a bad idea, but because it was so good an idea that the sultanate of Brunei stole it.

A more explicit narrative of maritime origins in a terrestrial context is found in Polynesia. It has different emphasis; yet the Pacific mythic cycle extends the implications of the basic Bajau account. It also significantly foresees a wider integration of sea-people and land-people. In much of the Pacific coastal peoples exploit the products of the sea as readily as they do the land. 'Sea people', in the entirely maritime way that Bajau Laut construe the concept, would be difficult to parallel in Oceanic cultures. People do not live permanently on the sea or use intermediaries to obtain what they need from the land in that way. None the less the concept of people who come from the sea, and are thereby in origin 'strangers' in relation to people of the land, is a fundamental one. As 'strangers', indeed, people more closely associated with the sea are not on the lowest ranks of society, as are the Bajau Laut within the Sulu sultanate of the Philippines, but are rather at the top, as powerful chiefs and divinities. Furthermore, it is not just a classification of people which is at stake but also of things and materials. The contrast between products obtained from the sea and those deriving from the land is also one of importance, particularly in ceremonial contexts.

In Fiji the mythic charter foresees the arrival of kingship from overseas.[40] It concerns a fair-skinned stranger of notable beauty who is the victim of an accident at sea. He is befriended by a shark which bears him to the shores of the island of Viti Levu. From there he goes inland and is given succour by a local chief, whose daughter in due course he marries. He is thereby tied by bonds of marriage to people of the islands; land and sea come together in a way that is foreseen in Bajau myth but there remains unconsummated. That versions of the narrative have wider currency in the Pacific islands is evidenced by a Hawaiian proverb to the effect that a chief is like a shark on land. In the part of Fiji where the myth was recorded the ruling clan is called the 'sharks'. The 'stranger' from the sea, a person who is external to the people of the land, comes to take a position of ruler-'ship' through a foundational act of marrying in. He is not just a stranger (in the sense of a foreigner), but by origin a stranger to the land itself. In the Fijian case the result is the creation of a new aristocratic dynasty. The union of people of the sea with people of the land, each appropriating the powers of the other, installs a powerful new element at the heart of the chieftaincy. The synthesis of the two generates an empowered new presence. In Fiji it goes further, for the stranger-king is also killed to be given rebirth as a divinity – as he is incorporated into the land, so he is also consumed by it. Both sides benefit. A new and authoritative entity is brought into existence by the fusion of sea-based and land-based principles, substance and materiality.

The ramifications of this are still evident. The installation rites of the new ruler of Lau in 1969 give a suggestive account of how myth is recapitulated in history.[41] The preliminaries of the investiture happened not on Lau itself but at Nayau Island. Thus when the new paramount ruler makes his first appearance in Lau he arrives by sea. The implication is that he is to that point unfamiliar with the land. He crosses the beach; and, as he processes, he does so led by chiefs of the land along a route lined with barkcloth, the so-called 'path of the god'. The barkcloth itself is not of native Fijian manufacture but Tongan. It is of the land, but still at this stage foreign. The new ruler proceeds to the chiefly house and then to the ceremonial ground. The central part of the investiture is the drinking of kava and at this stage the paramount chief has local bark-cloth tied to his arm. Barkcloth is not only a product exclusively produced on land: it is also the exclusive work of women. Once installed the chief is said to have taken possession of the 'barkcloth of the land'.[42] Elsewhere in Fiji, for instance at Bau, there are long pandanus-mat pathways for a similar purpose. The common element is that these should be women's 'land' products, embodiments of their persons, which are a ritualized mechanism for channelling, controlling and 'capturing' the potency of the external 'sea' chief – and by extension his original mythical entourage of sailors, navigators and other specialists. The agency of women, as in the mythic act of the stranger from the seas marrying in, is thereby acknowledged. The god from the sea has become the paramount chief of the land. Sea and land are wedded, and in their union the world is brought into cosmological balance. To the extent that similar ideas exist in Hawaii, the lack of such appropriate expressions of union, the disruption of the ritual cycle by Cook's prompt return, suggests the fuller context of his ultimate demise.

In Lau, this distinction between the land and the sea is used explicitly to classify people; but it is by no means straightforward. The ritual process of incorporating strangers from the sea clearly creates a situation where some people are of the sea in relation to longer-established clans who would be regarded by them as of the land. Yet they themselves are of the land in relation to succeeding arrivals. It works in several ways. A person may be 'sea' in relation to one clan but 'land' in relation to another. However, the land/sea categorization is less a distinction deployed statically in cultural contexts and more a fluid generative set of principles in whose synthesis powerful social and cultural imperatives arise. Land and sea are thereby to be interpreted less as absolute distinctions than as complementary categories. The geographical distinction between the land and the sea is thereby translated into a socio-cultural one between people with implications for human behaviour which go well beyond characteristic livelihood activities.

The implications are most evident in ritual process. Outside of that men and women in Fiji are shown to have no exclusive association with one realm rather than another; it is only that in particular contexts an association with one or the other is brought to bear. So, because of clan membership an association may be made between particular people and particular sea-based or land-based skills or predispositions. Someone of the land might more readily become seasick in a boat than someone associated with the sea. Some men may have inherited a particular affinity with, say, navigation and way-finding in the waters beyond the immediate shore. But whether they actually regularly set foot in a boat or exploit any assumed nautical expertise is another matter. Propensity is all that is implied.

Thus the categories of land-people and sea-people may make an actual distinction which follows differences in livelihood, cultural orientation and ethnicity. It may involve distinctions of language, diet, dress and other cultural differences beyond the simple particularity of occupational practice. Depending on seasons people may move back and forth between the categories. Or, again, the land/sea opposition may be deployed to establish distinctions within particular hierarchies which have no particular connection with the actual exercise of associated labour and skills. None the less, they make distinctions between people. However, in the Fijian example it is clearly in the conjunction of categories rather than in their separation that their full implications are recovered. From a maritime perspective, the beach has been definitively breached and the imagery of sea and land embedded in indigenous political theory.

six

The Sea on the Land

> *. . . the boat has not only been for our civilization, from the*
> *sixteenth century until the present, the great instrument*
> *of economic development but has been simultaneously the*
> *greatest reserve of the imagination. The ship is the hetero-*
> *topia par excellence. In civilizations without boats, dreams*
> *dry up, espionage takes the place of adventure, and the*
> *police take the place of pirates.*
>
> MICHEL FOUCAULT, 'Of other spaces' (1984)[1]

Always alert to sailor's language and usage, Richard Dana talked of cutting off the ears on cattle hides on the beach at San Diego as removing their 'flippers'. It seems an obvious metaphor for a mariner to use when referring in the colourful language of the sea to the large floppy ears of a land-based ruminant. Yet it is characteristic of a whole area of maritime practice which involves a cultural process of reversal between the things of the land and the things of the sea. The maritime and terrestrial worlds are linked, even constructed as separate in cultural terms. However, their separation is not such that one comes to be divorced from the other. In practice each expresses itself in terms of the other through a process of symbolic inversion. They mirror each other, but not through replication. Things are the same, but different. Moving definitively from the sea onto land, this final chapter asks how things are different. We begin with the interplay between maritime and terrestrial language.

Sailor talk

In the late 1990s the writer Redmond O'Hanlon set out to sea from the north-east of Scotland on a North Sea trawling boat in mid-winter. They were bound for the Icelandic fishing grounds with a hurricane in the offing. Even before setting out he was immediately made aware of the numerous customs to be observed, starting with a prohibition on wearing anything green. The restrictions proliferated as he learnt more. He was told:

> Your wife, for instance, whatever happens, she must *never* use the washing machine on the weekend before you go. Because it's like the sea, the whirlpool – she'll be washing your soul away.[2]

As mentioned earlier, women are not allowed on board or even to touch the guardrails. O'Hanlon learns he must also go back home if he sees a minister of religion on the way to a ship. He cannot leave harbour on a Friday. Before a new net is used a virgin should piss on it. Once on board a further series of taboos are activated. In relation to animals there are words which it is forbidden to use: these include rat, pig and ram. Likewise, the word 'egg' is forbidden. If a bird taps on the wheelhouse window, or if the ship's bell tolls of its own accord, it is a bad omen – it is said that 'the bell is the soul of the ship'.[3] Breaking any of these prohibitions spells misfortune – which, in the depths of winter and in extremes of weather, implies disastrous results to the haul of fish or the boat itself and its crew. There are, however, some remedies available: 'if you have offended, if you've said any of the words that may kill everybody – you simply touch cold iron, pronto. And there's plenty of cold iron on deck.'[4] Or if you have had an unlucky streak at fishing, you can 'burn the witch' – that is, take a lighted torch round the boat and smoke out the bad luck.

What O'Hanlon had stumbled upon is in fact a North Atlantic-wide set of taboos to do with the sea, many of which are linguistic. Thus, in addition to the use of certain words being discouraged when on board ship, a whole alternative vocabulary is in use. These are *noa* or 'normal' words, also called *godnemne* ('good name' in Norwegian), *lucky-words* in Shetland and *skoknamn* ('names of superstition', in Gotland).[5] So extensive has the practice of having two sets of vocabulary been that in Faroese it has amounted to two parallel languages, a sea-language and a land-based language, which is referred to as the 'kilnhouse' version. Some vocabularies had very extensive alternative nomenclatures: Christer Westerdahl identified eighteen words for 'horse', thirteen for 'pig', eleven for 'sheep' and seven for 'cow' on Shetland.[6] Faroese has as many as 22 words for 'cat'. Other animals characteristically included

in these lexicons were foxes and wolves, mice and rats, hares and rabbits, and otters. Birds often had special sea-names as, between the
languages of sea and land, did fish. Both ecclesiastical and civil authorities are also attributed *noa* words: clergy, sheriffs, bailiffs and the police
were all known by other names at sea. Places too might be referred to
differently in sea-going vocabulary.

Thus language – rather than simply sailing skills – comprises one of
the first elements of initiation into seafaring. Jack Cremer, an American
youth who ventured to sea in the early eighteenth century, later
remarked that his acceptance into the community of sailors could be
traced to the moment when his fellow seamen 'began to learn me to
call names, which was the first Rhudiment of that University'.[7] Sufficiently profuse was this seagoing vocabulary that the first English
dictionary of nautical language was written as early as the1620s by
Sir Henry Mainwaring and published in 1644. It incorporated both
the technical language of seamanship and what might otherwise be
termed sailor's slang. This was superseded in 1789 by the publication
of William Falconer's much larger *Universal Dictionary of the Marine* which
included an appendix on French sea-going language. By then the language in common usage had begun to reflect an experience of seas
beyond those off the coasts of northern Europe: the term 'banyan days',
for instance, was used for periods when supplies of meat had run
out.[8] The reference is to Indian vegetarianism. That sailor talk was a
language unto itself is enthusiastically endorsed in Admiral Smyth's
mid-nineteenth century dictionary which itself runs to over 700 pages.
He writes:

> The predilection for sea idiom is assuredly proper in a
> maritime people, especially as many of the phrases are at
> once graphic, terse, and perspicuous. How could the where-
> abouts of an aching tooth be better pointed out to the
> operative dentist than Jack's "'Tis the aftermost grinder
> aloft, on the starboard quarter."[9]

Beyond individual vocabulary, swearing is expected whilst praying
is discouraged. Indeed Marcus Rediker tells of a priest who, prohibitions notwithstanding, took to sea in squally conditions. Being worried
about the safety of the ship, he approached the captain for an assessment of their fate and was advised to go on deck and listen to the deck

hands as they struggled at their labours. When he returned he reported that they were all swearing profusely. That, the captain responded, was a good sign. Later, however, he went back on deck and found the seamen had turned to praying. On hearing this, the captain retorted: 'Oh, I am afraid if they have stopped swearing and started praying there is not hope for us.'[10]

Profanity represented the normal state of affairs. But such plain talk was not necessarily indicative of an abject state of continual defiance. It was simply the habit of ships. Sailors' English was, as Conrad – who knew the language well – remarked, terse and accurate, 'a flawless thing for its purpose'.[11] As we have seen, part of Dening's argument as to Captain Bligh's fate was based in part in his transgressions of expected linguistic practice.[12] As captain he was not supposed to indulge in bad language. That was for ordinary seamen. But his language was not just abusive; it was also hard to interpret. He was ambiguous rather than straight-talking; and through indulging ambiguity he relinquished authority. His fault was in abusing 'an instrument wrought into perfection by ages of experience', as Conrad remarked;[13] that is, he had transgressed the rules of language appropriately used at seas. Mainwaring's dictionary was intended, after all, not for the ordinary seaman but, as its preface explains, for officers, to 'make a man understand what other men say, and speak properly himself'.[14] And these and successive dictionaries record how few are the colourful terms referring to the captain of the ship himself: he is simply 'skipper'. He should be a figure of authority, not of fun. His use of language could affirm or undermine his leadership. Blight's fate, in Dening's insightful analysis, was sealed by the inept words issuing from his own mouth.

Apart from language, things associated with the land are not permitted on ship either and, as we have seen, even modern fishermen have to be attentive to their demeanour as well as their vocabulary. Many of the words in the seaman's parallel vocabulary refer to things which are also banned from ships. Yet boundary-crossing did occur. On Tudor ships, as work on the wreck of the *Mary Rose* has shown, dogs – usually terriers – seem to have been preferred to keep the population of rats in check. Ship's cats, however, were later regarded as essential and captains sailing round the coast of West Africa, where cats were not readily available, had cause to bemoan the loss of any brought with them from their home ports. Yet opinion on their more mystical impact varied. Some regarded them as agents of good fortune to the extent that in medieval times a shipwreck was not considered legally abandoned until the cat had left the foundering vessel. An alternative view, however, cast them in the role of agents of witchcraft. Thus, one of the sources used by Earle, Henry Fielding, gives a lively account of a kitten falling into the sea only for the boatswain to dive in after it and return holding the comatose kitten in his teeth. It duly revived. However, this proved to be a mixed blessing, for some of the sailors voiced the opinion that 'the drowning of a cat was the very surest way of raising a favourable wind'.[15] Dogs, though sometimes taboo aboard ship,[16] are useful in finding land at night or warning of it in a fog as they can hear and respond to the barely audible bark of a dog on land. In terms of food, the supplies brought on board from the land were always consumed in preference to the fish that would be caught at sea.

Yet clearly it is not just that the land is differently constructed at sea; so too has the usage of the sea penetrated aspects of the terrestrial domain. Again language is an obvious starting point. Admiral Smyth lists some of the vocabulary appropriate to the sea – what he calls Raleigh's 'ancient and fishlike'[17] – which has none the less found its way into 'landlubber' speech. He uses political discourse as illustration, remarking:

> Even our parliamentary orators, with a proper national bias, talk of swamping a measure, danger ahead, taking the wind out of an antagonist's sails, drifting into war, steering a bill through shoals of opposition or throwing it overboard, following in the wake of a leader, trimming to the breeze, tiding a question over a session, opinions above or below the gangway, and the like, so rife of late in St. Stephen's; even when a member 'rats' on seeing that the pumps cannot keep his party from falling to leeward, he is imitating the vermin that quit a sinking ship.[18]

We turn now to pursue the imaginative interpenetration of the sea in other domains.

Ships and architecture

In 1992 London acquired a new landmark. The Ark at Hammersmith in west London is unavoidable; it is most familiar to passersby from the view afforded on the flyover which connects west London to the motorway leading to Heathrow Airport. Conceptually, the flyover marks the 'water level' in relation to the ship-building which rises above it fanning out in a series of floors and platforms (or 'decks'). The architect, Robert Erskine, had Noah's Ark in mind. One idea had been to have a large ramp leading up to the main entrance like the access for the multitude of animals taken on board the biblical proto-type. A recessed space in the façade still alludes to that otherwise unrealized conception.

This, of course, is an exceptional building in a modern urban context; and it is meant to be. The reference to an ark immobilized on land realizes the ambition of the commission to construct an orig-inal and memorable architectural intervention in the skyline of west London. Surprise rather than familiarity is precisely the point. How a building can flare out like the hull of ship and not fall down is already an engineering challenge and to the ordinary viewer makes for an inherently unlikely structure, especially from the 'water level' of the flyover where the vertical columns which in reality support the out-wards curves of the structure are not visible. There are also other kinds of buildings in other places where an explicit reference to ships is entirely common and intentional.

The London Ark is an office building and has since been converted inside to increase the floor space available for that purpose. In many other places, however, it is ritual or sacred buildings which are con-ceived in terms of ships. Frequently it is the idea of ships as contained spaces and their crews as an integrated society (the subject of chapter Four above) that emerges on land in the form of metaphor to refer to congregations of various kinds. Sometimes it remains just that: a conceptual transformation of the experience of coming together in an enclosed conjunction of mutual self-reliance, played out more in linguistic terms than in architectural reference. But we have encoun-tered the idea that in some parts of Oceania things or creatures of the sea are conceptualized as metamorphosed into stone when on land, just as a remarkable boat-shaped rock formation on the slopes of Mount Ararat close to the Turkish/Iranian border has supported the biblical story of Noah and the Flood. For instance, stones on land and on beaches in parts of northern Australia are interpreted as the dried hardened remains of dugong and dolphin washed up by king tides and stranded there.[19] Yet these are natural phenomena that are given a particular significance. In the islands of South East Asia and the archipelagos of Indonesia, it may be asserted that a ceremonial centre is a boat. It too may contain a rock structure of some kind and, if not a mast, a tree of life where a reference to boat-like characteristics may be explicitly spelt out. However, there are some spectacular realizations of the physical implications of the analogy. The most dramatic is perhaps in the Tanimbar archipelago which lies to the south-west of Papua New Guinea.

Tanimbar myth describes a primordial time when the land was suspended in a perpetual darkness. The moon and the stars did not shine but were subsumed within the sun which was compressed against the horizon by the sky above. Likewise, there were no islands, for these were still part of the mainland; and there were no springs of fresh water. This timeless, undifferentiated state continued until the Tanimbar culture hero, Atuf, took his magic spear and stabbed the sun, breaking it into pieces and in the process created the moon and the stars. The sun was released from the weight of the heavens and was set on its passage through the sky and with the moon made day and night. Similarly, with his spear mounted on the prow of a boat Atuf sailed to the land, breaking it into headlands and islands. His spear stabbed into the ground, producing springs and streams. A creative, yet at the same time destabilizing energy was thus loosed upon the world.[20]

As in many parts of Oceania, a migratory history was thereby initiated. In the case of Tanimbarese communities, the turbulence unleashed in this primordial epoch caused them to take to their boats and flee their original homelands. Myth relates that, living in isolated villages, they remained fearful of the chaotic forces still active outside, which was associated with an escalation in inter-village warfare. Gradually these dispersed settlements began to come together in larger communities for common protection. Smaller villages joined each other and migrants who sailed into nearby anchorages in the continuing search for somewhere safe to settle were encouraged to stay. This nucleation of dispersed groups with their own migratory histories was given expression in a single common ritual centre within the village and through ritual offices distributed among formerly separated peoples.

12 Stone boat in the village of Sangaliat Dol, Tanimbar Islands.

The ritual site was constructed by creating a platform enclosed by stones and raised above the level of the surrounding village. In Tanimbar settlements it is conceptualized as a boat, but beyond that it is sometimes constructed as a version of a boat: a stone boat, immobile but architecturally referenced (illus. 12). In one case it is further furnished with anchors and chains salvaged from a Dutch shipwreck. Some of these stone structures even have versions of decorated prow boards of the kind prized by collectors of non-Western art, but in this case rendered in stone. The site at the centre of village affairs, the fixity of the boat and the permanence of the material used all cohere with the mythic programme by which a search for stability in a history of turmoil has been achieved. In Susan McKinnon's words the stone boat created

> a still anchorage in the midst of what was otherwise a
> maelstrom of motion and enmity. In so doing, it created a
> permanent place of access to the supernatural powers of
> *Ubíla'a* (the supreme god) and the ancestors. In effect, it
> united *Ubíla'a* and the ancestors and their descendants as
> the crew of a single boat whose shared history and purpose
> were permanently etched in stone.[21]

The stationary boat provides conceptual anchorage: it earths and controls dangerous external forces. Indeed, there is some evidence that things are taken further and the whole village is further conceptualized as yet another refraction of the boat with the ritual stone boat at its centre.

Tanimbar villages, formerly located on cliffs overlooking the sea, have now been relocated to beaches where churches have since been constructed. The stone boats remain on the abandoned sites above to be replaced in coastal villages by an open space with a flagpole. None the less, it continues to be referred to by the name given to the stone boat and to be the focus of village affairs. The boat imagery is also expressed in dance. When villagers go on ceremonial expeditions to renew alliances with neighbouring settlements there is a sense that they are recreating the voyages of their ancestors, exposing themselves again to the uncertainties of the migratory past. They do so bearing the name of the original boat on which their ancestors travelled. At the village with which alliance has been made a dance is performed; the dance formation itself replicates the shape of the boat's hull whilst the dancer at the front is called the 'prow' and the one at the rear, the 'rudder'. The leader in such ritual situations is referred to as the 'prow of the boat'. The drummers who take their place towards the 'bow' during the performance are thought of as the sails. In this way, hierarchy is expressed in terms of the positions different people take up in the model boat. The ship defines the community. The villagers commit themselves to the image of the crew within the boat and the hierarchies of the ship at sea. Equally the ritual roles which are allocated within the ceremonial cycle reflect those necessary to sail a ship.

An artefact of the sea thereby provides the template for social organization on land. In other words the relationships between the sea and the land are conceived of dialogically. This is clearly much more than an expression of an engagement with the sea or with ships as a significant and omnipresent part of the scene. The interplay between the mobility of the sea-going ship and the immobile stone version – or to reflect its complexity more completely, between the stillness within the moving vessel and the movement within the fixed village ship – is ultimately a narrative of renewal and ancestry. One aspect of the presence of a ship on land, then, is that it defines space and in so doing defines community, a phenomenon which in a variety of ways has become characteristic of many South East Asian societies.[22]

Churches and ships

However, an association between the image of ships and ritual centres as places of congregation is by no means limited to the islands of South East Asia. In Christian tradition ships and churches have a particular symbolic affinity. Etymology provides an immediate indication. The word 'nave' has two meanings in English. One is as a ship (Latin: *navis*, a ship), from which derive other obvious terms: navy, naval, navigation. Yet the 'nave' is also the body of the church. The meanings are not merely recent analogies, nor are they restricted to English alone. The conjunction of meaning is found in Italian, where it dates from at least 1250, and in Spanish, dating from the tenth century. In English the overlapping usage seems to date from the early twelfth century.

One argument for this etymological conjunction might, again, be that the church as a contained space is like the ship: each has its company or congregation, its hierarchies and its vocabulary of struggle against stormy challenges, whether moral or physical. Indeed hymnologies are replete with the implications of such metaphoric interchange where the perils of the sea are compared with the temptations and theological quandaries which beset attempts to live a Christian life. The ship tossed about on turbulent seas is a frequent metaphor deployed in sermons and theological contexts for the Church weathering a sea of disbelief and worldliness which none the less finds its way safely to harbour. The mast is likened to the cross, and indeed a ship with a cross for a mast is a common icon for contemporary Christian organizations. Hymns, like much literary writing, also deploy the idea of the sea as a fertile image for eternity. Noah's Ark, after all, contained within it the biological community from which life could be regenerated after the flood. In the Old Testament Noah's family navigated its path to salvation as Jesus protected St Peter's boat on the Sea of Galilee in the New Testament.

Yet we can go further than metaphor and textual imagery, for church architecture and its decoration often makes these connections direct. As an island, Anglesey off the north-west coast of Wales has a strong maritime context. It was the homeland of the Tudor dynastic line of Britain, a further aristocratic tradition with its roots beyond the mainland. Here – at Bull Bay, Amlwch – a remarkable Catholic church was built between 1933 and 1937 to the modernist design of Giuseppe Rinvolucri (illus. 13). The distinctive feature of Our Lady,

Star of the Sea is the body of the nave and sanctuary of the church which is in the form of an upturned ship's hull with its structural ribs prominent and interspersed with blue and white patterned glass. A hall beneath has porthole-shaped windows in keeping with the nautical references of the building.

A further connection is the use of recycled ships' timbers for church building and the involvement of shipwrights in the process. Rinvolucri's building was constructed round a concrete framework, but the construction of wooden vaulted ceilings in churches did often involve complex carpentry. One example may stand for many. Thus, Old Ship Church in Hingham, Massachusetts, was built in 1681. It is held to be the oldest church in the United States to have remained in continuous worship. It, too, has the form of an inverted ship and its soaring vaulted structure of seasoned oak is thought to have been constructed by ships' carpenters. The suggestion is not an improbable one. The technical accomplishment of being able to shape and carve the curved ribs of a ship was amongst the most prestigious of skills in medieval times and an overlap in coastal communities with church construction is entirely likely.

13 The Church of Our Lady, Star of the Sea, Anglesey. Completed in 1937 to the design of Giuseppe Rinvolucri.

14 Kappal Matha Church, Uvari, Tamil Nadu, India, 2006.

Other examples of this explicit architectural association can be found in, for example, Tamil Nadu at the coastal village of Uvari. Uvari is a significant place of Christian pilgrimage in southern India (though in practice its reputation attracts members of many faiths). The association comes from a tradition that in the mid-sixteenth century the crew of a Portuguese ship off the coast of the Bay of Bengal contracted cholera en masse. The ship's carpenter was put to work and carved a figure of St Anthony of Padua whose appearance amongst them, albeit in sculpted form, was enough to ensure that the whole crew recovered. They put into harbour at Uvari where the statue was set up, initially inside a hut where it continued to effect miracles and is still held to do so today. A church to house the ancient statue was built in the 1940s, where it was placed on the altar. On the seafront a church to St Mary was also built. The original site was affected by sea erosion and so was replaced in 1974 by the present Kappal Matha Church (the Church of Our Lady in Health). The church is a remarkable structure in the form of a large concrete ship with an aeroplane apparently landed on the roof. Viewed from the shore it seems to 'float' on the sea (illus. 14).[23]

Model ships are also known as 'adornments' in churches, notably in northern Holland, in Denmark and elsewhere in Scandinavia. They also occur in churches at places overseas which were frequented by seamen from those areas. Thus Cardiff in Wales has a Norwegian church constructed in 1868 in the dock area. It was built to serve a floating population of Norwegian seamen who came there notably after the outbreak of the Crimean War in 1853, which gradually spread from a conflict between Russia and Turkey to one which would suck in British and French shipping. Scandinavian fleets were well positioned to pick up the extra work as merchant ships from elsewhere were re-commissioned as transport ships. In Britain the Navigation Act of 1849/50 had imposed new requirements of classification and insurance which implied an updated fleet. The Norwegian ships in particular had been significantly upgraded. As a result Norwegian seamen travelled the globe on trading vessels. Seamen's missions were to be found in distant ports: 47 in Europe, 26 in the Americas, five in Africa and eight in Asia. The Norwegian Church in the dock area of Cardiff is one result of this dispersal of seamen from northern Europe. It was visited by large numbers of sailors passing through the port city. In the early years of the twentieth century as many as 70,000 sailors a year would use its reading room and worship there. The children's author Roald Dahl was christened in the church and he and his family were regular worshippers – his father ran the ship-broking business of Aadnessen & Dahl, based in Cardiff. A similar church was also set up along the coast at the docks in Swansea.

Planning for the reassembling of the Norwegian Church got underway in the 1980s as part of the redevelopment of Cardiff's dockland area. In the interim the church had become derelict and Dahl became president of the trust set up to fund and oversee the process. Amongst the items salvaged when the church was dismantled was a large model sailing ship, now restored to the re-consecrated church. It hung over the organ gallery facing the altar. Various explanations for the presence of such ships in Scandinavian and northern European churches have been advanced: that ships were appropriate decoration for a religious building in a sea-faring context; were mere sentimentality; or were offerings of thanks following successful completion of a sea voyage. Mostly, however, they have been described as ex-voto, that is, as an offering given to a church as the result of a vow. But this explanation may also be unsatisfactory, if indeed the more simplistic propositions fail to account for the widespread practice of hanging ships in northern European churches. Ex-voto offerings are more associated with Catholic practice than the traditions of the Reformed

Church where most of these images are now found. There is evidence that in a Catholic context they go back at least to the sixteenth century. Carpaccio's *Apparition of the Ten Thousand Martyrs* shows ships hanging from the rafters of a church in the context of altarpieces and religious paintings.[24] In the stricter of Reformed Church communities, of course, the use of any figurative imagery at all is discouraged. Ships seem to be the notable exception. And this is not limited to model ships hung from the ceilings of churches: there are also innumerable examples of ship imagery in stained-glass windows, on church weather vanes and on monuments in graveyards.

Take the case of a sanctuary, not in a major port city, but in a coastal town of several thousand largely Calvinist inhabitants. Maashuis was one such place in the seventeenth century, positioned on the estuary of the Meuse and dedicated as were many such on either side of the North Sea to the seasonal occupation of herring fishing. As it developed in prosperity the community undertook the construction of a new Reformed Church which was inaugurated in 1639. On the tenth anniversary of the event a group of navigators commissioned a painting to be set up in the church consisting of maritime scenes focusing on all the different kinds of fish caught in the surrounding seas and with a picture of the town itself. However, it also incorporated a text invoking God's protection of fishermen and praising the benefits of the enterprise of fishing. On a ledge above were placed two model ships.[25] The ensemble seems to have remained in place until the 1850s.

There is some evidence of Catholic practice in Holland in pre-Reformation times. A sanctuary near Rotterdam, for instance, was dedicated to the bearded female saint Wilgefortis and was used by herring fisherman to pray for good fortune before going on fishing expeditions. If things should go wrong, however, petitions would be made to the Virgin for protection against shipwreck, piracy or other woes. Often a wax image of a ship, a fish or a large candle would be donated to a seamen's sanctuary on safe return. If the image were of a ship it might, typically, be the shipowner or master who would undertake the offering. Sometimes the ex-voto image might be enhanced from what had been offered and a silver model be gifted in place of a simple wax version. Here the purposes are clearly those of protection and propitiation, the completion of the vow being some assurance of placing the ship and its master under God's protection on future voyages.

This Catholic practice however is somewhat different from the early Calvinist example from Mashuis. In these cases the sentiment represented by the votive image is essentially that of a personal petition for deliverance from danger. In the case of the Maashuis ensemble, however, it is a communal project, and apparently not instigated after the event but as a more general evocation of God's presence amongst seafaring peoples. Although initiated by a guild of navigators, the funding of the project was completed by the wider community. A corporate venture has become a communal one, moving it even further in character from the individualistic nature of ex-voto practice. It is also significant that it incorporates text. The restructuring of ritual in the Reformed Church involved a fundamental refocusing on text at the expense of image. Indeed, 'ritual' itself was simplified and stripped of its extensive symbolic content. Such text-based painted panels are referred to by Willem Frijhoff as 'talking pictures'.[26] They refer the devoted not to a figurative image but to biblical passages whose prayerful contemplation is seen to provide a less opportunistic, more complete access to God's protection. In other words the image of the ship in its ecclesiastical context has continuity with ex-voto precedent, but its capacity to symbolize has changed radically. In Calvinist space – thus emptied of religious imagery – the emphasis was on apostolic simplicity, on a direct unembellished route to godliness where textual enlightenment had precedence over iconic representations. In down-playing all the symbolic and ritual aspects of Catholic devotional practice, the Reformed tradition sought to create a symbolically neutral space. The ship is there not as an icon of salvation and deliverance, nor yet as visual metaphor of the church itself with its cargo of human souls, but to represent the ordinary everyday experience of a maritime community and connect it to biblical instruction. The Calvinist emphasis on the work ethic sustains the continued use of ship imagery, representing the livelihood and preoccupation of maritime populations. The ships hung from the rafters face the same way as the congregation. Both are housed in the nave – indeed the absence of the altar makes the association of the body of the church with the image of the ship more complete for the church effectively *is* the nave.

In other words, in historical terms the use of model ships or other imagery in churches evolved, but unlike other imagery was adapted in its semantic content, not removed. This is something which had always happened, even as ships created for display in a specifically

Catholic context were reconceived. Perhaps the best example of this is the two model ships at St Bavo's church in Haarlem. These are of a slightly different order, for their connection is not with fishing but with warfare. The Church militant is more of a Catholic image than one which has readily taken root in the Reformed tradition. In this instance the two models are associated with the Dutch involvement in the Fifth Crusade, in which William I of Holland participated. Amongst the Dutch contributions was their engagement in the attack on Damietta in Egypt in 1219. The English diarist John Evelyn noted the association on visiting Haarlem in 1641. Versions of the tradition later in the seventeenth century added a further detail: that the Dutch contribution to the attack included severing a large chain which had been strung across the port blocking entry. Additions were duly made to the models to reflect this developing mythology. A massive saw was added to the keels and one of the ships had two towers added representing Damietta with a chain linking them.[27] Thus, the models came to be adapted to accommodate this developing account of their significance – but the ships remained in an ecclesiastical context.

The ships in Calvinist churches were often themselves similarly remodelled, usually crudely, to keep them up to date with current maritime designs. To that extent they remained what the Reformed Church saw them as being, a reflection of the everyday, a mechanism for linking sacred space to daily space, godliness to the working environment. It was only when a community lost its connection to the sea and to seafaring practice that model ships found their way into museum collections and auction houses – where their role as ex-voto imagery was, ironically, reasserted in catalogues and labelling. The Norwegian example in Cardiff survived until the shipping connection with Norway faltered in the later part of the twentieth century. It was retrieved and still hangs there, but now in the context of a refurbishment of the building as The Norwegian Church Arts Centre.

Ships as terrestrial vessels

In these cases, then, the dominant image is of the boat as an instrument for asserting the ideal of communal fellowship and aspiration on land. This exploits the image of the ship as an embodied social space. No 'beach-crossing' is necessarily emphasized; and the ships themselves are either models or stone replicas. In other cases, however, the idea of the ship as a vessel of transport is emphasized with other implications for the agency of the ship itself. This has two aspects: the vessel as voyaging out and the vessel as voyaging in. We deal with the ship as a vessel of expulsion first.

We have already remarked that the sea consumes. What is consigned to its depths is permanently disposed of; it becomes irretrievable – for all time. Greek practice of disposing of polluted materials and images in deep sea locations takes advantage of this perception. However, an artefact, a replica ship, is also used among many coastal and riverine peoples for the same purpose of putting unwanted materials and spirits beyond human reach. James Frazer in that classic encyclopaedia of world-wide mythology and ritual *The Golden Bough* (1890, with a much expanded version 1906–15) gives some striking instances from the late nineteenth and early twentieth centuries. One example will serve for many. His account concerns an annual ceremony in the Nicobar Islands witnessed in 1897. To begin with two very large model canoes were made, fitted with sails and then loaded with quantities of leaves which were used in warding off evil spirits. Whilst this was being prepared exorcists paced the beach forbidding evil spirits to enter the village. The culmination of the events took place on the fourth day which was known as 'Expelling the Devil by Sails'. Frazer takes up the narrative:

> In the evening all the villagers assembled, the women bringing baskets of ashes and bunches of devil-expelling leaves. The leaves were then distributed to everybody, old and young. When all was ready, a band of robust men, attended by a guard of exorcists, carried one of the cars [canoes] down to the sea on the right side of the village graveyard, and set it floating in the water. As soon as they had returned, another band of men carried the other car to the beach and floated it similarly in the sea to the left of the graveyard. The demon-laden cars being now launched, the women threw ashes from the shore, and the whole crowd shouted, saying, 'Fly away, devil, fly away, never come again!' The wind and the tide being favourable, the canoes sailed quickly away; and that night all the people feasted together with great joy, because the devil had departed in the direction of Chowra.[28]

Many of the details of this ceremonial cycle are familiar in the contexts of expelling witchcraft elsewhere: the encircling of graveyards where ill-disposed spirits are often held to lurk, the use of ashes – the blackened remains of things whose form has reduced and transformed into powder which can safely be dispersed. On the island of Shetland, far off the north coast of Scotland, a nineteenth-century winter festival has become established. Up Helly Aa involves torching a full-size replica of a Viking longship. It has been described as the largest fire festival in Europe and is held in late January. In Lerwick, the main town of the island, one aspect of the festival is the lampooning of local people for various misdemeanours popularly held to have been committed in the intervening year in a 'bill' put up in a prominent place in the town – a practice which, as historian of the event Calum Brown points out, would in other circumstances give way to a claim in the courts for defamation of character. [29] The ship is dragged through the town by a gang of men dressed in appropriate costume under the leadership of a ritual figure, 'Guizer Jarl'. In the evening it is set alight. Elsewhere on the island similar events take place but here the ship is sent off seaward in a replication of one form of Viking burial practice. Similar elements are found in ceremonies which continue to the present day in, for example, the Philippines. Much as terrestrial myths of sea-peoples in South East Asia portray them as expelled from the land due to unworthiness, so here evil is dispelled by burning it in a ship or embarking it and sailing it off across the sea.

Arguably the more dramatic ritual gesture, however, is less the practice of using ships as an instrument of voyaging out and more in their role as a vessel for voyaging in. The image of the Ship of State is a metaphor that goes back to the times of Plato. Yet it is not just linguistic metaphor. In the early modern period the Ship of State was amongst the 'floats' taken in ceremonial procession at pageants (*ommegang*) in places like Brussels and Antwerp. These might be regular annual ceremonies to honour particular saints or associated with specific cults, or they might be part of the less regular process of 'Joyous Entry' staged to welcome a new ruler or governor to the city. A Ship of State was more appropriate to the latter events. Margit Thøfner provides an excellent account of such events, many of which might be infused with maritime reference. The ceremonial entry in 1585 of Alessandro Farnese, Duke of Parma and Governor of the Low Countries, into the important city port of Antwerp is one such. [30] His entrance had elements of a victory parade – after all, as Thøfner observes, one of the most heavily fortified cities of early modern Europe had fallen to his siege tactics. However, all was carefully stage-managed in a symbolic display which, whilst asserting Farnese's unchallenged supremacy, was at the same time conciliatory in tone. As he rode in Farnese was accompanied by his loyal troops and personal bodyguard, all resplendent in new livery. On entry he was met by the *ommegang* car of the 'Maid of Antwerp', closely associated with the Skippers' Guild of that city. She extended her golden keys in a submissive gesture. He in his turn pinned the keys to his chivalric robes, suggesting a relationship based on moral authority rather than repressive force. Other floats that were often brought out for display on such occasions are also listed as having been present at the event: the Giant of Antwerp, the Elephant, and two others with strong maritime resonances – the Neptune and the Whale and the Ship (illus. 15 and 16). These two have a range of possible meanings but at the very least assert in theatrical terms the dependence of Antwerp on the sea as its source of wealth and the anticipation that returning Habsburg rule will bring about a renaissance in its fortunes under their governance. The Ship itself was a very lavish affair furnished with several decks and three masts with ensigns and flags flying. It was escorted by four sea horses and pulled behind it the *plus ultra*, the Pillars of Hercules. *Plus ultra* ('further beyond', illus. 16) refers to the motto adopted by Charles I of Spain (otherwise the Holy Roman Emperor, Charles V). However, as we have seen above, in antiquity the Pillars of Hercules demarcated the limits of the known world and by tradition carried the alternative inscription '*non*' *plus ultra*. In the choreography of the floats the Ship

15 Anonymous, *Neptune and the Whale*, 1582, etching.

of State is portrayed as an instrument of expansionist empire with Antwerp added to the roster of conquest. It is pure visual metaphor.

But it is not just people that 'voyage in' and take up a terrestrial habitat. We know that in many South East Asian communities the role of the shaman-diviner is taken by ship's navigators – or, if not that, by specialists in ship construction.[31] Maritime expertise and familiarity with the world of spirits are also connected. The port of Tulear on the south-west coast of Madagascar is a harbour close to the Mozambique Channel where large ships dominate the coastal panorama. There, in the mid-1990s, a young Masikoro man had become ill and the source of his affliction was identified as being spirit possession (*tromba*). Each *tromba* spirit has its own personality and identity, many of them in contemporary times having exotic origins. The Masikoro *tromba* was identified as being that of a foreign sailor and the mechanism for getting it to 'come out' and heal the man was, as everywhere in Madagascar, that of inducing it to speak. Three material elements were central to achieving this. One was suitable attire and to that end a white costume of a generic naval kind was prepared. A second was a zebu cow to sacrifice as part of the ceremony. And the third was a suitable vessel for the spirit. To that end a model ship was constructed and placed on a table in front of the initiate throughout the night-long ceremony

16 Gillis Hendricx and Hieronymus Cock, *Ship of State and 'Plus Ultra'*, 1559, hand-coloured etching and copper engraving.

17 Spirit possession with large model ship. Tulear, Madagascar, 1990s.

(illus. 17). All the action took place facing the ship, and incense was burnt in front of it, the initiate inhaling the smoke. The perfumes attract the spirit. As dawn broke the spirit finally spoke through the initiate in a cathartic, excited language which, though not coherent speech, seemed to be a mix of French and Swahili, which needed to be interpreted by an attendant spirit medium. The sacrifice of the zebu completed the ceremony.

Different *tromba* have different personalities and each has its own accessories. A maritime reference is by no means a requisite of possession even in these coastal communities. However, the role of the ship in this ceremony is worth further reflection. If above we have talked about the ship as an embodied space by virtue of the human skill invested in its operation, the purpose here is to invest the ship with a spirit presence. A conversion takes place. The person possessed is made the object of cure; meanwhile the object, the ship, is personified. In the moment of transference between the two states – as person becomes object and object becomes person – language becomes fractured, behaviour ecstatic. Attracted by the ship and the maritime environment thus created the troublesome spirit ceases to afflict the possessed, who thereafter may reassemble the props which entice back the spirit to effect cures for others. The possessed has become the healer.

Similar ideas of exotic spirits arriving from the seas are central to belief and practice in relation to Mami Wata ('Mother Water' or

'Mistress Water') and related spirit divinities, whose spread in a number of parts of the world is one of the most remarkable stories of twentieth-century globalization. This is a phenomenon which is known from many of the coastal states of West Africa from Sierra Leone right round to the Democratic Republic of Congo and Angola and has also spread extensively in the African diaspora in the Caribbean and to Bahia province in Brazil. The starting point was the production of a chromolithograph of a South East Asian snake charmer commissioned in the 1880s by an entrepreneur in Hamburg for his own promotional purposes.[32] The image showed one Malamdamatjaute who performed her snake-charming acts in Germany but whose image was more widely circulated in accessible poster form to Paris, the United States and eventually West Africa, carried there no doubt by German shipping interests. In West Africa this image of a lightish-skinned familiar of large snakes possessed of long wavy black hair and exotic clothing had a particularly strong resonance. The lithograph was taken to be a photograph capturing one of the emanations of a spirit of the waters and associated in many cases with Mami Wata, an exotic divinity sometimes rendered in the form of a mermaid – an association made all the more plausible by the fact that the lithograph was only a half-figure, leaving what happened below the waist for local speculation.

Its significance was by no means the same everywhere the image travelled; indeed its interpretation may vary from individual to individual as readily as from place to place. Henry Drewal has documented many of Mami Wata's visual transformations on both sides of the Atlantic. Mami Wata may be associated with bringing good fortune and wealth, with fertility; she may attract sexual partners to devotees, cure and protect. Those drawn to her may not be able to escape the sacrifice her devotion frequently requires. Her context is usually the complex of beliefs and practices associated with Vodun in West Africa or Vodou in places such as Haiti. Sometimes she is associated with a male divinity, Papi Wata, who is portrayed as her consort. Amongst the Fon in the Republic of Benin she is distinguished as a salt-water divinity in contrast to fresh-water divinities. She may be elided with Christian belief, associated with other popular images such as al-Buraq, the Prophet Mohammed's magical winged horse, or identified with Hindu deities, notably Lakshmi, whose image is identified with her in parts of West Africa. To some Christians she is regarded as a seductive evil spirit. She

18 Long John Mbazuigwe, sculpted masquerade headpiece, This Igbo piece shows Mami Wata paddled in her spirit canoe by attendants. Nigeria, 1950s.

appears variously in wood and ceramic sculpture, often on shrines, on perfume bottle labels, on masks and headdresses, in paintings both on canvas and its equivalents and on murals, flags, signboards, mirrors, trays and even on album covers. One fine ensemble from the Igbo in Nigeria represents her being paddled by her attendants in a 'spirit canoe', apparently a large but presumably light superstructure intended to top a masquerade costume.[33] (Illus. 18) Such images use the ship as a mechanism to express the idea of external influences voyaging in, or in the Igbo case allude to the community formed round the exotic seaborne image of Mami Wata. Ships on land may be ambiguous, but the ship itself comes to embody the idea of a vehicle for the restoration of health, a symbol of deliverance from illness and misfortune.

The vessels of the dead

We have encountered a range of contexts in which ships are an appropriate conceptual vehicle on land – they define space and in that sense can define as communities those who gather within them. They may be associated with voyaging 'in' and localizing external elements or they may be an instrument of expelling things. But is this all? As Foucault suggested, the image of the ship itself is a potent part of the terrestrial imaginary. In defiance of its weight a vessel constructed on land of skin, wood or metal, unwieldy in a terrestrial setting, contrives to float readily on the surface of the water and ride the waves where lighter objects would otherwise be swamped and sink. If it seems intuitively improbable that they would float on water at all, they are distinctly immobile when *not* on water. None the less ships do have a presence on the land beyond the circumstances of their manufacture. They should not be there other than for repair or over-wintering; but that is precisely the point. When they are found on land they are potentially transgressive intruders – and it is that very symbolic quality which is often exploited.

There are very few examples of cultures that systematically bury (or have buried) their dead at sea. True, sailors on Western commercial or naval vessels who die on the high seas will often have their bodies committed to the sea to remove the potential taint of death from the ship and, no doubt, to avert the difficulties of storing the deceased remains on board during what might be a long voyage. That, however, might be regarded as an exceptional circumstance. One of the few examples of a coastal people systematically burying their dead at sea is reported amongst inhabitants of islands off the coast of central Queensland. Here, it is speculated, the intention would seem to be to make an offering to the spirits of the sea.[34]

Death itself, of course, is an ambiguous occurrence, as the anthropological treatment of the subject makes entirely evident. It is at once a polluting event yet, when properly handled through ritual process, the dead as ancestors come to have potentially regenerative and beneficial effects for their living descendants. In many cultures the involvement of ships in mortuary processes is an aspect of this. The transference between the two states of the living and dead may be conceived as a journey or a voyage. Ships may be invoked, metaphorically or physically, to transport the dead between one state and the other. A number of coastal islands act as cemeteries, from the Cimitero di San Michele in the lagoon in Venice, to the Isla de Sacrificios in the Gulf of Mexico, and Nosy Faly off the north-west coast of Madagascar. Burying in these places involves a journey over water. And once there ships are also sometimes referenced in the burial procedures themselves. Thus, amongst the Bajau Laut the boat-hearse was distinguished from boats on everyday fishing trips. It had a white flag at the bow if the deceased was a man and at the stern if it was a woman. The body itself was laid out lengthwise with the head facing the bow. Once at the cemetery island the body was carried to the grave held high whilst the deceased's immediate family moved back and forth underneath the corpse, representing the final parting of the dead from the world of the living. If the deceased were a fisherman then, although his boat would not be pressed into service as a coffin, it would be dismantled by carpenters and the sideboards and keel used to make a coffin. The boat is thus in that sense buried with the dead as are parts of his property.[35] In many Austronesian languages the word for 'ship' can also mean 'coffin'.[36]

Thus those occasions on which coffins use ships' timbers for the construction of funeral biers, such as occurred with the funeral of Admiral Lord Nelson, have more than sentimental value. The most spectacular examples, however, are those funerary procedures which involve the burial of complete ships. The classic Old English epic poem *Beowulf*, fully 3,182 lines in length, is bracketed by two funerary scenes. The poem opens with a description of the burial of Beowulf's father, Shield Sheafson, floated out to sea in his ship surrounded by the treasure and trappings of warriorhood. Seamus Heaney's recent translation recaptures the imaginative poetic description of the original:

> They stretched their beloved lord in his boat,
> laid out by the mast, amidships,
> the great ring-giver. Far-fetched treasures
> were piled upon him, and precious gear.
> I never heard before of a ship so well furbished
> With battle-tackle, bladed weapons
> and coats of mail. The massed treasure
> was loaded on top of him: it would travel far
> on out into ocean's sway.
> They decked his body no less bountifully
> with offerings than those first ones did
> who cast him away when he was a child
> and launched him alone out over the waves.[37]

Contemporaneous Scandinavian literature, both mythic and legalistic or directly observational, records further examples of such practice.

Beowulf's own funeral, with which the poem ends, is a cremation on a promontory which affords a sight of the sea. The funerary pyre is 'hung with helmets, heavy war-shields / and shining armour'.[38] Above the pyre, by his command, a mound is built which is at once a memorial to his achievements and an aid to navigation for seamen approaching the coast in search of a safe haven:

> Then the Geat people began to construct
> a mound on a headland, high and imposing,
> a marker that sailors could see from afar
> and in ten days they had done their work.
> It was their hero's memorial . . .[39]

This, too, is a method of disposing of the dead which is authenticated in other literary sources.

At around the time that *Beowulf* was being composed, however, another form of funeral which brings the two practices together had developed in England and more extensively in Scandinavia. This was the burial of notable people in large ships on land, surmounted by an earthen mound. Upwards of 250 such ship-burials are recorded in Europe, with several in East Anglia dating from the early years of the seventh century AD, including one at Snape of a fourteen-metre-long boat and another at Sutton Hoo which involved a ship fully 24 metres in length.

At Sutton Hoo the dramatic nature of these finds is enhanced by the tantalizing fact that the famous ship itself survives only as a carcass imprinted in the earth and now only observable in photographs taken at the time of its excavation and in a model replica subsequently constructed at what is now the National Trust Visitor Centre near the site. The excavation of this skeletal boat, such that its impression in the earth and the defining lines of the ship's rivets were retained, was itself an impressive feat. The famous photograph reproduced here shows the excavated Mound 1 (illus. 19); however the previous year excavations at Mound 2 had discovered ships' rivets indicative of a second ship originally buried at the site. As the Second World War approached the excavation was backfilled and the mound itself eventually rebuilt to provide visitors with a sense of its original height. Given this, it is perhaps surprising that more has not been made in archaeological interpretations of the fact that it is a *ship* in which the burial has taken place.

19 The imprint of a ship as excavated in a burial mound at Sutton Hoo, Suffolk in 1939.

Indeed the same is true of contemporaneous literature; for the practice of ship-burial attracts less attention in the Scandinavian sagas than might be expected for so spectacular a method of disposing of the dead. At least one commentator has speculated that it was so familiar a practice at least in Viking lands that it was no more necessary for the writer of the period to dwell on the fact of ship-burial 'than it would be for a modern writer to say that a person was buried in a coffin'.[40]

In reality, Sutton Hoo is a site of national, and indeed international, significance less because of the ship – intriguing as its presence is – than because of the treasures with which it was associated, the richest ever found together at such a site. There was gold and silverware, garnets, bronze work, enamel, and the famous Sutton Hoo helmet subsequently reconstructed and now displayed in the British Museum.[41] To bury in a ship of that size, to drag it – no doubt wet and thereby additionally heavy – up the hill from the river estuary below, is indeed a dramatic gesture. But the use of the ship itself remains largely unexplained. The ship – the implication seems to be – is exceptional because the deceased is exceptional. Could it be the burial site of one of the kings of East Anglia listed in the Venerable Bede's *A History of the English Church and People* (*c.* 731)? Might it possibly be the burial place of Raewald – as immediately suggested by the Anglo-Saxon scholar H. M. Chadwick when he visited the site, an idea subsequently endorsed by the British Museum curator behind the voluminous report of the finds, Rupert Bruce-Mitford?[42] Or, is it the cemetery of an emergent elite family, possibly with connections to the similar burial site at nearby Snape?

Although some tentative explanations have been put forward, the literature on the numerous Scandinavian ship-burials is hardly more definitive than those on Sutton Hoo. There have probably been more words expended on Sutton Hoo than virtually any other archaeological site in Europe. Yet the presence of the ship remains largely unexplained. The thrust of the argument and the range of examples in this book suggest some additional ways to think about the question. Having spent most of the book out at sea, bringing the topic back on land provides a fitting way to conclude.

Why bury a ship on top of a hill?

So finally, why bury a ship on top of a hill? The tricky part of the Sutton Hoo question, of course, revolves round the ship rather than the hill. The use of promontories as sites for monuments with a mix of symbolic and navigational significance is well-enough rehearsed and the *Beowulf* poetic cycle clearly endorses such locations in a funerary context. Cunliffe has pointed out that the building of imposing structures on remote coastal promontories cannot have been done with the aim of creating defensive bastions, as their very remoteness militates against such a role. He sees them rather as 'a defined enclave at the interface between land and sea'.[43] A location overlooking the sea is meaningful both in symbolic and practical terms.

So, why the ship? Two obvious observations arise. Firstly, it has been suggested that its inclusion in the burial is simply an expression of the wealth of the deceased and the regard in which he was held. More vaguely, there is a familiar assumption that it is an appropriate vessel in which to accommodate a deceased leader of distinction in a maritime culture. The idea of it being a mode of transport between the world of the living and that of the dead is not improbable. Yet even so it is exceptional even in that context. Much has been made of the fact that it is not just ships but also sometimes chariots and even horses which are found in association with some elite burials in the period. As modes of transport their presence might seem entirely explicable. The idea of a ship transporting the dead leader into the afterlife is a conventional enough proposition deriving in part from the interpretation of Ancient Egyptian, Greek and Roman funerary ideas. One important difference, however, is that, unlike chariot- and horse-burials, the ship is literally out of its intended domain. The chariot and the horse as buried in Anglo-Saxon graves remain in their proper terrestrial context. For chariot-burial to be equivalent to ship-burial, the chariot-burial would have to take place *at sea*, which as far as we know did not happen. Thus ship-burial is a singular dramatic ritual gesture, made more so by the substantial physical challenge implied in getting it to the top of a hill in the first place.

The conclusion to which we have been moving is that a ship on land is a liminal object in and of itself.[44] It has 'crossed the beach' and is now in the wrong place. A ship should voyage out to sea and back again but is not supposed to travel on land. It is constructed, usually, close to the sea, launched often with great ceremonial and thereafter consigned to the water. On land it has richness in an imaginative sense because it is anomalous. Thus where it is deployed as a referent on land it takes on the wider symbolic characteristics we have been discovering in this chapter.

In a funerary context it is linked to another liminal condition. Death itself implies liminality. It introduces a disruption of the social order. But beyond that it also entails cosmological imbalance. The ritual prescriptions placed on the living through the death of a member of the community constitute one part of this. The dead themselves also exist in a liminal condition, no longer classed amongst the living but not yet conveyed to the afterlife. The implications are especially pertinent in the case of a great leader, which from the magnificence of his funerary goods, the person buried at Sutton Hoo must certainly have been.

If, then, the ship is an agent of transport, it is not just between the world of the living and that of the dead, a movement from life to afterlife. It is also arguably part of a larger symbolic project: an attempt to restore elemental stability. The burial of the ship can be seen as less a terrestrial appropriation of the sea than an offering of the things of the sea to the land. Clearly direct evidence of the ideas underlying such burials is not easily available from archaeological sources alone. As seen earlier, in Fiji, the 'chief from the sea' is 'killed' in a ritual sense to be reborn as of the land – he drinks kava to kill him and is revived by drinking water. The model is that of sacrifice. It is tempting to suggest that in ship-burial the entity from the sea is similarly surrendered to create the circumstances of an appeasement of the land, an attempt to establish a complementarity between the two domains. It is part of the critical enterprise to re-establish that existential order threatened by the spectre of aristocratic death.

It is only when we fully comprehend the extent to which the sea is constituted as a domain in its own right – separated from the land symbolically, socially and practically – that the fuller significance of any such reconciliation of the sea to the land emerges. If we started by separating the maritime and the terrestrial, we end by seeing that in bringing them together again lies the possibility of bringing about a restoration of cosmological balance.

References

Introduction

1 Jonathan Raban, *Coasting* (London, 1987), p. 220.
2 Ian J. McNiven, 'Saltwater People: Spiritscapes, Maritime Rituals and the Archaeology of Australian Indigenous Seascapes', *World Archaeology*, 'Seascapes', xxxv/3 (2003), pp. 329–49; N. Sharp, *Saltwater People: The Waves of Memory* (Crows Nest, NSW, 2002).
3 C. Sather, *The Bajau Laut* (Oxford, 1997).
4 Stan Hugill, *Sailortown* (London, 1967).
5 As discussed in Nicholas Thomas, 'Licensed Curiosity: Cook's Pacific Voyages', in *The Cultures of Collecting*, ed. John Elsner and Roger Cardinal (Cambridge, MA, 1994), pp. 116–36.
6 As quoted in Felipe Fernández-Armesto, *Pathfinders: A Global History of Exploration* (Oxford, 2006), pp. 308–9.
7 Victor Hugo, *The Toilers of the Sea*, trans. James Hogarth [1866] (New York, 2002), p. 186.
8 Jonathan Raban, *The Oxford Book of the Sea* (Oxford, 1992), p. 506.
9 Ibid., p. 508.
10 François Rabelais, *The Histories of Gargantua and Pantagruel*, trans. with an introduction by J. M. Cohen [1532–4] (London, 1955), pp. 566–8.
11 John Mack, *The Museum of the Mind: Art and Memory in World Cultures* (London, 2003), pp. 41–2.
12 Braudel was a historian in the French tradition of the *Annales d'histoire économique et sociale* who cut his scholarly teeth on the archival sources relating to the sixteenth century for the Mediterranean area, as summarized in John Burrow, *A History of Histories: Epics, Chronicles, Romances and Inquiries from Herodotus and Thucydides to the*

Twentieth Century (London, 2007), pp. 483ff.

13 F. Braudel, *The Mediterranean and the Mediterranean World in the Age of Philip II*, trans. Siân Reynolds [1949] (London, 1973).

14 Here the historian K. N. Chaudhuri has been strongly influenced by Braudel's analysis in asserting the interconnectedness of Indian Ocean histories; see K. N. Chaudhuri, *Trade and Civilisation in the Indian Ocean* (Cambridge, 1985); and *Asia before Europe: Economy and Civilisation of the Indian Ocean from the Rise of Islam to 1750* (Cambridge, 1990).

15 The most comprehensive revisions of Braudel's views occur in P. Horden and N. Purcell, *The Corrupting Sea: A Study of Mediterranean History* (Oxford, 2000). Their critique has a number of starting points. Most significant is disquiet about the deterministic cast of the argument. Their approach takes place at the level of micro-ecologies seeking to set them in the context of wider and more extensive networks. Horden and Purcell in their turn have stimulated a lively and insightful debate partly around the theme of the very local nature of their analysis, within the context of a large geographical expanse (see, for instance, the contributions to W. V. Harris, ed., *Rethinking the Mediterranean* (Oxford, 2005)).

16 N.A.M. Rodger, *The Wooden World: An Anatomy of the Georgian Navy* (London, 1986); *The Safeguard of the Sea: A Naval History of Britain, 660–1649* (London, 1997); and *The Command of the Sea: A Naval History of Britain, 1649–1815* (London, 2004).

17 An anthology of recent historical writings – Jerry H. Bentley, Renate Bridenthal and Kären Wigen, eds, *Seascapes: Maritime Histories, Littoral Cultures and Transoceanic Exchanges* (Honolulu, HI, 2007) – seeks to address what the editors see as this fragmented body of emergent scholarship by assembling a series of essays round particular themes: different constructs that pervade maritime studies (islands and littorals, ships and seascapes themselves); the transmarine empires; the sociological dimension of seafaring; and finally the world of pirates and smugglers. This leads to discussion of – amongst other seas – the North Pacific, the waters of South East Asia, the Atlantic and Indian Oceans and the Caribbean. The logic for taking such a comparative approach is worth rehearsing, for it contrasts strongly with the very specific ambitions of the Mediterranean studies to which we have referred.

18 As, for instance, Fernández-Armesto amongst others has convincingly demonstrated in his *Pathfinders*.

19 The essays in a recent volume edited by Bernard Klein and Gesa Mackenthun – *Sea Changes: Historicizing the Ocean* (London, 2004) – argues for such an expanded conception.

20 There are a number of dedicated journals which focus on maritime subjects, of which the most prominent are *The Mariners' Mirror*, the journal of The Society for Nautical Research (and thus with a wider remit than maritime archaeology alone), which has been in continuous production since 1911, and the *International Journal of Nautical Archaeology* (founded in 1972).

21 Barry Cunliffe, *Facing the Ocean: The Atlantic and its Peoples, 8000 BC to AD 1500* (Oxford, 2001).

22 See for example *World Archaeology*, 'Seascapes', xxxv/3 (2003). The range of essays in this volume look at the experience of the sea from the perspective of peoples as distant from each other as those of different parts of Europe, Newfoundland, East Africa, South East Asia, Australia and New Zealand. There is no historical connection between the regions discussed but the cross-cultural approach is strongly suggestive of the richness of an attention to seascapes. A notable example is Chris Ballard, Richard Bradley, Lise Nordenborg Myhre and Meredith Wilson, 'The Ship as Symbol in the Prehistory of Scandinavia and Southeast Asia', *World Archaeology*, 'Seascapes', xxxv/3 (2003), pp. 385–403.

23 Paul Rainbird, 'Islands out of Time: Towards a Critique of Island Archaeology', *Journal of Mediterranean Archaeology*, XII/2 (1999), pp. 218–36; and *The Archaeology of Islands* (Cambridge, 2007). See also Cyprian Broodbank, 'The Insularity of Island Archaeologists: Comments on Rainbird's "Islands out of Time"', *Journal of Mediterranean Archaeology*, XII/2 (1999), pp. 235–9; Geoffrey Irwin, 'Commentary on Paul Rainbird, "Islands Out of Time: Towards a Critique of Island Archaeology"', *Journal of Mediterranean Archaeology*, XII/2 (1999), pp. 252–4; William F. Keegan, 'Comment on Paul Rainbird's "Islands out of Time: Towards a Critique of Island Archaeology"', *Journal of Mediterranean Archaeology*, XII/2 (1999), pp. 255–8; Peter van Dommelen, 'Islands in History', *Journal of Mediterranean Archaeology*, XII/2 (1999) pp. 246–51.

24 It was not always so. The physicist Horace Lamb, speaking late in life at the British Association for the Advancement of Science meetings of 1932, remarked:

I am an old man now, and when I die and go to Heaven there are two matters on which I hope for enlightenment. One is quantum electrodynamics, and the other is the turbulent motion of fluids. And about the former I am really rather optimistic.

(As quoted in Jonathan Raban, *Passage to Juneau: A Sea and its Meanings* (London, 1999), p. 291).

25 An instructive research programme, 'Ocean's Connect', was run by Duke University, North Carolina, over a period from 1997 and drew on a large range of expertise to explore a remapping of international relations focusing on the maritime world. The project eventuated in a number of outcomes including the publication of a special issue of the *Geographical Review*, LXXXIX/2 (April 1999) on the topic. This programme led to a number of sustainable propositions concerning the place of islands in maritime empires and the transoceanic spread of ideas, such as that of the Masonic Brotherhood for instance (see Jessica Harland-Jacobs, '"Hands across the Sea": The Masonic Network, British Imperialism, and the North Atlantic World', *Geographical Review*, LXXXIX/2 (April 1999), pp. 237–53).

26 Philip E. Steinberg, 'Lines of Division, Lines of Connection: Stewardship in the World Ocean', *Geographical Review*, LXXXIX/2 (1999), pp. 254–64.

27 An excellent source on such history is Alain Corbin's *The Lure of the Sea: The Discovery of the Seaside in the Western World, 1750–1840*, trans. Jocelyn Phelps (Cambridge, 1994).

28 See Eric Hirsch and Michael O'Hanlon, eds, *The Anthropology of Landscape: Perspectives on Place and Space* (Oxford, 1995). Likewise, the insightful work of Chris Tilley on the sensory aspects of the perception of landscape have yet to be systematically explored in a maritime context other than in Rainbird's archaeological work; see Christopher Tilley, *A Phenomenology of Landscape: Paths, Places and Monuments* (Oxford, 1994). Ingold's influential thinking about the environment, though it does seek to give some account of maritime experience, has inevitably had to rely principally on terrestrial accounts of man's engagement with his surroundings; see Timothy Ingold, *The Perception of the Environment: Essays in Livelihood, Dwelling and Skill* (London, 2000).

29 As quoted in Horden and Purcell, *The Corrupting Sea*, p. 7.

30 In the mid-twentieth century the American anthropologist Ward Goodenough made a pioneering study of native astronomy in the

Carolines in what is now the Republic of Micronesia; see his *Native Astronomy in the Central Carolines* (Philadelphia, PA, 1953). Since the observation of the heavens is at the heart of navigation by night, such reporting is firmly rooted in the Carolinian experience of the sea. Thomas Gladwin followed up with work amongst the peoples of Puluwat Atoll focusing on navigational knowledge. Indeed, the title of his resulting monograph, *East is a Big Bird* (Cambridge, MA, 1970), refers to the rising point of the star Altair in the east which provides Micronesian navigators with their cardinal direction, Altair being part of the constellation known locally as 'Big Bird'.

31 David Lewis, *We, the Navigators: The Ancient Art of Landfinding in the Pacific* (Honolulu, HI, 1972). See also David Lewis, *The Voyaging Stars: Secrets of the Pacific Island Navigators* (New York, 1978).

32 Joseph Conrad, *The Nigger of the 'Narcissus' and Other Stories*, ed. J. H. Stape and Allan H. Simmons, with an introduction by Gail Fraser [1897] (London, 2007), p. 8.

33 C.L.R. James, *Mariners, Renegades and Castaways: The Story of Herman Melville and the World We Live In* (London, 1985).

34 Raban, *The Oxford Book of the Sea*, pp. 5–7.

35 Rachel Carson, *The Sea Around Us* (London, 1951); *Under the Sea-wind: A Naturalist's Picture of Ocean Life* (Oxford, 1953); and *The Edge of the Sea* (London, 1955).

36 Richard Collins, *The Land as Viewed from the Sea* (Bridgend, 2004); see also John Mack, 'The Land Viewed from the Sea', *Azania*, XLII (2007), pp. 1–14.

37 As quoted in Raban, *Passage to Juneau*, p. 6.

38 James, *Mariners, Renegades and Castaways*, p. 35.

39 Richard Henry Dana Jr, *Two Years before the Mast: A Personal Narrative of Life at Sea* [1840] (New York, 1981).

40 Raban, *The Oxford Book of the Sea*, p. 23.

41 Richard Holmes, *Coleridge: Darker Reflections* (London, 1989), chap. 8.

42 Redmond O'Hanlon, *Trawler* (London, 2004).

43 Stephen Crane, 'The Open Boat', in *The Red Badge of Courage and Other Stories* [1899] (London, 2005), p. 219.

44 O'Hanlon, *Trawler*, p.8.

45 Joseph Conrad, 'A Smile of Fortune: Harbour Story', in *'Twixt Land and Sea* (London, 1912), p. 15.

46 See, for example, the discussion in Evelyn Edson, *Mapping Time and Space: How Medieval Mapmakers Viewed their World* (London, 1997).

47 For instance, David Cordingly's informative article for *The Grove Dictionary of Art* (1896) follows convention and talks only of European and American artists – and then frequently only of their pictures of their own native seas.

48 Alain Corbin, *The Lure of the Sea: The Discovery of the Seaside in the Western World, 1750–1840*, trans. Jocelyn Phelps (Cambridge, 1994), pp. 34–40.

49 F. B. Cockett, *Early Sea Painters 1660–1730: The Group Who Worked in England under the Shadow of the Van de Veldes* (Woodbridge, 1995)

50 F. B. Cockett, *Peter Monamy, 1681–1749, and his Circle* (Woodbridge, 2000); David Cordingly, *Marine Painting in England, 1700–1900* (London, 1974)

51 Geoffrey Quilley and John Bonehill, eds, *William Hodges 1744–1797: The Art of Exploration* (New Haven, CT, 2004); see also Geoffrey Quilley, 'The Art of the Cook Voyages', in *The History of British Art*, ed. David Bindman (London, 2008).

52 Sarah Monks, 'Turner Goes Dutch', in *Turner and the Masters*, ed. David Solkin, exh. cat., Tate Britain, London (2009), pp. 73–85.

53 See Luke Herrmann, 'Turner and the Sea', *Turner Studies*, I/I (1981), pp. 4–18; Andrew Wilton, *Turner and the Sublime* (London, 1980).

1 Different Seas?

1 Victor Hugo, *The Toilers of the Sea*, trans. James Hogarth [1866] (New York, 2002), p. 251.

2 David Abulafia, 'Mediterraneans', in *Rethinking the Mediterranean*, ed. William V. Harris (Oxford, 2005), p. 68.

3 Robert S. Lopez, *The Commercial Revolution of the Middle Ages, 950–1350* (Englewood Cliffs, NJ, 1971) pp. 20, 23, 95, 113–17, 136; see also the exploration of the phrase in David Abulafia, 'Mediterraneans', pp. 76–80.

4 Abulafia, 'Mediterraneans', pp. 82–5.

5 Ibid., pp. 85–90.

6 Paul W. Blank, 'The Pacific: a Mediterranean in the Making?' *Geographical Review*, LXXXIX/2 (1999), pp. 265–77.

7 H. J. Mackinder, *Britain and the British Seas* (London, 1902).

8 Captain Vancouver, as quoted in Jonathan Raban, *Passage to Juneau: A Sea and its Meanings* (London, 1999), p. 49.

9 On the Sahara as a terrestrial version of the Mediterranean, see for example Abalafia, 'Mediterraneans', pp. 75–6.

10 Commander W. E. May, *A History of Marine Navigation* (Henley-on-Thames, 1973).

11 The summary here is derived from the insightful work of John H. Pryor, *Geography, Technology, and War: Studies in the Maritime History of the Mediterranean, 649–1571* (Cambridge, 1988), chap. 1. It is also discussed in P. Horden and N. Purcell, *The Corrupting Sea: A Study of Mediterranean History* (Oxford, 2000), pp. 137–43.

12 Mary Beard, *The Parthenon* (London, 2002)

13 Horden and Purcell, *The Corrupting Sea*, map 12, p. 141.

14 Justin Pollard and Howard Reid, *The Rise and Fall of Alexandria: Birthplace of the Modern Mind* (New York, 2006), pp. 26–7.

15 M'hamad Hassine Fantar, *Carthage, The Punic City*, trans. Justin McGuinness (Tunis, 1998).

16 Barry Cunliffe, *Facing the Ocean: The Atlantic and its Peoples, 8000 BC to AD 1500* (Oxford, 2001), p. 89; and more generally on the Phoenician expansion of interest out of the Mediterranean, see pp. 297–302.

17 Ibid., pp. 91–2, 306–8; for a fuller assessment, see also Barry Cunliffe, *The Extraordinary Journey of Pytheas the Greek* (London, 2001).

18 E.G.R. Taylor, *The Haven-Finding Art: A History of Navigation from Odysseus to Captain Cook* (London, 1971), p. 45. The term Thule was used in medieval times to express the idea of a land at the limits of the world. It was until recently the name by which the main town in northern Greenland was known (now Qaanaaq) and also the term for groups of Inuit living there.

19 Cunliffe, *Facing the Ocean*, p. 307.

20 Ibid., p. 475

21 For a discussion see G. J. Marcus, *The Conquest of the North Atlantic* (Woodbridge, 1980), chap. 5.

22 John M. Synge, *The Aran Islands,* with drawings by Jack B. Yates [1906] (Belfast, 1988), p. 129.

23 Taylor, *The Haven-Finding Art*, p. 76.

24 Amongst much writing about the Vikings, wide-ranging and scholarly overviews include P. Foote and D. Wilson, *The Viking Achievement* (London, 1980); J. Graham-Campbell, *The Viking World* (London, 1989); and G. Jones, *A History of the Vikings* (Oxford, 1980). See also Cunliffe, *Facing the Ocean*, chap. 11.

25 Cunliffe, *Facing the Ocean*, pp. 503–5.

26 Taylor, *The Haven-Finding Art*, chap. 4.

27 Richard Henry Dana Jr, *Two Years before the Mast: A Personal Narrative of*

Life at Sea [1840] (New York, 1981), pp. 448–9.

28 A number of books by Felipe Fernández-Armesto document the Iberian exploration of the Atlantic: *Columbus and the Conquest of the Impossible* (London, 1974); *Before Columbus: Exploration and Colonisation from the Mediterranean to the Atlantic, 1229–1492* (Basingstoke, 1987); *Columbus* (Oxford, 1991). A more general account of maritime exploration is *Pathfinders: A Global History of Exploration* (Oxford, 2006).

29 Fernández-Armesto, *Pathfinders*, p. 159.

30 Ibid., p. 156.

31 See Luciana de Lima Martins, 'Mapping Tropical Waters: British Views and Visions of Rio de Janeiro', in *Mappings*, ed. Denis Cosgrove (London, 2001), pp. 148–68; and Nicholas Thomas, *Discoveries: The Voyages of Captain Cook* (London, 2003), pp. 43–5.

32 G. R. Tibbetts, *Arab Navigation in the Indian Ocean before the Coming of the Portuguese, being a translation of Kitāb al-Fawā'id fī uṣūl al-baḥr wa'l-awā'id of Ahmad b. Mājid al-Najdī*, with an introduction notes and a glossary, Oriental Translation Fund, n.s. XLII [1490] (London, 1971). Where the reference is to the translated text we use Ibn Mājid's name and refer to the *Fawā'id*; where it is to notes and commentary we use Tibbetts as the source and *Arab Navigation* as the title. Both, of course, appear in a single volume. See also G. R. Tibbetts, 'Arab Navigation in the Red Sea', *Geographical Journal*, CXXVII/3 [1961], pp. 322–34.

33 *Mājid, Fawā'id*, p. 243.

34 Ibid., pp. 243–68.

35 Ibid., p. 249.

36 Ibid.

37 As quoted in Fernández-Armesto, *Pathfinders*, p. 212.

38 Tibbetts, *Arab Navigation*, p. 368.

39 G. F. Hourani, *Arab Seafaring in the Indian Ocean in Ancient and Early Medieval Times* (Princeton, NJ, 1995), p. 130.

40 See *The Periplus of the Erythrean Sea by an unknown author with some extracts from Agatharkhids 'On the Erythraean Sea'*, trans. and ed. G.W.B. Huntingford (London, 1980).

41 Hourani, *Arab Seafaring*, p. 18.

42 H. Neville Chittick, 'East Africa and the Orient: Ports and Trade before the Arrival of the Portuguese', in *Historical Relations across the Indian Ocean* (Paris, 1980), p. 13.

43 P. Sinclair, 'The Origins of Urbanism in East and Southern Africa: A Diachronic Perspective', in *Islamic Art and Culture in sub-Saharan Africa*,

ed. K. Ådahl and B. Sahlstrom (Uppsala, 1995), pp. 99–109.

44 Mark Horton, 'Mare Nostrum, a New Archaeology in the Indian Ocean', *Antiquity*, 71 (1997), pp. 753–5.

45 Notably K. N. Chaudhuri, *Asia before Europe: Economy and Civilisation of the Indian Ocean from the Rise of Islam to 1750* (Cambridge, 1990)

46 For an authoritative summary see Peter Mitchell, *African Connections: Archaeological Perspectives on Africa and the Wider World* (Walnut Creek, CA, 2005), pp. 99–133.

47 See Fernández-Armesto, *Pathfinders*, pp. 174–82.

48 For a review see Peter Worsley, *Knowledges: What Different Peoples Make of the World* (London, 1997).

49 As quoted in Derek Wilson, *A Brief History of The Circumnavigators: The Pioneer Voyagers who Set Off Around the Globe* (London, 1989), pp. 196–7.

50 Ibid., p. 218.

51 Raban, *Passage to Juneau*, p. 96.

52 Ibid., pp. 96–7.

2 Concepts of the Sea

1 W. H. Auden, *The Enchafèd Flood* (London, 1951), pp. 18–19.

2 Epeli Hau'ofa, 'Our Sea of Islands' in *A New Oceania, Rediscovering our Sea of Islands*, ed. E. Waddell, V. Naidu and E. Hau'ofa (Suva, Fiji, 1993), p. 8.

3 Auden, *The Enchafèd Flood*, p. 21.

4 C. Sather, *The Bajau Laut* (Oxford, 1997), p. 102.

5 Epeli Hau'ofa, 'The Ocean in Us', in *The Contemporary Pacific*, X/2, (1998), p. 403.

6 N. Sharp, *Saltwater People: The Waves of Memory* (Crows Nest, NSW, 2002), p. 27.

7 Ibid.

8 Hau'ofa, 'The Ocean in Us', p. 409.

9 Ian J. McNiven, 'Saltwater People: Spiritscapes, Maritime Rituals and the Archaeology of Australian Indigenous Seascapes', *World Archaeology*, XXXV/3 (2003), pp. 329–49.

10 Ibid., p. 334.

11 Sather, *The Bajau Laut*; Benedict Sandin, *The Sea Dyaks of Borneo before White Rajah Rule* (London, 1967).

12 See Tom R. Zuidema, 'Shaft-tombs and the Inca Empire', *Journal of the Steward Anthropological Society*, IX (1977), pp. 133–78; Allison C. Paulsen,

'The Thorny Oyster and the Voice of God: Spondylus and Strombus in Andean Prehistory', *American Antiquity*, 39 (1974), p. 397.

13 N.A.M. Rodger, *The Command of the Ocean: A Naval History of Britain, 1649–1815* (London, 2004).

14 N.A.M. Rodger, *The Safeguard of the Sea: A Naval History of Britain, 660–1649* (London, 1997), pp. 19–21.

15 Rodger, *The Command of the Ocean*, pp. 2–4.

16 Susan Mckinnon, 'Tanimbar Boats', in *Islands and Ancestors: Indigenous Styles of Southeast Asia*, ed. J. P. Barbier and D. Newton (New York, 1988), pp. 152–69. See also Pierre-Yves Manguin, 'Shipshape Societies: Boat Symbolism and Political Systems in Insular Asia', in *Southeast Asia in the 9th to 14th Centuries*, ed. David G. Marr and A. C. Milner (Singapore, 1986), pp. 187–213.

17 Bruce Chatwin, *The Songlines* (London, 1987).

18 McNiven, 'Saltwater People', p. 331.

19 A. C. Haddon, ed., *Reports of the Cambridge Anthropological Expedition to Torres Straits*, vol. v, 'Sociology, Magic and Religion of the Western Islanders' (Cambridge, 1904), pp. 355–6.

20 McNiven, 'Saltwater People', p. 333.

21 Ibid., p. 336.

22 The *United Nations Convention on the Law of the Sea* was passed in 1982 and published in 1983.

23 Hau'ofa, 'The Ocean in Us', p. 406.

24 Jules Verne, *Twenty Thousand Leagues under the Sea*, trans. and with an introduction and notes by William Butcher [1869] (Oxford 1998), pp. 68–9.

25 Haddon, ed., *Reports*, p. 289.

26 R. Astuti, *People of the Sea: Identity and Descent among the Vezo of Madagascar* (Cambridge, 1995).

27 Astuti, *People of the Sea*, p. 47.

28 See ibid., chap. 3.

29 Ibid., p. 48.

30 Ibid., pp. 62–3.

31 Robert Louis Stevenson, 'The English Admirals', *Cornhill Magazine*, 38 (July 1878), p. 36.

32 Marcia Yonemoto, 'Maps and Metaphors of the "Small Eastern Sea" in Tokugawa Japan (1603–1868)', *Geographical Review*, LXXXIX/2 (1999), pp. 173–6.

33 Yonemoto, 'Maps and Metaphors', pp. 171–2.

34 Ibid., pp. 181–3.

35 Ibid., p. 185.

36 Timothy Clark, *100 Views of Mount Fuji*, exh. cat., British Museum, London (2001).

37 N. C. Rousmanière and W. Jeffett, *Hiroshi Sugimoto*, exh. cat., Sainsbury Centre for Visual Arts, Norwich (1997); H. Sugimoto, *Sugimoto*, exh. cat. Contemporary Arts Museum, Houston, and Hara Museum, Tokyo (1996).

38 Muneshige Narazaki, *Hokusai: The Thirty-six Views of Mount Fuji*, English adaption by John Bester (Tokyo, 1968); see also Matthi Forrer, *Hokusai: Prints and Drawings*, exh. cat., Royal Academy of Arts, London (1991); Katsushika Hokusai, *One Hundred Views of Mount Fuji*, with intro. and commentaries by Henry Smith (London, 1988); Richard Lane, *Hokusai: Life and Work* (London, 1989).

39 Alfred Gell, 'The Language of the Forest: Landscape and Phonological Iconism in Umeda', in *The Anthropology of Landscape: Perspectives on Place and Space*, ed. Eric Hirsch and Michael O'Hanlon (Oxford, 1995), pp. 237.

40 See, for instance, Evelyn Edson, *Mapping Time and Space: How Medieval Mapmakers Viewed their World* (London, 1997), pp. 38–50.

41 Thomas O'Loughlin, 'Living in the Ocean', in *Studies in the Cult of Saint Columba*, ed. Cormac Bourke (Dublin, 1997), p. 13.

42 Ibid., p. 17.

43 Ibid., p. 11.

44 P. J. Rhodes, *A Commentary on the Aristotelian 'Athenaion Politeia'* (Oxford, 1981), p. 646.

45 Astrid Lindenlauf, 'The Sea is a Place of No Return in Ancient Greece', *World Archaeology*, XXXV/3 (2003), pp. 416–33; and, on this point particularly, see pp. 419–23.

46 Wyatt MacGaffey, 'BaKongo Cosmology', *The World and I*, 9 (1988), pp. 512–21.

47 Lindenlauf, 'The Sea is a Place of No Return', p. 424.

48 Ian Baucom, 'Hydrographies', *Geographical Review,* LXXXIX/2 (1999), pp. 301–13.

49 Ibid., p. 303.

50 Auden, *The Enchafèd Flood*, p. 122, n. 1.

51 Herman Melville, *Moby-Dick or The Whale* [1851] (New York, 2001), p. 4.

52 Alain Corbin, *The Lure of the Sea: The Discovery of the Seaside 1750–1840*, trans. Jocelyn Phelps (London, 1994).

53 Corbin, *The Lure of the Sea*, p. 17.

54 Edmund Burke, *A Philosophical Enquiry into the Origin of Our Ideas of the Sublime and the Beautiful*, ed. J. T. Boulton [1757] (London, 1958).

55 Corbin, *The Lure of the Sea*, p. 72.

56 Ibid., pp. 66ff.

57 As quoted in ibid., p. 123.

58 Victor Hugo, *The Toilers of the Sea*, trans. James Hogarth [1866] (New York, 2002), p. 296.

59 Ibid., p. 97.

60 Ibid., p. 101

61 Ibid., p. 97.

62 Joseph Conrad, *Typhoon and Other Tales*, ed. with an introduction and notes by Cedric Watts (Oxford, 2002). 'Typhoon' was begun in 1899 and finished in 1902.

63 Jonathan Raban, *Passage to Juneau: A Sea and its Meanings* (London, 1999), p. 8.

64 Andrew Wilton, *Turner and the Sublime* (London,1980) p. 103, n. 70.

65 Wilton, *Turner and the Sublime*, p. 99.

66 Joseph Conrad, *The Nigger of the 'Narcissus' and Other Stories*, ed. J. H. Stape and Allan H. Simmons, with an introduction by Gail Fraser (London, 2007), p. 24.

67 Luke Herrmann, 'Turner and the Sea', *Turner Studies*, 1/1 (1981), pp. 4–18.

68 William Makepeace Thackeray, 'De Juventute', in *Roundabout Papers* [1863] (London, 1887), p.72.

69 Ibid.

70 I am very grateful to Sarah Monks for developing this perspective in conversation and for sharing her thoughts on Turner which are built into her own forthcoming book.

3 Navigation and the Arts of Performance

1 Victor Hugo, *The Toilers of the Sea*, trans. James Hogarth [1866] (New York, 2002), p. 190.

2 David Lewis, *We, the Navigators: The Ancient Art of Landfinding in the Pacific*, 2nd edn (Honolulu, HI, 1994), pp. 245–9.

3 As quoted in Commander W. E. May, *A History of Marine Navigation* (Henley-on-Thames, 1973), p. 4.

4 Although Ibn Mājid talks of his encounters with 'the Franks', he makes

no claims himself to having taught them any of his skills. The Portuguese make reference to having been instructed by 'Malemo canaqua', usually translated as 'Mu'allim Kanaka'. A *mu'allim* is a 'master of navigation', a title rather than a named person. 'Kanaka' is also a generic appellation, a term later used of Pacific Island mariners as a whole in the imprecise parlance of international seafaring. An Arab historian writing in 1582 mentions Ibn Mājid specifically and recounts the story that the chief of the 'Franks', *al-amīlandī* (or 'Admiral'), befriended the Arab navigator, made him drunk and thereby learnt of the best route to India – straight across the Indian Ocean rather than going northwards and around the coast where the seas were too rough.

5 Lewis, *We, the Navigators*, p. 9.

6 G. R. Tibbetts, *Arab Navigation in the Indian Ocean before the Coming of the Portuguese, being a translation of Kitāb al-Fawā'id fī uṣūl al-baḥr wa'l-qawā'id of Aḥmad b. Mājid al-Najdī*, with an introduction notes and a glossary, Oriental Translation Fund, n.s. XLII [1490] (London, 1971).

7 This is one of about forty works of Ibn Mājid which have survived into modern times. However, this by no means represents the totality of his written output for we know that other documents have been lost because of some cross-referencing and quotation from works that are not otherwise represented in the archives (there are some thirteen such references to missing texts in the *Fawā'id* alone). The archives are principally those in the Bibliothèque Nationale de France and in St Petersburg.

8 Tibbetts, *Arab Navigation*, p. 290.

9 Ibn Mājid, *Fawā'id*, pp. 69–70.

10 We know he was an Arab, born probably around 1432, possibly of Shi'a descent and perhaps from Djulfar in southern Arabia. He came from a family of illustrious master navigators who, like him, wrote navigational treatises and with whom he served his apprenticeship. His father indeed wrote a piece of navigational poetry, the *al-Ḥijjazya*, which his son was to redraft and improve. The family specialism was in the navigation of the Red Sea, though Ibn Mājid was to greatly extend this range.

11 Ibn Mājid, *Fawā'id*, p. 71; Tibbetts, *Arab Navigation*, p. 14.

12 Tibbetts, *Arab Navigation*, pp. 44–6.

13 Richard Burton, *First Footsteps in Africa* [1856] (London, 1966), pp. 3–4.

14 Tibbetts, *Arab Navigation*, p. 12.

15 Ibn Mājid, *Fawā'id*, p. 65.

16 G. J. Toomer, 'Ptolemy and his Greek Predecessors', in *Astronomy before the Telescope*, ed. Christopher Walker (London, 1999), pp. 76–82.

17 Joseph Needham, 'Navigation in Medieval China', in *The Haven-Finding Art: A History of Navigation from Odysseus to Captain Cook*, ed. E.G.R. Taylor (London, 1971), pp. 264–78.

18 Daniel Defoe, *The Storm* [1704] (London, 2005) p. 21.

19 For a detailed discussion see Tibbetts, *Arab Navigation*, pp. 398–421.

20 May, *A History of Marine Navigation*, p. xiii.

21 Needham, 'Navigation in Medieval China', p. 275.

22 C. Sather, *The Bajau Laut* (Oxford, 1997), p. 102.

23 Taylor, *The Haven-Finding Art*, p. 83. The discussion in this paragraph is derived from this source.

24 Ibn Mājid, *Fawā'id*, p. 240.

25 Ibid.

26 Barry Cunliffe, *Facing the Ocean: The Atlantic and its Peoples* (Oxford, 2001), pp. 81–2.

27 Lewis, *We, The Navigators*, pp. 119–20.

28 Gísli Pálsson, 'Enskilment at Sea', *Man*, n.s., XXIX/4 (1994), p. 903.

29 Ernest Hemingway, *The Old Man of and the Sea* [1952] (London, 2000), p. 75.

30 Thomas Gladwin, *East Is a Big Bird: Navigation and Logic on Puluwat Atoll* (Cambridge, MA, 1970), p. 171.

31 John Mack, *The Museum of the Mind: Art and Memory in World Cultures* (London, 2003), p. 35.

32 Timothy Ingold, 'Technology, Language, Intelligence', in *Tools, Language and Cognition in Human Evolution*, ed. D. Genter and T. Ingold (Cambridge, 1993), p. 462; see also Pálsson, 'Enskilment at Sea', pp. 93ff.

33 Lewis, *We, The Navigators*, pp. 201–5.

34 Ibid., p. 202.

35 Cunliffe, *Facing the Ocean*, p. 79.

36 As quoted in Nicholas Thomas, *In Oceania: Visions, Artefacts, Histories* (London, 1997), p. 1. The opening chapter itself is subtitled 'Tupaia's Map'.

37 Thomas, *In Oceania*, p. 1; Nicholas Thomas, *Discoveries: The Voyages of Captain Cook* (London, 2003), pp. 80–81. As this book was being finished I came across an important article by Anne Salmond: 'Their Body is Different, Our Body is Different: European and Tahitian

Navigators in the 18th Century', *History and Anthropology*, XVI/2 (2005), pp. 167–86. This includes a fuller account of Tupaia's early life which is derived from a mid-nineteenth century missionary source. The argument about the embodiment of navigational knowledge at times parallels that advanced here.

38 David Turnbull, 'Cook and Tupaia, a Tale of Cartographic *Méconnaissance?*', in *Science and Exploration in the Pacific: European Voyages to the Southern Oceans in the Eighteenth Century*, ed. Margarette Lincoln (Woodbridge, 1998), p. 126.

39 As quoted in Turnbull, 'Cook and Tupaia', p. 128.

40 As quoted in Thomas, *In Oceania*, p. 1.

41 As quoted in Turnbull, 'Cook and Tupaia', p. 129.

42 Steven Hooper, *Pacific Encounters, Art and Divinity in Polynesia 1760–1860* (London, 2006), p. 178.

43 Thomas, *Discoveries*, p. 76.

44 Harold B. Carter , 'Note on the Drawing by an Unknown Artist from the Voyage of HMS *Endeavour*', in *Science and Exploration in the Pacific*, ed. Margarette Lincoln, p. 133.

45 Carter, 'Note on the Drawing', p. 134. The portfolio of Tupaia's suspected works now runs to sixteen drawings.

46 Lewis, *We, The Navigators*, p. 343.

47 Thomas, *In Oceania*, p. 4.

48 Turnbull, 'Cook and Tupaia' p. 117 n1.

49 Horatio Hale, *Unites States Exploring Expedition during the years 1838, 1839, 1840, 1841, 1842 under the command of Charles Wilkes, USN: Ethnography and Philology* (Philadelphia, PA, 1846), p. 122.

50 Lewis, *We, The Navigators*, pp. 87–8.

51 Ibid., p. 88.

52 Ibid., p. 84.

53 Ibid., p. 235.

54 Ibid., p. 127.

55 Ibid., p. 290.

56 Ibid., pp. 195–223.

57 Ibid., p. 218.

58 Ibid., pp. 252–6.

59 Gladwin, *East Is a Big Bird*, p. 204.

60 Lewis, *We, The Navigators*, pp. 245–9; A. Gell, 'How to Read a Map: remarks on the practical logic of navigation', *Man*, n.s., 20 (1985), pp. 284–6.

61 Tim Ingold, *Lines: A Brief History* (London, 2007), pp. 15–16; see also chap. 3.

62 Jonathan Raban, *Coasting* (London, 1987), p. 119.

63 Richard Henry Dana, Jr, *Two Years before the Mast: A Personal Narrative of Life at Sea* [1840] (New York, 1981), p. 426.

64 Jerome K. Jerome, *Three Men in a Boat (To Say Nothing of the Dog)* [1889] (London, 2004), pp. 106–7.

65 Joseph Conrad, *'Twixt Land and Sea Tales* (London, 1912), p. 107.

66 Joseph Conrad, *The Nigger of the 'Narcissus' and Other Stories*, ed. J. H. Stape and Allan H. Simmons with an introduction by Gail Fraser [1897] (London, 2007), p. 27.

67 Dana, *Two Years before the Mast*, p. 161.

4 Ships as Societies

1 Richard Henry Dana, Jr, *Two Years before the Mast* [1840] (New York, 1986), p.77.

2 James Boswell, *The Life of Samuel Johnson*, ed. with an introduction by David Womersley [1791] (London, 2008), p. 186.

3 Michel Foucault, 'Des espaces autres', *Architecture, Mouvement, Continuités* (October 1984), trans. Fay Miskowiec at http://foucault.info/documents/heteroTopia/foucault.heteroTopia.en.html

4 Dana, *Two Years before the Mast*, p. 77.

5 Redmond O'Hanlon, *Trawler* (London, 2004).

6 Dana, *Two Years before the Mast*, p. 37.

7 Ibid., p. 369.

8 Ibid., p. 44.

9 Ibid., p. 143.

10 Ibid., p. 40.

11 As quoted in Marcus Rediker, *Between the Devil and the Deep Blue Sea: Merchant Seamen, Pirates and the Anglo-American Maritime World, 1700–1750* (Cambridge, 1987), p. 11.

12 Peter Earle, *Sailors: English Merchant Seamen 1650–1775* (London, 2007), p. 34.

13 Dana, *Two Years before the Mast*, p. 458.

14 Ibid., p. 470.

15 Pablo E. Pérez-Mallaína, *Spain's Men of the Sea: Daily Life on the Indies Fleets in the Sixteenth Century*, trans. Carla Rahn Phillips (Baltimore, MD, 1998), pp. 55–62.

16 Pérez-Mallaína, *Spain's Men of the Sea*, p. 58.

17 I am grateful to Steven Hooper for pointing out this derivation.

18 David A. Chappell, 'Ahab's Boat: Non-European Seamen in Western Ships of Exploration and Commerce', in *Sea Changes: Historicizing the Ocean*, ed. Bernard Klein and Gesa Mackenthun (London, 2004), p. 85.

19 Stan Hugill, *Sailortown* (London, 1967), parts iii and iv.

20 N.A.M. Rodger, *The Command of the Sea: A Naval History of Britain, 1649–1815* (London, 2004). On pp. 394–5 mention is made of a black seaman transferred to relieve him of racism from fellow crew members.

21 Earle, *Sailors*, p. 204.

22 Cynthia Fansler Behrman, *Victorian Myths of the Sea* (Athena, OH, 1977), p. 72.

23 Chappell, 'Ahab's Boat', p. 75.

24 C.L.R. James, *Mariners, Renegades and Castaway: The Story of Herman Melville and the World We Live In* [1953] (London, 1985), p. 25.

25 Herman Melville, *Moby-Dick or The Whale* [1851] (New York, 2001), pp. 131–2.

26 James, *Mariners, Renegades and Castaways*, p. 26.

27 Behrman, *Victorian Myths of the Sea*, chap. 5.

28 Melville, *Moby-Dick*, p. 12.

29 Ibid., p. 22.

30 Ibid.

31 Ibid., p. 606.

32 Ibid., p. 159.

33 Pérez-Mallaína, *Spain's Men of the Sea*, p. 63.

34 Chappell, 'Ahab's Boat', p. 77.

35 Earle, *Sailors*, p. 21.

36 Ibid.

37 Ibid., p. 204.

38 Hugill, *Sailortown*, p. xxi

39 Melville, *Moby-Dick*, p. 517.

40 J. M. Acheson, 'Anthropology of Fishing', *Annual Review of Anthropology*, 10 (1981), p. 279.

41 Thomas Gladwin, *East Is a Big Bird: Navigation and Logic on Puluwat Atoll* (Cambridge, MA, 1970), chap. 2.

42 Richard Feinberg, *Polynesian Seafaring and Navigation* (Kent, OH, 1988), chap. 6.

43 G. R. Tibbetts, *Arab Navigation in the Indian Ocean before the Coming of the*

Portuguese, *being a translation of Kitāb al-Fawā'id f ī uṣūl al-baḥr wa'l-qawā'id of Aḥmad b. Mājid al-Najdī*, with an introduction notes and a glossary, Oriental Translation Fund n.s. XLII [1490] (London, 1971), pp. 58–9.

44 Alan Villiers, *Sons of Sindbad: an account of sailing with the Arabs in their dhows, in the Red Sea, round the coasts of Arabia, and to Zanzibar and Tanganyika ; pearling in the Persian gulf ; and the life of the shipmasters and the mariners of Kuwait* (London, 1940) p. 346.

45 G. F. Hourani, *Arab Seafaring in the Indian Ocean in Ancient and Early Medieval Times*, revised and expanded by John Carswell (Princeton, NJ, 1995), p. 113; see also Tibbetts, *Arab Navigation*, pp. 60–61.

46 Mājid, *Fawā'id*, p. 192.

47 Feinberg, *Polynesian Seafaring and Navigation*, p. 131.

48 See the front cover of Hourani, *Arab Seafaring*.

49 Hourani, *Arab Seafaring*, caption p. 98.

50 Mark Horton, 'Artisans, Communities and Commodities; medieval exchanges between Northwestern India and East Africa', *Ars Orientalis* (2007), 34, pp. 64–83.

51 Dana, *Two Years Before the Mast*, p. 463.

52 Greg Dening, *Mr Bligh's Bad Language: Passion, Power and Theatre on the Bounty* (Cambridge, 1992), pp. 115–16.

53 Rodger, *The Command of the Sea*, p. 450.

54 Herman Melville, *Melville's Billy Budd*, ed. F. Barron Freeman [1891], (Cambridge, MA, 1948), p. 153.

55 Dening, *Mr. Bligh's Bad Language*, p. 114.

56 Ibid., p. 156.

57 Rodger, *The Command of the Sea*, p. 490.

58 Melville, *Moby-Dick*, pp. 158–60.

59 Ibid., p. 166.

60 Ibid.

61 Ibid., p. 164.

62 Ibid., p. 590.

63 Gladwin, *East Is a Big Bird*, p. 47.

64 O'Hanlon, *Trawler*, p. 8.

65 Cordingly, *Seafaring Women: Adventures of Pirate Queens, Female Stowaways and Sailors' Wives* (New York, 2007).

66 Ibid., pp. 92–3.

67 Ibid., pp. 55–6; Rodger, *The Command of the Sea*, p. 507.

68 Cordingly, *Seafaring Women*, chap. 4.

69 Captain Charles Johnston, *A General History of the Robberies & Murders of*

the Most Notorious Pirates, with an introduction by David Cordingly [1724] (London, 1998).

70 Joseph Conrad, *Nostromo: A Tale of the Seaboard* [1923] (London, 1947), chap. 10.

71 Originally published in Joseph Conrad,'*Twixt Land and Sea Tales* (London, 1912); subsequently reprinted in Joseph Conrad, *Typhoon* (London, 2002).

72 Conrad, *Typhoon*, p. 197.

73 Ibid., p. 198.

74 Silvia Rodgers, 'Feminine Power at Sea', *rain*, no. 64 (1984), p. 3.

75 Earle, *Sailors*, p. 102.

76 Cordingly, *Seafaring Women*, chap. 9.

77 Rodgers, 'Feminine Power at Sea', pp. 2–4.

5 Beaches

1 Greg Dening, *Beach Crossings: Voyaging across Times, Cultures and Self* (Carlton, Victoria, 2004), pp. 16–17.

2 Vanessa Smith, 'Crusoe in the South Seas: Beachcombers, Missionaries and the Myth of the Castaway', in *Robinson Crusoe: Myths and Metamorphoses*, ed. Lieve Spaas and Brian Stimpson (Basingstoke, 1996), pp. 64–5.

3 Daniel Defoe, *Robinson Crusoe, An Authoritative Text, Contexts and Criticism*, 2nd edn, ed. Michael Shinagel [1719] (New York, 1994), p. 44.

4 Ibid., p. 126.

5 The BBC Radio programme *Desert Island Discs*, which uses such a construct as its premise, was conceived as long ago as 1942 and is still running weekly.

6 Ford Madox Ford, *The Cinque Ports: A Historical and Descriptive Record* (London, 1900), p. 183.

7 Paula Girshick Ben Amos, 'Symbolism in Olokun Mud Art', *African Arts*, VI/4 (1973), pp. 28–31.

8 Marshall Sahlins, *Islands of History* (Chicago, IL, 1985), chap. 4.

9 Nicholas Thomas, *Discoveries: The Voyages of Captain Cook* (London, 2003), p. 384.

10 Thomas, *Discoveries*, p. 387.

11 John Mack, 'The Land Viewed from the Sea', *Azania*, XLII (2007), pp. 1–14.

12 Pierre Vérin, *The History of Civilisation in Northern Madagascar* (Rotterdam, 1986), p. 380.

13 Richard Henry Dana Jr, *Two Years before the Mast: A Personal Narrative of Life at Sea* [1840] (New York, 1981).

14 Ibid., p. 202.

15 Ibid., pp. 202ff.

16 Ibid., p. 219.

17 Ibid., pp. 221–2.

18 Ibid., p. 315.

19 Robert Louis Stevenson, 'The Beach of Falesá' in *South Sea Tales,* ed. Rosyln Jolly [1892] (Oxford, 1996).

20 Paul Rainbird, *The Archaeology of Islands* (Cambridge, 2007), p. 51.

21 Marcus Rediker, *Between the Devil and the Deep Blue Sea: Merchant Seamen, Pirates and the Anglo-American Maritime World, 1700–1750* (Cambridge, 1987), p. 11.

22 Thomas, *Discoveries*, p. 15.

23 M. N. Pearson, 'Brokers in Western Indian Ports: Their Role in Servicing Foreign Merchants', *Modern Asian Studies*, 22 (1988), pp. 455–72 .

24 Pearson, 'Brokers in Western Indian Ports', p. 464, quoting a Portuguese source, João de Barros.

25 As cited in Pearson, 'Brokers in Western Indian Ports', p. 462.

26 Ibid.

27 Victor Hugo, *The Toilers of the Sea*, trans. James Hogarth [1866] (New York, 2002), p. 146.

28 Mark Horton and John Middleton, *The Swahili: The Social Landscape of a Mercantile Society* (Oxford, 2000), pp. 14–17.

29 François Rabelais, *The Histories of Gargantua and Pantagruel*, trans. and with an introduction by J. M. Cohen [1532–4] (London, 1955), p. 491.

30 Rita Astuti, *People of the Sea: Identity and Descent among the Vezo of Madagascar* (Cambridge, 1995)

31 Astuti, *People of the Sea*, p. 44

32 C. Sather, *The Bajau Laut* (Oxford, 1997), p. 13.

33 Sather, *The Bajau Laut*, p. 103.

34 See, for instance, Sebastian Hope, *Outcasts of the Islands: The Sea Gypsies of South East Asia* (London, 2002).

35 This paraphrases Sather, *The Bajau Laut*, pp. 19–20.

36 Sather, *The Bajau Laut*, p. 95.

37 Ibid., p. 92.

38 Astuti, *People of the Sea*, p. 164 n. 6.

39 Sather, *The Bajau Laut*, p. 17.

40 Sahlins, 'The Stranger-King: or, Dumézil among the Fijians' in *Islands*

of History, p. 79.

41 The account is that written down in 1980 through discussion with participants by Steven Hooper. It is on this documentation that Sahlins's account in 'The Stranger-King' is based. I am also grateful to him for bringing it to my attention.

42 Sahlins, 'The Stranger-King', p. 85.

6 The Sea on the Land

1 Michel Foucault, 'Des espaces autres', *Architecture, Mouvement, Continuités* (October, 1984), trans. Fay Miskowiec at http://foucault.info/documents/heteroTopia/foucault.heteroTopia.en.html

2 Redmond O'Hanlon, *Trawler* (London, 2004), p. 8.

3 Ibid., p. 99.

4 Ibid., p. 10.

5 Christer Westerdahl, 'Seal on Land, Elk at Sea: The Ritual Landscape at the Seaboard', *International Journal of Nautical Archaeology*, 34/1 (2005), p. 2.

6 Ibid., p. 4.

7 As quoted in Marcus Rediker, *Between the Devil and the Deep Blue Sea: Merchant Seamen, Pirates and the Anglo-American Maritime World, 1700–1750* (Cambridge, 1987), p. 162.

8 J. H. Parry, 'Sailors' English', *The Cambridge Journal*, 2 (1948–9), pp. 663.

9 Admiral W. H. Smyth, *The Sailor's Word-Book: An Alphabetical Digest of Nautical Terms, Including Some More Especially Military And Scientific, But Useful to Seamen; As Well As Archaisms of Early Voyagers, Etc.* [1865] (London, 1991), p. 7.

10 Rediker, *Between the Devil and the Deep Blue Sea*, p. 169.

11 Parry, 'Sailors' English', p. 670.

12 Greg Dening, *Mr. Bligh's Bad Language: Passion, Power and Theatre on the Bounty* (Cambridge, 1992).

13 Parry, 'Sailors' English', p. 670.

14 Ibid., p. 662.

15 Peter Earle, *Sailors: English Merchant Seamen 1650–1775* (London, 2007), p. 95.

16 Westerdahl, 'Seal on Land, Elk at Sea', p. 8.

17 Smyth, *The Sailor's Word-Book*. p. 7.

18 Ibid., p. 6.

19 Ian J. McNiven, 'Saltwater People: Spiritscapes, Maritime Rituals and the Archaeology of Australian Indigenous Seascapes', *World*

Archaeology, XXXV/3 (2003), p. 337.

20 Mckinnon, Susan, 'Tanimbar Boats', in *Islands and Ancestors: Indigenous Styles of Southeast Asia*, ed. J. P. Barbier and D. Newton (New York, 1988), pp. 158–9.

21 Mckinnon, 'Tanimbar Boats', p. 161.

22 Pierre-Yves Manguin, 'Shipshape Societies: Boat Symbolism and Political Systems in Insular Asia', in *Southeast Asia in the 9th to 14th Centuries*, ed. David G. Marr and A. C. Milner (Singapore, 1986), pp. 187–213; see also Chris Ballard et al., 'The Ship as Symbol in the Prehistory of Scandanavia and Southeast Asia', *World Archaeology*, XXXV/3 'Seascapes' (2003), p. 391–3.

23 Soma Basu, 'Of Waves and Worship', *The Hindu* (27 May 2006)

24 Patricia Fortini Brown, *Venetian Narrative Painting in the Age of Carpaccio* (London, 1988), p. 187.

25 Willem Frijhoff, *Embodied Belief: Ten Essays on Religious Culture in Dutch History* (Hilversum, 2002), p. 222

26 Ibid.

27 Ibid., p. 226.

28 Sir James George Frazer, *The Golden Bough: A Study in Magic and Religion*, 3rd edn, pt vi: 'The Scapegoat' (London, 1966), pp. 201–2.

29 Calum G. Brown, *Up-helly-aa: Custom, Culture and Community in Shetland* (Manchester, 1998), p. 2.

30 Margit Thøfner, *A Common Art: Urban Ceremonial in Antwerp and Brussels during and after the Dutch Revolt* (Zwolle, 2007); see especially on this point pp. 149–56.

31 Manguin, 'Shipshape Societies: Boat Symbolism and Political Systems in Insular Asia', p. 198.

32 The authoritative scholarship on this phenomenon is that of Henry John Drewal, *Mami Wata: Arts for Water Spirits in Africa and its Diasporas* (Los Angeles, CA, 2008), pp. 49–52. For a further review of the phenomenon see also Drewal, ed., *Sacred Waters: Arts for Mami Wata and Other Divinities in Africa and the African Atlantic World* (Bloomington, IN, 2008). I am grateful for his generous help with a number of aspects of this book.

33 Drewal, *Mami Wata*, p. 114.

34 Ian J. McNiven, 'Saltwater People: Spiritscapes, Maritime Rituals and the Archaeology of Australian Indigenous Seascapes', *World Archaeology*, XXXV/3 (2003), p. 336.

35 C. Sather, *The Bajau Laut* (Oxford, 1977), pp. 283–4.

36 Manguin, 'Shipshape Societies', p. 196; see also Ballard et al., 'The Ship as Symbol', p. 392.

37 Seamus Heaney, trans., *Beowulf* (London, 1999), lines 34–47.

38 Ibid., lines 3139–40.

39 Ibid., lines 3156–60.

40 Albany F. Major, 'Ship Burials in Scandinavian Lands and the Beliefs that Underlie Them', *Folklore*, 35/2 (1924), pp. 123.

41 Angela Evans, *The Sutton Hoo Ship Burial* (London, 1986)

42 Rupert Bruce-Mitford, *The Sutton Hoo Ship Burial* (London, 1975–83). See also Martin Carver, *Sutton Hoo: A Seventh-century Princely Burial and its Context*, with contributions by Angela Evans (London, 2005); Martin Carver, *Sutton Hoo: Burial Ground of Kings?* (London, 1998).

43 Barry Cunliffe, *Facing the Ocean: The Atlantic and its Peoples, 8000 BC to AD 1500* (Oxford, 2001), p. 10.

44 As Westerdahl, for instance, tentatively suggests; see 'Seal on Land, Elk at Sea', p. 3.

Bibliography

Abulafia, David, 'Mediterraneans' in *Rethinking the Mediterranean*,
    ed. W. V. Harris (Oxford, 2005), pp. 64–93
Abulafia, David, ed., *The Mediterranean in History* (London, 2003)
Acheson, J. M., 'Anthropology of Fishing', *Annual Review of Anthropology*,
    10 (1981), pp. 275–316
Allen, J. de Vere, *Swahili Origins: Swahili Culture and the Schungwaya Phenomenon*
    (London, 1993)
Armitage, David, *The Ideological Origins of the British Empire* (Cambridge, 2000)
Astuti, Rita, *People of the Sea: Identity and Descent among the Vezo of Madagascar*
    (Cambridge, 1995)
Auden, W. H., *The Enchafèd Flood, or Romantic Iconography of the Sea* (London,
    1951)
Bachelard, Gaston, *Water and Dreams: An Essay on the Imagination of Dreams*,
    trans. Edith Farrell (Dallas, TX, 1942)
Bailyn, Bernard, *Atlantic History: Concept and Contour* (Cambridge, MA, 2005)
Ballard, Chris, Richard Bradley, Lise Nordenborg Myhre and Meredith
    Wilson, 'The Ship as Symbol in the Prehistory of Scandinavia
    and Southeast Asia', *World Archaeology*, XXXV/3, 'Seascapes' (2003),
    pp. 385–403
Banfield, John, *The Sea* (London, 2005)
Barnes, Robert, *Sea Hunters of Indonesia: Fishers and Weavers of Lamalera* (Oxford,
    1996)
Basu, Soma, 'Of Waves and Worship', *The Hindu* (27 May 2006)
Baucom, Ian, 'Hydrographies', *Geographical Review*, LXXXIX/2 (1999),
    pp. 301–13
Beard, Mary, *The Parthenon* (London, 2004)
Behrman, Cynthia Fansler, *Victorian Myths of the Sea* (Athens, OH, 1977)

Belloc, Hilaire, *The Cruise of the Nona* (London, 1925)

Ben Amos, Paula Girshick, 'Symbolism in Olokun Mud Art', *African Arts*, VI/4 (1973), pp. 28–31

Bender, Bert, *Sea-Brothers: The Tradition of American Sea Fiction from Moby-Dick to the Present* (Philadelphia, PA, 1988)

——, 'Sea and Ocean Basins as Frameworks of Historical Analysis', *Geographical Review*, LXXXIX/2 (1999), pp. 215–24

Bentley, Jerry H., 'Sea and Ocean Basins as Frameworks of Historical Analysis', *Geographical Review*, LXXXIX/2 (1999), pp. 215–24

Bentley, Jerry H., Renate Bridenthal and Kären Wigen, eds, *Seascapes: Maritime Histories, Littoral Cultures and Transoceanic Exchanges* (Honolulu, HI, 2007)

Blank, Paul W., 'The Pacific: A Mediterranean in the Making?', *Geographical Review*, LXXXIX/2 (1999), pp. 265–77

Bose, Sugata, *A Hundred Horizons: The Indian Ocean in the Age of Global Empire* (Cambridge, MA, 2006)

Boswell, James, *The Life of Samuel Johnson*, ed. with an introduction David Womersley [1791] (London, 2008)

Boxer, C. R., *The Dutch Seaborne Empire, 1600–1800* (London, 1965)

Brandt, Anthony, ed., *The Tragic History of the Sea: Shipwrecks from the Bible to Titanic* (Washington, DC, 2006)

Braudel, F., *The Mediterranean and the Mediterranean World in the Age of Philip II*, trans. Siân Reynolds (London, 1973)

Breen, C. and P. Lane, 'Archaeological Approaches to East Africa's Changing Seascapes', *World Archaeology*, XXXV/3 (2003), pp. 469–89

Broodbank, Cyprian, 'The Insularity of Island Archaeologists: Comments on Rainbird's "Islands out of Time"', *Journal of Mediterranean Archaeology*, 12/2 (1999), pp. 235–9

Brown, Calum G., *Up-helly-aa: Custom, Culture and Community in Shetland* (Manchester, 1998)

Brown, Patricia Fortini, *Venetian Narrative Painting in the Age of Carpaccio* (London, 1988)

Bruce-Mitford, Rupert, *The Sutton Hoo Ship Burial* (London, 1975–83)

Buisseret, David, *The Mapmakers' Quest: Depicting New Worlds in Renaissance Europe* (Oxford, 2003)

Burke, Edmund, *A Philosophical Enquiry into the Origin of Our Ideas of the Sublime and the Beautiful*, ed. J. T. Boulton [1757] (London, 1958)

Burrow, John, *A History of Histories: Epics, Chronicles, Romances and Inquiries from Herodotus and Thucydides to the Twentieth Century* (London, 2007)

Burton, Richard, *First Footsteps in Africa* [1856] (London, 1966)

Carson, Rachel, *The Sea Around Us* (London, 1951)

——, *Under the Sea-wind: A Naturalist's Picture of Ocean Life* (Oxford, 1953)

——, *The Edge of the Sea* (London, 1955)

Carter, Harold B., 'Note on the Drawings by an Unknown Artist from the Voyage of HMS *Endeavour*', in *Science and Exploration in the Pacific: European Voyages to the Southern Oceans in the Eighteenth Century*, ed. Margarette Lincoln (Woodbridge, 1998), pp. 133–4

Carter, Paul, 'Dark with Excess of Bright: Mapping the Coastlines of Knowledge', in *Mappings*, ed. Denis Cosgrove (London, 2001), pp. 125–47

Cartier, Carolyn, 'Cosmopolitics and the World Maritime City', *Geographical Review*, LXXXIX/2 (1999), pp. 278–89

Carver, Martin, *Sutton Hoo: Burial Ground of Kings?* (London, 1998)

——, *Sutton Hoo: A Seventh-century Princely Burial and its Context*, with contributions by Angela Evans (London, 2005)

Casdon, Lionel, *The Ancient Mariners: Seafarers and Sea Fighters of the Mediterranean in Ancient Times* (Princeton, NJ, 1991)

Chappell, David A., 'Ahab's Boat, Non-European Seamen in Western Ships of Exploration and Commerce' in *Sea Changes: Historicizing the Ocean*, ed. Bernard Klein and Gesa Mackenthun (London, 2004), pp. 75–89

Chatwin, Bruce, *The Songlines* (London, 1987)

Chaudhuri, K. N., *Trade and Civilisation in the Indian Ocean* (Cambridge, 1985)

——, *Asia before Europe: Economy and Civilisation of the Indian Ocean from the Rise of Islam to 1750* (Cambridge, 1990)

Chittick, H. Neville, 'East Africa and the Orient: Ports and Trade before the Arrival of the Portuguese', in *Historical Relations across the Indian Ocean*, (Paris, 1980), pp. 13–22

Clark, Timothy, *100 Views of Mount Fuji*, exh. cat., British Museum (London, 2001)

Cockett, F. B., *Early Sea Painters 1660–1730: The Group Who Worked in England under the Shadow of the Van de Veldes* (Woodbridge, 1995)

——, *Peter Monamy, 1681–1749, and his Circle* (Woodbridge, 2000)

Coleridge, Samuel Taylor, *The Collected Works of Samuel Taylor Coleridge* (Princeton, NJ, 2001)

Collins, Richard, *The Land as Viewed from the Sea* (Bridgend, 2004)

Conrad, Joseph, *Nostromo: A Tale of the Seaboard* [1923] (London, 1947)

——, *Typhoon and Other Tales*, ed. with an introduction and notes by Cedric Watts [1903] (Oxford, 2002)

——, *The Nigger of the 'Narcissus' and Other Stories*, ed. J. H. Stape and Allan H. Simmons with an introduction by Gail Fraser [1897] (London, 2007)

——, *'Twixt Land and Sea Tales* (London, 1912)

——, *The Mirror of the Sea* (London, 1906)

Constantakopolou, Christy, *The Dance of the Islands: Insularity, Networks, the Athenian Empire and the Aegean World* (Oxford, 2007)

Cooke, Miriam, 'Mediterranean Thinking: from Netizen to Medizen', *Geographical Review*, LXXXIX/2 (1999), pp. 290–300

Cooney, Gabriel, 'Seeing the Land from the Sea', *World Archaeology*, 35/3, 'Seascapes' (2003), pp. 323–8

Coote, J., ed., *The Faber Book of the Sea* (London, 1989)

——, ed., *The Faber Book of Tales of the Sea* (London, 1991)

Corbin, Alain, *The Lure of the Sea: The Discovery of the Seaside in the Western World, 1750–1840*, trans. Jocelyn Phelps (Cambridge, 1994)

Cordingly, David, *Marine Painting in England, 1700–1900* (London, 1974)

——, *Heroines and Harlots: Women at Sea in the Age of Sail* (London, 2002)

——, *Seafaring Women: Adventures of Pirate Queens, Female Stowaways, and Sailors' Wives* (New York, 2007)

Cosgrove, Denis, ed., *Mappings* (London, 2001)

Cosgrove, Denis, and Stephen Daniel, eds, *The Iconography of Landscape: Essays on the Symbolic Representation, Design and Use of Past Environments* (Cambridge, 1988)

Crane, Stephen, 'The Open Boat' in *The Red Badge of Courage and Other Stories* [1899] (London, 2005), pp. 211–41

Crumlin-Pedersen, O., and B. M. Thye, eds, *The Ship as Symbol in Prehistoric and Medieval Scandinavia* (Copenhagen, 1995)

Cunliffe, Barry, *The Ancient Celts* (Oxford, 1997)

——, *Facing the Ocean: The Atlantic and its Peoples 8000 BC to AD 1500* (Oxford, 2001)

——, *The Extraordinary Journey of Pytheas the Greek* (London, 2001)

Dahl, O., *Malgache et Maanjan, une comparison linguistique* (Oslo, 1951)

Dana, Richard Henry Jr, *Two Years before the Mast: A Personal Narrative of Life at Sea* [1840] (New York, 1981)

Dant, Tim, 'Playing with Things: Objects and Subjects in Windsurfing', *Journal of Material Culture*, 3/1 (1998), pp. 75–95

De Souza, Philip, *Seafaring and Civilization: Maritime Perspectives on World History* (London, 2001)

Defoe, Daniel, *The Storm* [1704] (London, 2005)

——, *Robinson Crusoe, An Authoritative Text, Contexts and Criticism*, 2nd edn, ed. Michael Shinagel [1719] (New York, 1994)

——, *The King of Pirates*, foreword by Peter Ackroyd [1719] (London, 2002)

Dening, Greg, *Islands and Beaches: Discourse on a Silent Land: Marquesas 1774–1880* (Chicago, IL, 1980)

——, *Mr Bligh's Bad Language: Passion, Power and Theatre on the Bounty* (Cambridge, 1992)

——, 'Deep Times, Deep Spaces. Civilizing the Sea', in *Sea Changes. Historicizing the Ocean*, ed. Bernard Klein and Gesa Mackenthun (London, 2004), pp. 13–35

——, *Beach Crossings: Voyaging across Times, Cultures and Self* (Carlton, Victoria, 2004)

Deutsch, Jan-Georg, and Brigitte Reinwald, eds, *Space on the Move: Transformations of the Indian Ocean Seascape in the Nineteenth and Twentieth Century* (Berlin, 2002)

Dewar, R. E., and H. T. Wright, 'The Cultural History of Madagascar', *Journal of World Prehistory*, 7 (1993), pp. 417–66

Dick-Read, R., *The Phantom Voyagers: Evidence of Indonesian Settlement in Africa in Ancient Times* (Winchester, 2005)

Drewal, Henry John, *Mami Wata: Arts for Water Spirits in Africa and its Diasporas* (Los Angeles, CA, 2008)

——, ed., *Sacred Arts: Arts for Mami Wata and Other Divinities in Africa and the African World* (Bloomington, IN, 2008).

Earle, Peter, *Sailors: English Merchant Seamen 1650–1775* (London, 2007)

Edmond, R., and V. Smith, eds, *Islands in History and Representation* (London, 2003)

Edson, Evelyn, *Mapping Time and Space: How Medieval Mapmakers Viewed their World* (London, 1997)

Eliade, M., *Shamanism: Archaic Techniques of Ecstasy* (London, 1964)

Evans, Angela, *The Sutton Hoo Ship Burial* (London, 1986)

Fantar, M'hamad Hassine, *Carthage, The Punic City*, trans. Justin McGuinness (Tunis, 1998)

Feinberg, Richard, *Polynesian Seafaring and Navigation* (Kent, OH, 1988)

Fernández-Armesto, Felipe, *Columbus and the Conquest of the Impossible* (London, 1974)

——, *Before Columbus: Exploration and Colonization from the Mediterranean to the Atlantic, 1229–1492* (Basingstoke, 1987)

——, *Columbus* (Oxford, 1991)

——, *Pathfinders: A Global History of Exploration* (Oxford, 2006)

Ferrand, G. (with additional material by P. Vérin), 'Madagascar', in *The*

Encyclopedia of Islam, ed. C. E. Bosworth, E. van Donzel, B. Lewis and Ch. Pellat, 5 (Leiden, 1986), pp. 939–45

Foote, P., and D. Wilson, *The Viking Achievement* (London, 1980)

Ford, Ford Madox, *The Cinque Ports: A Historical and Descriptive Record* (Edinburgh, 1900)

Forrer, Matthi, *Hokusai: Prints and Drawings*, exh. cat., Royal Academy of Arts, London (1991)

Foucault, Michel, 'Des espaces autres', *Architecture, Mouvement, Continuités* (October 1984), trans. Fay Miskowiec at http://foucault.info/documents/heteroTopia/foucault.heteroTopia.en.html

Frazer, Sir James George, *The Golden Bough: A Study in Magic and Religion*, 3rd ed, pt VI, 'The Scapegoat' (London, 1966)

Frijhoff, Willem, *Embodied Belief: Ten Essays on Religious Culture in Dutch History* (Hilversum, 2002)

Gell, Alfred, 'How to Read a Map: remarks on the practical logic of navigation', *Man*, n.s., 20 (1985), pp. 271–86

——, 'The Language of the Forest: Landscape and Phonological Iconism in Umeda', in *The Anthropology of Landscape: Perspectives on Place and Space*, ed. Eric Hirsch and Michael O'Hanlon (Oxford, 1995), pp. 232–54

Gladwin, Thomas, *East Is a Big Bird: Navigation and Logic on Puluwat Atoll* (Cambridge, MA, 1970)

Golding, William, *To the Ends of the Earth: A Sea Trilogy Comprising 'Rites of Passage' 'Close Quarters' and 'Fire Down Below'* (London, 1991)

Goodenough, Ward H., *Native Astronomy in the Central Carolines* (Philadelphia, PA, 1953)

Gosden, Chris and Christina Pavlides, 'Are islands insular? Landscape v. seascape in the case of the Arawe Islands, Papua New Guinea', *Archaeologia Oceania*, 29 (1994), pp. 162–71

Graham-Campbell, J., *The Viking World* (London, 1989)

Greenhill, Basil, and Anne Gifford, eds, *Women under Sail: Letters and Journals Concerning Eight Women Travelling or Working in Sailing Vessels between 1829 and 1949* (Newton Abbot, 1970)

Haddon, A. C., *Reports of the Cambridge Anthropological Expedition to Torres Strait*, 5: 'Sociology, Magic and Religion of the Western Islanders' (Cambridge, 1904)

Hale, Horatio, *United States Exploring Expedition during the years 1838, 1839, 1840, 1841, 1842 under the command of Charles Wilkes, U.S.N: Ethnography and Philology* (Philadelphia, PA, 1846)

Harland-Jacobs, Jessica, '"Hands across the Sea": The Masonic Network,

British Imperialism, and the North Atlantic World', *Geographical Review*, LXXXIX/2 (1999), pp. 237–53

Harris, W. V., ed., *Rethinking the Mediterranean* (Oxford, 2005)

Hau'ofa, Epeli, 'Our Sea of Islands', in *A New Oceania, Rediscovering our Sea of Islands*, ed. E. Waddell, V. Naidu and E. Hau'ofa (Suva, Fiji, 1993), pp. 2–16

——, 'The Ocean in Us', *The Contemporary Pacific*, 10/2 (1998)

Heaney, Seamus, trans., *Beowulf* (London, 1999)

Hemingway, Ernest, *The Old Man and the Sea* [1952] (London, 2000)

——, On the Blue Water: A Gulf Stream Letter', *Esquire*, April 1936, p. 31f. Reprinted in *By-Line: Ernest Hemingway*, ed. William White [1936] (New York, 1968), pp. 236–44

Hennington, Henning, *Crossing the Equator: Sailor's Baptisms and other Initiation Rites* (Munksgaard, 1961)

Herrmann, Luke, 'Turner and the Sea', *Turner Studies*, 1/1 (1981), pp. 4–18

Hirsch, Eric, and Michael O'Hanlon, eds, *The Anthropology of Landscape: Perspectives on Place and Space* (Oxford, 1995)

Hobman, B., *Sarimanok* (Paris, 1985)

Hokusai, Katsushika, *One Hundred Views of Mount Fuji*, intro. and commentaries by Henry Smith (London, 1988)

Hole, C., 'Superstition and Beliefs of the Sea', *Folklore*, 78 (1967), pp. 184–9

Holmes, Richard, *Coleridge: Darker Reflections* (London, 1989)

Hooper, Steven, 'Who are the Chiefs? Chiefship in Lau, Eastern Fiji', in *Leadership and Change in the Western Pacific: Essays Presented to Sir Raymond Firth on the Occasion of his Ninetieth Birthday*, ed. Richard Feinberg and Karen Ann Watson-Gegeo (London, 1996), pp. 239–71

——, *Pacific Encounters: Art and Divinity in Polynesia, 1760–1860* (London, 2006)

Hope, Sebastian, *Outcasts of the Islands: The Sea Gypsies of South East Asia* (London, 2002)

Horden, P., and N. Purcell, *The Corrupting Sea: A Study of Mediterranean History* (Oxford, 2000)

Horton, Mark, 'The Swahili Corridor', *Scientific American*, 257 (1987), pp. 76–84

——, 'Mare Nostrum: A New Archaeology in the Indian Ocean', *Antiquity*, 71 (1997), pp. 753–55

——, 'Artisans, Communities and Commodities: Medieval Exchanges between Northwestern India and East Africa', *Ars Orientalis*, 34 (2007), pp. 65–83

Horton, Mark, and John Middleton, *The Swahili: The Social Landscape of a Mercantile Society* (Oxford, 2000)

Hourani, G. F., *Arab Seafaring in the Indian Ocean in Ancient and Early Medieval Times*, revised and expanded by John Carswell (Princeton, NJ, 1995)

Hugill, Stan, *Sailortown* (London, 1967)

Hugo, Victor, *The Toilers of the Sea*, trans. James Hogarth [1866] (New York, 2002)

Hulme, Peter, 'Cast Away: The Uttermost Parts of the Earth', in *Sea Changes: Historicizing the Ocean*, ed. Bernard Klein and Gesa Mackenthun (London, 2004), pp. 187–201

Humphrey, C., and J. Laidlaw, *The Archetypal Actions of Ritual* (Oxford, 1994)

Hutchins, Edwin, *Cognition in the Wild* (Cambridge, MA, 1995)

Ingold, Timothy, 'Technology, Language, Intelligence', in *Tools, Language and Cognition in Human Evolution,* ed. D. Genter and T. Ingold (Cambridge, 1993)

——, *The Perception of the Environment: Essays in Livelihood, Dwelling and Skill* (London, 2000)

——, *Lines: A Brief History* (London, 2007)

Insoll, Timothy, *The Land of Enki in the Islamic Era: Pearls, Palms and Religious Identity in Bahrain* (London, 2005)

Irwin, Geoffrey, 'Commentary on Paul Rainbird, "Islands Out of Time: Towards a Critique of Island Archaeology"', *Journal of Mediterranean Archaeology*, 12/2 (1999), pp. 252–4

James, C.L.R., *Mariners, Renegades and Castaways: The Story of Herman Melville and the World We Live In* (London, 1985)

James, Simon, *The Atlantic Celts: Ancient People or Modern Invention?* (London, 1999)

Jerome, Jerome K., *Three Men in a Boat (To Say Nothing of the Dog)* [1889] (London, 2004)

Johnston, Captain Charles, *A General History of the Robberies & Murders of the Most Notorious Pirates*, with an introduction by David Cordingly [1724] (London, 1998)

Jones, G., *A History of the Vikings* (Oxford, 1980)

Keegan, William F., 'Comment on Paul Rainbird's "Islands out of Time: Towards a Critique of Island Archaeology"', *Journal of Mediterranean Archaeology*, 12/2 (1999), pp. 255–8

King, D., 'Islamic Astronomy', in *Astronomy before the Telescope*, ed. C. Walker (London, 1999), pp. 143–74

Klein, Bernard, ed., *Fictions of the Sea: Critical Perspectives on the Ocean in British Literature and Culture* (Aldershot, 2002)

——, 'Staying Afloat. Literary Shipboard Encounters from Columbus to Equiano', in *Sea Changes: Historicizing the Ocean*, ed. Bernard Klein and Gesa Mackenthun(London, 2004), pp. 91–109

Klein, Bernard, and Gesa Mackenthun, eds, *Sea Changes: Historicizing the Ocean* (London, 2004)

Koechlin, B., *Les Vezo du sud-ouest de Madagascar: Contribution à l'étude de l'eco-systeme de semi-nomades marins* (Paris, 1975)

Kristiansen, K., 'Centre and Periphery in Bronze Age Scandinavia', in *Centre and Periphery in the Ancient World*, ed. M. Rowlands, M. Larsen and K. Kristiansen (Cambridge, 1987), pp. 74–95

Lane, Richard, *Hokusai: Life and Work* (London, 1989)

Larsen, Kjersti, *Where Humans and Spirits Meet: The Politics of Rituals and Identified Spirits in Zanzibar* (Oxford, 2008), pp. 68–70

Laurier, Eric, 'Replication and Restoration: Ways of Making Maritime Heritage', *Journal of Material Culture*, 3/1 (1998), pp. 21–50

Lee, J., and T. Ingold, 'Fieldwork on Foot: Perceiving, Routing, Socializing', in *Locating the Field: Space, Place and Context in Anthropology*, ed. S. Coleman and P. Collins (Oxford, 2006), pp. 67–85

Lenček, Lena, and Gideon Bosker, *The Beach: The History of Paradise on Earth* (London, 1998)

Lewis, David, *We, the Navigators: The Ancient Art of Landfinding in the Pacific*, 2nd edn (Honolulu, HI, 1994)

——, *The Voyaging Stars: Secrets of the Pacific Island Navigators* (New York, 1978)

Lewis, Martin W., 'Dividing the Ocean Sea', *Geographical Review*, LXXXIX/2 (1999), pp. 188–214

Lewis, Martin W. and Karen Wigen, 'A Maritime Response to the Crisis in Area Studies', *Geographical Review*, LXXXIX/2 (1999), pp. 161–8

Lincoln, Margarette, ed., *Science and Exploration in the Pacific: European Voyages to the Southern Oceans in the Eighteenth Century* (Woodbridge, 1998)

Lindenlauf, Astrid, 'The Sea is a Place of No Return in Ancient Greece', *World Archaeology*, 35/3 (2003), pp. 416–33

Lopez, Robert S., *The Commercial Revolution of the Middle Ages, 950–1350* (Englewood Cliffs, NJ, 1971)

Lundberg, A., 'Time Travels in Whaling Boats', *Journal of Social Archaeology*, 3 (2003), pp. 312–33

MacGaffey, Wyatt, 'BaKongo Cosmology', *The World and I*, 9 (1988), pp. 512–21

Mack, John, *Madagascar, Island of the Ancestors* (London, 1986)

——, 'Islamic Influences: The View from Madagascar', in *Islamic Art and Culture in sub-Saharan Africa*, ed. K. Ådahl and B. Sahlstrom (Uppsala, 1995), pp. 123–37

——, *Museum of the Mind: Art and Memory in World Cultures* (London, 2003)

——, 'The Land Viewed from the Sea', *Azania*, XLII (2007), pp. 1–14

Mackenthun, Gesa, 'Chartless Voyages and Protean Geographies: Nineteenth-century American Fictions and the Black Atlantic', in *Sea Changes: Historicizing the Ocean*, ed. Bernard Klein and Gesa Mackenthun (London, 2004), pp. 131–48

Mackinder, H. J., *Britain and the British Seas* (London, 1902)

McGrail, Sean, *Studies in Maritime Archaeology* (Oxford, 1997)

Mckinnon, Susan, 'Tanimbar Boats', in *Islands and Ancestors: Indigenous Styles of Southeast Asia*, ed. J. P. Barbier and D. Newton (New York, 1988), pp. 152–69

McNiven, Ian J., 'Saltwater People: Spiritscapes, Maritime Rituals and the Archaeology of Australian Indigenous Seascapes', *World Archaeology*, 35/3 (2003), pp. 329–49

McPherson, Kenneth, *The Indian Ocean: A History of People and the Sea* (Oxford, 1993)

Mājid al-Najdī, Aḥmad b., see Tibbetts, G. R.

Major, Albany F., 'Ship Burials in Scandinavian Lands and the Beliefs that Underlie them', *Folklore*, 35/2 (1924), pp. 113–50

Mancke, Elizabeth, 'Early Modern Expansion and the Politicization of Oceanic Space', *Geographical Review*, LXXXIX/2 (1999), pp. 225–36

Manguin, Pierre-Yves, 'Shipshape Societies: Boat Symbolism and Political Systems in Insular Asia', in *Southeast Asia in the 9th to 14th Centuries*, ed. David G. Marr and A. C. Milner (Singapore, 1986), pp. 187–213

Marcus, G. J., *The Conquest of the North Atlantic* (Woodbridge, 1986)

Marshall, M. W., *Ocean Traders: from Portuguese Discoveries to the Present Day* (London, 1986)

Martins, Luciana de Lima, 'Mapping Tropical Waters: British Views and Visions of Rio de Janeiro', in *Mappings*, ed. Denis Cosgrove (London, 2001), pp. 148–68

May, Commander W. E., *A History of Marine Navigation* (Henley-on-Thames, 1973)

Melville, Herman, *Melville's Billy Budd* (the complete text of the novel and of the unpublished short story), ed. F. Barron Freeman [1891] (Cambridge, MA, 1948)

——, *Moby-Dick or The Whale*, with a foreword by Nathaniel Philbrick [1851] (London, 2001)

Middleton, J., *The World of the Swahili: An African Mercantile Civilization* (New Haven, CT, 1992)

Mitchell, Peter, 'Towards a Comparative Archaeology of Africa's Islands', *Journal of African Archaeology*, 2, (2004), pp. 229–50

——, *African Connections: Archaeological Perspectives on Africa and the Wider World* (Oxford, 2005)

Monks, Sarah, 'Turner Goes Dutch', in David Solkin, ed., *Turner and the Old Masters*, exh. cat., Tate Britain (London, 2009), pp. 73–85

Narazaki, Muneshige, *Hokusai: The Thirty-six Views of Mount Fuji*, Eng. adaption by John Bester (Tokyo, 1968)

Needham, Joseph, 'Navigation in Medieval China', in *The Haven-Finding Art: A History of Navigation from Odysseus to Captain Cook*, ed. E.G.R. Taylor (London, 1971), pp. 264–78

Newby, Eric, *The Last Grain Race* (Boston, MA, 1956)

Nimmo, H. Arlo, *The Sea People of Sulu: A Study of Social Change in the Philippines* (Aylesbury, 1972)

Nurse, D., *The Swahili: Reconstructing the History and Language of an African Society, 800–1500* (Philadelphia, PA, 1985)

O'Brien, Patrick, *Master and Commander* (London, 2002)

O'Hanlon, Redmond, *Trawler* (London, 2004)

O'Loughlin, Thomas, 'Living in the Ocean', in *Studies in the Cult of Saint Columba*, ed. Cormac Bourke (Dublin, 1997)

Ong, W. J., *Orality and Literacy: The Technologizing of the World* (London, 1982)

Orchiston, Wayne, 'From the South Seas to the Sun: The Astronomy of Cook's Voyages', in *Science and Exploration in the Pacific: European Voyages to the Southern Oceans in the Eighteenth Century*, ed. Margarette Lincoln (Woodbridge, 1998), pp. 55–72

Pálsson, Gísli, 'Enskilment at Sea', *Man*, n.s., XXIX/4 (1994), pp. 901–27

Parry, J. H., 'Sailors' English', *The Cambridge Journal*, 2 (1948–9), pp. 660–70

Paulsen, Allison C., 'The Thorny Oyster and the Voice of God: Spondylus and Strombus in Andean Prehistory', *American Antiquity*, 39 (1974), p. 397

Payne, Christiana, *Where the Sea Meets the Land: Artists on the Coast in Nineteenth-century Britain* (Bristol, 2007)

Pearson, M. N., 'Brokers in Western Indian Ports: Their Role in Servicing Foreign Merchants', *Modern Asian Studies*, 22 (Cambridge, 1988), pp. 455–72

——, *Port Cities and Intruders: The Swahili Coast, India and Portugal in the Early*

Modern Era (Baltimore, MD, 1998)

——, *The World of the Indian Ocean, 1500–1800: Studies in Economic, Social and Cultural History* (Aldershot, 2005)

Pérez-Mallaína, Pablo E., *Spain's Men of the Sea: Daily Life on the Indies Fleets in the Sixteenth Century*, trans. Carla Rahn Phillips (Baltimore, MD, 1998)

The Periplus of the Erythraean Sea by an unknown author with some extracts from Agatharkhi s 'On The Erythraean Sea', trans. and ed. G.W.B. Huntingford (London, 1980)

Philbrick, Nathaniel, *In the Heart of the Sea: The Epic True Story that Inspired Moby Dick* (London, 2000)

Pollard, Justin, and Howard Reid, *The Rise and Fall of Alexandria* (London, 2006)

Prentice, Rina, *A Celebration of the Sea: The Decorative Art Collections of the National Maritime Museum* (London, 1994)

Pryor, John H., *Geography, Technology, and War: Studies in the Maritime History of the Mediterranean, 649–1571* (Cambridge, 1988)

Pryor, John H., and Elizabeth M. Jeffreys, *The Age of the Dromon: the Byzantine Navy ca. 500–1204 with an appendix translated from the Arabic of Muhammad ibn Mankali by Ahmad Shboul* (Leiden, 2006)

Quilley, Geoffrey, 'Missing the Boat: the place of the maritime in the history of British visual culture', *Visual Culture in Britain*, vol. 1/2 (2000), pp. 79–92

——, *Art for the Nation: The Oil Paintings Collections of the National Maritime Museum* (London, 2006)

——, 'The Battle of the Pictures: Painting the History of Trafalgar', in *Trafalgar in History: A Battle and its Afterlife*, ed. David Cannadine (London, 2006), pp. 121–38

——, 'The Art of the Cook Voyages', in *The History of British Art*, ed. David Bindman (London, 2008)

——, and Kay Dian Kriz, eds, *An Economy of Colour: Visual Culture and the Atlantic World, 1660–1830* (Manchester, 2003)

——, and John Bonehill, eds, *William Hodges 1744–1797: The Art of Exploration* (New Haven, CT, 2004)

Raban, Jonathan, *Coasting* (London, 1987)

——, *The Oxford Book of the Sea* (Oxford, 1992)

——, *Passage to Juneau: A Sea and its Meanings* (London, 1999)

Rabelais, François, *The Histories of Gargantua and Pantagruel*, trans. and with an introduction by J. M. Cohen [1532–4] (London, 1955)

Rainbird, Paul, 'Islands out of Time: Towards a Critique of Island Archaeology', *Journal of Mediterranean Archaeology*, 12/2 (1999), pp. 218–36

——, *The Archaeology of Micronesia* (Cambridge, 2004)

——, *The Archaeology of Islands* (Cambridge, 2007)

Rediker, Marcus, *Between the Devil and the Deep Blue Sea: Merchant Seamen, Pirates and the Anglo-American Maritime World, 1700–1750* (Cambridge, 1987)

Rhodes, P. J., *A Commentary on the Aristotelian* Athenaion Politeia (Oxford, 1981)

Rodger, N.A.M., *The Wooden World: An Anatomy of the Georgian Navy* (London, 1986)

——, *The Safeguard of the Sea: A Naval History of Britain, 660–1649* (London, 1997)

——, *The Command of the Sea: A Naval History of Britain, 1649–1815* (London, 2004)

Rodgers, Silvia, 'Feminine Power at Sea', RAIN, no. 64 (1984), pp. 2–4

Rousmanière, N. C., and W. Jeffett, *Hiroshi Sugimoto*, exh. cat., Sainsbury Centre for Visual Arts, Norwich (1997)

Russell, M., *Visions of the Sea: Hendrick C. Vroom and the Origins of Dutch Marine Painting* (Leiden, 1983)

Sahlins, Marshall, *Culture and Practical Reason* (Chicago, IL, 1976).

——, *Islands of History* (Chicago, IL, 1985)

Salmond, Anne, 'Their Body is Different, Our Body is Different: European and Tahitian Navigators in the 18th Century', *History and Anthropology*, XVI/2 (2005), pp. 167–86

Sandin, Benedict, *The Sea Dyaks of Borneo before White Rajah Rule* (London, 1967)

Sather, C., *The Bajau Laut* (Oxford, 1997)

Sekula, Allan, *Fish Story* (Rotterdam, 1995)

Sinclair, P., 'The Origins of Urbanism in East and Southern Africa: A Diachronic Perspective', in *Islamic Art and Culture in sub-Saharan Africa*, ed. K. Ådahl and B. Sahlstrom (Uppsala, 1995), pp. 99–109

Sharp, Lesley A., *The Possessed and the Dispossessed: Spirits, Identity and Power in a Madagascar Migrant Town* (Berkeley, CA, 1993)

Sharp, N., *Saltwater People: The Waves of Memory* (Crows Nest, NSW, 2002)

Smith, Bernard, *European Vision and the South Pacific* (New Haven, CT, 1985)

Smith, Bernard, 'The Artwork', in *The Art of the First Fleet*, ed. Bernard Smith and Alwyne Wheeler (New Haven, CT, 1985), pp. 198–287

Smith, Vanessa, 'Crusoe in the South Seas: Beachcombers: Missionaries and the Myth of the Castaway', in *Robinson Crusoe: Myths and Metamorphoses*, ed. Lieve Spaas and Brian Stimpson (Basingstoke, 1996), pp. 62–77

Smith, Vanessa, 'Costume Changes. Passing at Sea and on the Beach', in *Sea Changes: Historicizing the Ocean*, ed. Bernard Klein and Gesa Mackenthun (London, 2004), pp. 37–53

Smyth, Admiral W. H., *The Sailor's Word-Book: An Alphabetical Digest of Nautical Terms, Including Some More Especially Military And Scientific, But Useful to Seamen; As Well as Archaisms of Early Voyagers, Etc.* [1865] (London, 1991)

Spaas, Lieve, and Brian Stimpson, eds, *Robinson Crusoe: Myths and Metamorphoses* (Basingstoke, 1996)

Steinberg, Philip E., 'Lines of Division, Lines of Connection: Stewardship in the World Ocean', *Geographical Review*, LXXXIX/2 (1999), pp. 254–64

Stevenson, Robert Louis, 'The English Admirals'. *Cornhill Magazine*, 38 (July 1878), p. 36

——, *South Sea Tales*, ed. Roslyn Jolly (Oxford, 1996)

——, *Treasure Island*, introduction by David Cordingly [1883] (New York, 2001)

Sugimoto, H., *Sugimoto*, exh. cat. Contemporary Arts Museum, Houston, and Hara Museum, Tokyo (1996)

Synge, John M., *The Aran Islands,* with drawings by Jack B. Yates [1906] (Belfast, 1988)

Taylor, E.G.R., *The Haven-Finding Art: A History of Navigation from Odysseus to Captain Cook* (London, 1971)

Thackeray, William Makepeace, 'De Juventute', in *Roundabout Papers* [1863] (London, 1887), pp. 68–82

Thøfner, Margit, *A Common Art: Urban Ceremonial in Antwerp and Brussels during and after the Dutch Revolt* (Zwolle, 2007)

Thomas, Nicholas, 'Licensed Curiosity: Cook's Pacific Voyages', in *The Cultures of Collecting*, ed. John Elsner and Roger Cardinal (Cambridge, MA, 1994), pp. 116–36

——, *In Oceania: Visions, Artefacts, Histories* (Durham, NC, 1997)

——, *Discoveries: The Voyages of Captain Cook* (London, 2003)

Tibbetts, G. R., *Arab Navigation in the Indian Ocean before the Coming of the Portuguese, being a translation of Kitāb al-Fawā'id fī uṣūl al-baḥr wa'l-qawā'id of Ahmad b. Mājid al-Najdī*, with an introduction, notes and a glossary, Oriental Translation Fund, n.s., XLII [1490] (London, 1971)

——, 'Arab Navigation in the Red Sea', *Geographical Journal*, 127/3 (1961), pp. 322–34

Tilley, Christopher, *A Phenomenology of Landscape: Paths, Places and Monuments* (Oxford, 1994)

Toomer, G. J., 'Ptolemy and his Greek Predecessors' in *Astronomy before the Telescope*, ed. Christopher Walker (London, 1999), pp. 68–91

Toren, Christina, 'Seeing the Ancestral Sites: Transformations in Fijian Notions of the Land', in *The Anthropology of Landscape: Perspectives on*

Place and Space, ed. Eric Hirsch and Michael O'Hanlon (Oxford, 1995), pp. 163–83

Turnbull, David, 'Cook and Tupaia, a Tale of Catographic *Méconnaisance?*', in *Science and Exploration in the Pacific: European Voyages to the Southern Oceans in the Eighteenth Century*, ed. Margarette Lincoln (Woodbridge, 1998), pp. 117–31

Tvedt, Terje, and Terje Oestigaard, eds, *A History of Water*, III: *The World of Water* (London, 2006)

United Nations, *The Law of the Sea* (New York, 1983)

van Dommelen, Peter, 'Islands in History', *Journal of Mediterranean Archaeology*, XII/2 (1999), pp. 246–51

Vérin, P., *The History of Civilisation in North Madagascar* (Rotterdam, 1986)

Verne, Jules, *Twenty Thousand Leagues under the Sea*, trans. and with an introduction and notes by William Butcher [1869] (Oxford 1998)

Villiers, Alan, *Sons of Sindbad: an account of sailing with the Arabs in their dhows, in the Red Sea, round the coasts of Arabia, and to Zanzibar and Tanganyika; pearling in the Persian Gulf; and the life of the shipmasters and the mariners of Kuwait* (London, 1940)

——, *Joseph Conrad, Master Mariner* (Rendlesham, 2006)

Vryonis, S., ed., *The Greeks and the Sea* (New York, 1993)

Walker, Christopher, ed., *Astronomy before the Telescope* (London, 1999)

Ward, R. Gerard, 'Earth's Empty Quarter? The Pacific Islands in a Pacific Century', *Geographical Journal*, 155/2 (1989), pp. 235–46

Warren, James Francis, 'The Global Economy and the Sulu Zone: Connections, Commodities and Culture', in *Sea Changes: Historicizing the Ocean*, ed. Bernard Klein and Gesa Mackenthun (London, 2004), pp. 55–74

Westerdahl, Christer, 'The Maritime Cultural Landscape', *International Journal of Nautical Archaeology*, XXI/1 (1992), pp. 5–14

——, 'Seal on Land, Elk at Sea: The Ritual Landscape at the Seaboard', *International Journal of Nautical Archaeology*, XXXIV/1 (2005), pp. 2–23

White, Walter Grainge, *The Sea Gypsies of Malaya: An Account of the Nomadic Mawken People of the Mergui Archipelagi with a Description of their Ways of Life, Customs, Habits, Boats, Occupations* (London, 1922)

Wilson, Derek, *The Circumnavigators: The Pioneer Voyagers Who Set Off Around the Globe* (London, 1989)

Wilton, Andrew, *Turner and the Sublime* (London, 1980)

Worsley, Peter, *Knowledges: What Different Peoples Make of the World* (London, 1997)

Wright, H. T., 'Early Communities on the island of Mayotte and the coasts of Madagascar', in *Madagascar: Society and History*, ed. C. Kottak, A. Southall and P. Vérin (Durham, NC, 1984), pp. 53–87

——, 'Early Seafarers of the Comoro Islands: The Dembeni Phase of the IXth–Xth Centuries AD', *Azania*, 19 (1984), pp. 13–59

Yonemoto, Marcia, 'Maps and Metaphors of the "Small Eastern Sea" in Tokugawa Japan (1603–1868)', *Geographical Review*, LXXXIX/2 (1999), pp. 169–87

Zuidema, Tom R., 'Shaft-tombs and the Inca Empire', *Journal of the Steward Anthropological Society*, 9 (1977), pp. 133–78

Acknowledgements

In the course of the wide-ranging research this project has implied I have benefited from casual conversations and more formal interactions with many colleagues. I originally rehearsed some of the arguments that might be advanced in a western Indian Ocean context in an article published subsequent to a conference on the island of Zanzibar in 2006 organized by the British Museum and the British Institute in Eastern Africa in collaboration with the Zanzibari authorities. Dr Stephanie Wynne-Jones organized this and published some of the contributions in a special issue of the journal *Azania* the following year. I am grateful to her for her initiatives and to a number of participants in that conference for the encouragement to carry on developing its themes.

Many other people have assisted subsequently. The help of the staff, the resources and the focused working environment of the London Library for periods based there was important at various stages. I am otherwise very grateful for the resources and expertise offered by the Sainsbury Research Unit Library at my own university, the University of East Anglia, where Pat Hewitt and her staff have gone well beyond routine helpfulness in the advice and the tenacity with which they have sought out often obscure publications for me. David Barrie, Arts advocate but also a knowledgeable navigator in his own right, has been an insightful commentator on aspects of the emerging text. I have also benefited from the conversation and comments of another friend of long-standing, Henry Drewal, who at a significant stage in the production of this manuscript took up a Visiting Fellowship in my university department. Although we were working in quite different areas at the time, this allowed us to explore some of the evident convergence of our ideas. Lucy Blue and Stephanie Jones at the University of Southampton both allowed me to try out ideas at an early stage at the research seminars they organize focusing on different aspects of maritime studies. Parts of the book were also rehearsed in research seminars at University College London, and the universities of Oxford, Cambridge and Lampeter, whilst my own students and colleagues offered much useful comment and provided references and ideas deriving from a wide range of literature and examples. Steven Hooper, in particular, has been a constant source of useful advice on Polynesian maritime experience. Margit Thøfner introduced me to the pageants in the Low Countries in the early modern period which often had a maritime theme. A doctoral student, Sokratis Kioussis, took time out to help me understand Greek perspectives on the sea and another colleague, Aristotoles Barcelos Neto, provided helpful discussion and references. I have also been encouraged by the arrival on our faculty of Sarah Monks who at lectures and more informally has made helpful comments on my less expert understanding of European traditions of marine painting. Others have also been generous and responsive to my sometimes last-minute enquiries about recondite details. A school of 'World Art Studies', whatever else its merits, does provide a wealth and diversity of informed colleagues with whom to discuss what might otherwise seem obscure and unnoticed niceties. Michael Leaman, his colleagues at Reaktion Books and an anonymous reader have helped shape the final text. I also thank many not otherwise mentioned here who provided ready responses to my enquiries. Sue Hedges has helped by chasing down photographic permissions and Katy Mack has prepared the Index. The book was completed in draft during two consecutive periods of leave in 2008 and I am especially grateful to my colleagues and the authorities at the University of East Anglia for granting and supporting research leave for that year and to the Leverhulme Trust which granted me a Fellowship for the second half of the period.

In recent years my experience of being under sail has been as an occasional, if inexpert, 'crew' of a small yacht sailed by my brother-in-law off the Welsh coast at Aberdovey. However any claim to wider skill is undoubtedly down to my father who introduced us to the experience of sailing in Strangford Lough in Northern Ireland over many summers and who himself ventured beyond, sailing to Scotland, the Isle of Man and down the east coast of Ireland. Some of that early experience has evidently informed what follows. My brother Geoffrey has reminded me of many incidents from those days. I dedicate this book to our father's memory.

Photo Acknowledgements

The author and the publishers wish to express their thanks to the below sources of illustrative material and/or permission to reproduce it

Asher and Co. BV, Ijmuiden: p. 206; © Bibliothèque nationale de France. The Shefer collection, Ms arabe 5847, fol. 119v: p. 154; © The British Library Board. Add. 15508 f.12: p. 122; © The Trustees of the British Museum: p. 177; © Centre for Maritime Archaeology, University of Southampton: p. 199; Henry J. Drewal: p. 210; Jeremy Marre: p. 208; © Platin-Moretus Museum/Stedlijk Pretenkabinett, Antwerp, Belgium: p. 207; © Hiroshi Sugimoto, courtesy the Pace Gallery, New York. Also courtesy of the Robert and Lisa Sainsbury Collection, University of East Anglia, Norwich, Photographer James Austin: p. 86; © Tate, London 2011: p. 102.

Index